Eloquent Obsessions

ELOQUENT

OBSESSIONS

Writing Cultural Criticism

Edited by MARIANNA TORGOVNICK

DUKE UNIVERSITY PRESS   Durham and London 1994

© 1994 Duke University Press
All rights reserved
Printed in the United States of America on acid-free paper ∞
Typeset in Joanna by Tseng Information Systems, Inc.
Library of Congress Cataloging-in-Publication Data appear
on the last printed page of this book.
The text of this book originally was published without the
present introduction or index, and without the essays by
Davidson, Tompkins, or Edmundson as volume 91, no. 1
of the South Atlantic Quarterly. The essays by Graff, Torgovnick,
and Jonaitis and Inglis have been revised for this edition.
The essay by Nancy K. Miller is © 1992 by Nancy K. Miller.

Contents

Introduction

MARIANNA TORGOVNICK

M any of the essays in this volume began as obsessions. Something in the writer's background or experience took hold in the imagination, so that the essay grew from the core of experience—often from an important bit of family or personal history, a text or movement that influenced an education or career, profoundly controversial politics. Asked "Why are you writing about this topic?" writers in this volume would be unlikely to respond: because Foucault showed its importance in systems of domination and control; because it's a hot topic right now; because I needed to write something; or, I don't know. Instead, the answers would most likely be framed in terms of some strongly felt experience, deeply held conviction, long-term interest, or problem that has irritated the mind. Explanations that return to childhood or youth would be common, conviction and passion abound. As the essays took shape, the thinker's rigor and the writer's craft came into play: testing convictions, supplying facts, honing the prose. Writing cultural criticism involves not wild or strange obsessions, but eloquent ones—examined, reasoned, persuasive, and shaped.

Take, for example, Alice Yaeger Kaplan's "The American Stranger." Kaplan unpeels the layers of her association with Albert Camus's novel, placing it in generational contexts. She reflects on how she was taught the book and how it crystallizes what "French" or "Algerian" means to a contemporary "American." Also in a generational mode, Nancy K. Miller's "Decades" traces her evolving relationship to feminist criticism and the stages by which it came to feel like home. Writing as a native Southerner, Linda Orr returns to her childhood home in order to explain her suspicions about narrators in Southern fiction. Cathy N. Davidson also writes about the South, but as a newcomer who wants to reproduce in North Carolina memories of Japan; she affirms feeling most alive when living between cultures—but also interrogates that feeling.

This mood of questioning, of writing between cultures, of being both insider and outsider, is exemplary in cultural criticism. So too is movement into the past to explain the present. In *The Historical Novel*, Lukács says that the impulse behind historical fiction is to examine the past as "the concrete precondition for the present"—an elegant and rich formulation. A similar view inhabits the essays in this volume. The past is seen as the concrete precondition of the present; the present as the concrete precondition of the future. The writers do not present seamless or single-voiced arguments. But they affirm connections between thought and action, the social and personal, the individual and communal, the "I" and the "we." "Saving Their Lives," the title of Jane Tompkins's essay on male identity in contemporary culture, is an apt metaphor for the motivation behind many of the essays, which want to make things happen—want, more precisely, to make things better.

Do I advocate obsession as a model for writing about culture? Not necessarily. But not necessarily not. The coolness, the aloofness (dare I say the tedium?) of much of what passes for cultural criticism strikes me as inappropriate at some fundamental level. The day that writing about culture becomes just another academic activity, dusty and dry, severed from the lives of writers and society, it will be just another academic field and not the site of potential and excitement that it is today. For the basic premise of cultural criticism is that writers have something to say about society and that society will listen. The circuit between writer and society is the lifeblood of cultural criticism. Without it, the enterprise would be meaningless.

———

In the last two centuries, in England and the United States, people who wrote literature often also wrote cultural criticism: Samuel Johnson, Thomas Carlyle, Matthew Arnold, John Stuart Mill, Zora Neale Hurston, and George Orwell, for example. They set a high standard of writing which was matched in a different way by critics who focused more specifically on cultural life: Margaret Fuller, W. E. B. Du Bois, Edmund Wilson, Hannah Arendt, Lionel Trilling, and Raymond Williams are some additional great names from the past. These writers cover a variety of topics, and "culture" means a variety of things to them: literature and the arts (German Kultur), educational traditions and philosophies, fads and fashions, political or historical events and movements, moods and manners, the spoken and unspoken assumptions of social conduct.

Eloquent Obsessions: Writing Cultural Criticism draws upon all these meanings of "culture." In addition to the essays previously mentioned, it includes essays on a wide range of specific texts and phenomena: subway graffiti (Sayre), museum exhibitions (Jonitis and Inglis), National Geographic magazine (Collins and Lutz), and "green" criticism (Ross). It includes also broad definitions of culture (Dominguez) and discussions of how to write about it (Graff, Edmundson, and Torgovnick).

Though the essays are rich in theory, readers can profitably read them without being versed in current theoretical debates. Almost all the writers have confined critical references to endnotes or incorporated technical arguments in a way that makes overt mention unnecessary. This is reader-friendly theory. Above all, it aims for communication from writer to reader. Simply put, the collection offers writerly models for writing about culture—models that are intellectually and socially responsible, but attuned to the critic's voice and the reader's ear.

One of my ambitions for this volume is that it will encourage writerly models for writing about culture. There are six convictions underlying this collection of essays.

Writing about culture is personal. Writers find their material in experience as well as books, and they leave a personal imprint on their subjects. They must feel free to explore the autobiographical motivation for their work, for often this motivation is precisely what generates writers' interests in their topics. Much of the work being done under the rubric of multiculturalism shows this. It is not that writers necessarily "write as" African Americans, or Italian Americans, or Cuban Americans—for not all members of groups have identical experiences, and ethnic identity is not destiny. But formative experiences strongly shape intellectual temper and a writer's instinct for what counts. There is nothing sadder than writing that is "multicultural" but also dutiful and dull.

Writing about culture is informed. A lot of research can go into writing about culture, and probably should when the history of a specific institution is involved. Catherine Lutz and Jane Collins's article about *National Geographic* exemplifies how research can be distilled into lively and readable form. Just because writing about culture comes from the heart does not mean that it comes off the top of the head. Single, random bits of evidence from personal experience can be powerful in such writing—but they may not always be enough.

Writing about culture is text or phenomenon based. In other words, the choice of subject is wide open but there must still be a cultural subject and not writing for writing's sake—which is a different kind of enterprise. Broader notions of "text" pertain—and these come from European traditions from Walter Benjamin to Roland Barthes. They are here to stay. From now on, "texts" means not just printed matter and not just films or movies, the first texts to break the print barrier. It includes photographs, institutions, trends and fads, and personalities.

Writing about culture suspends distinctions between high and mass culture. It's not that writers do not know the difference between Ernest Hemingway and Edgar Rice Burroughs but that it has become productive to take both levels of culture seriously. No one is obligated to work on just one level or the other. Movement between levels is common and to be expected.

Writing about culture wants to make a difference. Which is to say, a difference in the culture. Writing in this mode usually does not hide its political sympathies and opinions, though it may still remain open to other views. Writers believe that criticism can and has made things happen. Writers target areas where they can promote ends they believe progressive.

Writing about culture should be aimed, at least some of the time, at a general, educated audience. This premise follows directly from the last, that writing about culture makes a difference. To effect social change, criticism has to make itself felt. Granted that certain movements (feminism and gay rights, for example) have received a significant boost from academic writing. Granted that academics can be movers and shakers in culture. Writing that wants to affect social attitudes and change or heighten awareness still has to find broader venues—as it usually does.

As you read this volume, I hope you listen to the voices in and behind the essays. The collection has been written for readers, written for pleasure, written to pass on views on matters of weight, significance, passion, and even obsession.

The American Stranger

ALICE YAEGER KAPLAN

I begin with a memory of one of the standard rites of French pedagogy.[1] You start out by drawing a time line. You go up to the blackboard, and it's dramatic, and you say, "This is the imperfect: the imperfect is for description; it's for events that haven't finished." The time it takes to say this is just about the time it takes to drag your chalk line, slowly, all the way across the board. You explain, chalk in hand, that the imperfect is used to describe feelings, state of being; it's used to describe background, landscape, and ongoing thoughts. All sorts of things with no definite beginning and end. Then you pause, take hold of your chalk piece like a weapon, and you stab that blackboard line at one point, then at another. This is the *passé composé*, this staccato: a point on the imperfect line of experience, a discrete action in the past with a beginning and an end that you can name.

> I was walking to the parking lot [unfinished action] when I tripped [sudden discrete action].
> It was nice out that day [description: *il faisait beau*], so we went [narrative event] to the park.

The *passé composé-imparfait* time line is found in French grammar texts (Figure 1) as well as in the most sophisticated reference works.[2] Life has description and life has plot. French divides it up in such a way that you always know what tense to use. The air was still as glass when the tornado touched down. Was—imperfect; touched—*passé composé*.

For many years, Albert Camus's *L'Etranger* was the text used for teaching these past time sequences.[3] The novel is written in the *passé composé*

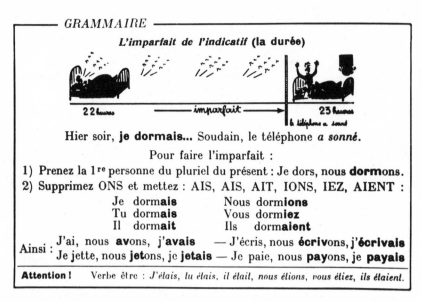

Figure 1. *Learning the tenses. From G. Mauger,* Cours de langue et de civilisation française à l'usage des étrangers, I *(1er et 2ème degrés) (Paris, 1953). Collection publiée sous le patronage de l'Alliance Française.*

and *imparfait*; it does not employ the *passé simple*, the French tense used for official history, although the *passé simple* was the standard past tense in the French novel well into the twentieth century. I would guess that there is a generation of American writers of French prose in this country who got their sense of how to narrate in the past from Camus's novel. I would guess, too, that Camus's substitution of the conversational for the historical tenses may well have determined the way the book has been taught. Teachers of *L'Etranger* have always emphasized Meursault's physical/metaphysical experience, and have bracketed the historical context of the novel.

When I was asked to give a lecture on the teaching of French literature in the United States, I thought immediately of *L'Etranger* as the text that stood for French education, a text that was utterly familiar to me and yet irritating, because of how little I really knew about it beyond its immediate texture. I kept thinking about how *L'Etranger* functioned in the American education system: how inviting it is, with its sparse vocabulary and verb sequences, for the student just coming to literature, yet how much more there is to tell about it.

Germaine Brée and Carlos Lynes published a textbook edition of L'Etranger with an American publisher, Appleton-Century-Crofts, in 1955. The text was in French, with an introduction in English and a French-English glossary at the end. As of July 1988, when it was in its forty-first printing, the book had sold "in the hundreds of thousands of copies"—although the company refuses to reveal actual sales figures.[4] Germaine Brée states in a letter that she and Lynes received a specially bound volume when the book sold 35,000, or, as she added, "was it 350,000?"[5] And the Brée/Lynes edition is only one of several French language editions available. The 1957 French Livre de Poche edition of L'Etranger, capitalizing on the fact that it had become a popular novel among students, depicted on its cover a boy who looks more like a sixteen-year-old Arthur Rimbaud than Meursault, a man old enough for his mother to have died in an old age home. As recently as 1979, the British rock group The Cure translated a single scene of L'Etranger into the present of adolescent nihilism: "I can turn and walk away or I can fire the gun / Staring at the sky, staring at the sun / Whichever I choose it amounts to the same / Absolutely nothing / I'm alive. I'm dead. I'm the Stranger. Killing an Arab."[6]

For American students of my generation—and still, perhaps—L'Etranger was the first novel we read in French. The flagship book. Our own pleasure at knowing how to read French was mirrored by it. It's no wonder that of all the mountains of essays written about L'Etranger, the one that has always appealed to me most is Renée Balibar's, which focuses on the important role of the novel in the French national education system. When I listen to Camus reading L'Etranger in a 1950s recording, I don't hear an author; I hear a teacher. A French teacher.

This is the story we learn in school. A white guy, a petty bureaucrat in a French company in Algiers, kills an Arab on the beach. He is tried for murder. Testimony reveals, among other things, that he went to a Fernandel movie the day after his mother's funeral. And to the beach. About the murder, he claims, when pressed, that the heat of the sun made him do it. He is condemned, his head to be cut off on a public square in the name of the French people.

The man's emotional life begins only as he realizes he's about to die. He is happy as he watches the sun rise and fall in the slit in his cell. And he can just see the water, just see the beach. In his cell, about to be guillotined for the murder of an Arab on a sunny day, the Stranger says: "I think that I slept because I woke with stars on my face. I felt ready to relive everything." I felt: *je me suis senti* (*passé composé*) and not the expected, *je me sentais* (*imparfait*). Feelings are usually supposed to be in the imperfect. But the whole point of the book, the point that this nuance of tense expresses all by itself, is that nothing in the Stranger's life lasts long enough to be written in the imperfect. He is in prison and he is going to die. Life for the Stranger is existential: everyone who reads *L'Etranger* learns the big word, even though it's not a word that Camus himself would have used in 1940 when he was finishing the book. We also learn that "Stranger" can mean foreigner—like us, learning French—or it can mean, in a purely psychological sense, an alien or outsider. In the novel the narrator is both: he is a foreigner in Algiers, estranged from his habitual language. He can't muster up the conventionality to tell his girlfriend that he loves her, or to cry at his mother's funeral.

The tools I had for understanding the story weren't sociological ones; they were the tenses and the conditionals. I read that book at age fourteen and I taught it for the first time at age twenty-five—without having ever seen Marengo or Algiers on a map.

What happens to history when reading is done as an attempt to learn a language? What happens to context when you learn a foreign language? Does context have to be the foreign context? Is there time for "theirs" and "yours"? And is there any energy left, after looking up all the words in the back of the book, for any context at all? On the other hand, is history in French studies at best a distraction from the pain of grammar?

======

It is macabre that so many American students have practiced French on this story of an existential joy, the joy of the Stranger in his prison, facing a death that is achieved through the indifferent murder of an Arab.

We were taught to admire Meursault's indifference, his deadpan manner, his silences, all expressed in his use of the *passé composé* to mean "nothing lasts." Something about the paucity of imperfect verbs in the novel says, "this is literature—not habit." And yet its narrative is almost imbecilic: staccato actions in the *passé composé* without the imperfect longing or desire that usually provides the motivation, the glue between the parts of a story. Examples in a grammar book raised to the level of art.

"Je n'ai jamais eu de véritable imagination" ("I never had any real imagi-nation"), says Meursault, as he's trying to imagine his own death.[7] That denial of imagination was part of the aura that existential literature gave out; it was marked by both constant awareness of death and indifference to context—beach or cell. We cut our teeth on it, we learned to teach the murder of an Arab. *Cliff's Notes*, 1965 edition, theme topics and ques-tions for discussion: "What does his habit of not relating events to one another tell us about his character? How does this influence what hap-pens to him?" *Cliff's Notes*, 1979 edition, finally, in the review questions: "Meursault is a Frenchman living in Algeria; of what importance is this fact?" That's the question nobody asked me.

=====

Outside the rituals of the French department, I have always wondered, would it have been any different? I recently interviewed three women who read *The Stranger* in college between 1957 and 1970. They are profes-sional readers, all three of them professors of English. They do not share with me the experience of learning the time line; the *passé composé/imparfait* distinction fades in the English translations.[8]

The first woman I talked to read *The Stranger* in 1957 at Bryn Mawr Col-lege. She bought it and read it on her own—not, she claims, because she's such an overachiever but because of visceral peer pressure. "It was in the air; every self-respecting undergraduate was talking about it," she remem-bers. "In the class of 1961, if you hadn't read *The Stranger*, you didn't exist." She still has strong feelings about the book: "Here's this story about a guy whose mother dies and he doesn't care. And then he kills another man and he doesn't care. And then he himself is condemned to death and he still doesn't care. I couldn't figure out why I was supposed to care, actually. I hated it, and I feared it because it was supposed to be deep and philo-sophical. And deep and philosophical went along with lack of feeling—and I hated and feared that."

The two 1960s readers shared a different reaction. One read Camus in New York, one in Chicago; their professors were politically active. Both read *The Stranger* along with Frantz Fanon's *Wretched of the Earth*; they saw the movie called *The Battle of Algiers*, which told the story of the Algerian Revolution. Each of them remembers Camus's novel as a story of social alienation and subsequent liberation. One recalls reading *The Stranger* lying on her parents' couch in Brooklyn and gravitating toward the concept of alienation; in her case, The Stranger was taught "in an enormous room where we all spread out with four or five seats each between us, liking the loneliness of the space." The other connects The Stranger specifically to the assassination of Black Panther Fred Hampton by Chicago Police in 1969 and to the student body's support of the Panther cause. She evokes a scene in which Meursault, the poor white, draws back from the blinding light of the sun and recognizes the Arab he has killed. The Arab became a character in her novel, his body like Fred Hampton's body. Meursault and the Arab, for both these readers, were emblems of two different kinds of alienation: white bourgeois alienation (their own) and the alienation of the colonized subject. In a 1960s American context, the war in Vietnam (and the identification of some American students with the Viet Cong) was the event that bridged the gap between the two kinds of alienation and the two subjects—Meursault and the Arab. If you had the right consciousness, you could make a coalition.

I thought that reading the novel in English might give readers a chance to think politically about The Stranger. And yet for these former students it wasn't so much Camus's text they seemed to be encountering, but their own situation, with The Stranger's neutrality encouraging them to project their world onto the blankness of the novel.

———

What does context, the Algerian context, add to our knowledge of L'Etranger?

Rereading the 1955 Brée/Lynes textbook introduction, I am amazed at how easily the specificity of Algiers, L'Etranger's placeness, was blurred by the charm of picturesque description:

> Algiers, in which Camus lived most of his life up to 1939, provides the setting for L'Etranger. This large, modern seaport is built in a wide semi-circle around the water's edge; its houses climb the steep slope of the rugged African coast. Surrounding the casbah (fort) is the picturesque old Arab town, with its narrow, noisy streets and its motley population tightly packed into the high, terraced houses. Once the stronghold of pirates—Cervantes long remained a captive there—the old quarter has retained some of the violence and lawlessness of its past. As the city grew, modern "European" sections were built, and

the neighboring hills are now dotted with gleaming white buildings and sunlit villas.[9]

"As the city grew": an organic explanation for colonization. No sense that there were two cities, one administering the other. The city just "grew," and as it grew it improved, and the gleaming white and sunlit adjectives came to govern the narrow, noisy, and lawless ones. European sections "were built": the verb is passive, because there is no agency here. The city is double, Arabic and European, and the description can only naturalize that double quality. Sartre's Algeria, in his "Explication" of 1947, isn't even double: Algeria is "the other side of the line," "the other side of the ocean," "the perpetual summer." Neither French nor American criticism predating the Algerian struggle for independence makes race, class, and uneven development part of Meursault's world.

After decolonization, for a brief, excited period in the 1960s and 1970s, critics wanted to make *L'Etranger* an allegory for national liberation or independence, as though Camus had been telling the story of revolution. This was certainly wishful thinking. In the France of the 1990s, the emphasis has shifted. Camus has become the model of the "rights of man" writer, an antitotalitarian liberal, "good cop" to the "bad cop" Sartre with his Marxist-communist sympathies.[10] Julia Kristeva has written about Meursault as a key figure for understanding foreignness in a France forever transformed by North African immigration. It doesn't matter, she writes, that Meursault killed an Arab—it could have been anyone. Meursault, not the Arab, is the figure of foreignness in her reading.[11] But if the identity of Meursault's victim doesn't matter, *L'Etranger* is in danger of becoming a symbolic monument to foreignness, without the political specificity that race and class convey. Monument building can become a way of prettying up the past, or forgetting it.

Students may or may not learn the following facts about the place, Algeria, and the author, Albert Camus.

Algeria is located in North Africa, on the Mediterranean Sea. The indigenous peoples of Algeria, the Berbers, were colonized in the seventh century by Arabs. Then the French colonized the Arabs in 1840. The Algeria of the 1940s, the country represented in *L'Etranger*, was considered French territory; administration and education were French-run. Linguistically, the community was mixed. French was the official language. The colonized people spoke Arabic and Berber. Arabic was not taught in schools until 1936, when it was introduced as a "foreign" language. Europeans—of French, Italian, and Spanish origin—developed their own *patois* or *pataouète*, a mix of French, Spanish, Italian, and Arabic with its own rhythmic identity and enriched vocabulary.[12] Algeria wouldn't become independent from France until twenty years after the publication of L'Etranger, after an eight-year struggle for independence led by the National Liberation Front (FLN).

Although Albert Camus is known as a French intellectual, the facts of his life are inseparable from Algerian history and geography in crucial ways. Camus was born into poverty in Belcourt, a lower-middle-class neighborhood bordering on the Casbah, the Moslem district of Algiers. He did not speak Arabic. He lived in Algeria until he was an adult. His mother was deaf and illiterate. Camus was educated in the French school system, where, as of 1944, only 8 percent of the "natives" attended, even at the primary school level.[13] Camus excelled in school; his teachers urged him to go on to lycée. Tuberculosis probably kept him from becoming an academic. He lived in Algeria until World War II. He worked in theater. He joined, then left, the Communist party. He worked as a reporter and investigated the condition of the Kabyls, the Berber people who inhabited the mountainous regions of the country. He worked as a courtroom reporter. He moved to France at the outbreak of World War II, where he finished L'Etranger.

Camus did not live to see the decolonization of Algeria, but at the beginning of the struggle, when faced with taking sides, he could not support the National Liberation Front, although he agonized over the issue. In one famous statement, he referred to his mother: "I must also denounce a terrorism which is exercised blindly, in the streets of Algiers for example, and which some day could strike my mother or my family. I believe in justice, but I shall defend my mother above justice." [14]

In sociological terms, the hero of L'Etranger was not a foreigner, as the title étranger might denote; he was a colonizer: a "petit colonisateur" working in an office. A petty colonizer is a person of small financial means—the term would cover both Raymond the thug and Meursault the bureaucrat. According to Albert Memmi's definition, the petty colonizer shares the worldview of the politically or financially empowered colonizers, but because he does not enjoy economic privilege, he lives in close proximity to the colonized and is tempted by sedition and racial violence.[15] The geography of Algiers—the segregation and proximity of colonizer to colonized, with the Arab Casbah smack up against the lower-middle-class European neighborhood where Raymond and Meursault lived—makes the temptations vivid. One imagines the two characters walking by the Casbah to get home.

These are basic facts that every student of *L'Etranger* ought to know, but until recently, most never got.

===

Because I didn't know these facts, I had no sense of how shocking it was that when the Stranger's boss asked him if he wanted to go work in the Paris office, the Stranger didn't jump for joy. This must be, for the French reader, the ultimate sign of a man lacking all normal ambition and desire.

Nor did I understand that as a Frenchman living in Algeria, Camus would not have known how to speak Arabic. There is the scene in *L'Etranger* where Raymond almost shoots at two Arabs but Meursault stops him. One of them is playing a flute. The sound the Arab makes, three notes, sticks in Meursault's head, a sound he can't understand, a charm, and also a goad that leads him back onto the beach. The Arabs don't speak; their sound is represented by a musical instrument. This is not just an exotic detail. It is a symptom, in the text, of the fact that Meursault—and Camus—couldn't have understood them even if they had spoken.

Then there is the question of how to evaluate the "law" in the novel. *L'Etranger* teaches that Meursault died because he killed an Arab. But when you read colonial testimonies, this no longer seems like unequivocal justice. I was never curious about Meursault's punishment until I read Fanon's *Wretched of the Earth*. In the part of the book devoted to accounts of mental illness among victims of the Algerian war, a fourteen-year-old Arab boy who has just murdered his European schoolmate tries to get the FLN psychiatrist, Fanon, to explain to him why Europeans were never jailed for murdering Arabs.[16] (That the lynching of African-Americans went unpunished at the same time in the American South is a coincidence that can be useful in teaching the novel.) In a dangerous way, Camus misrepresents the workings of Algerian justice in *L'Etranger*, even though he had worked as a court reporter for the *Alger Républicain* and knew the colonial legal system intimately. The courtroom testimony scenes are the only places in which the text calls attention to the discrepancy between its legal premise and colonial society's norms. But this discrepancy has no thematic or political longevity. The dead Arab himself is not the issue. Meursault's "true" crime is that he doesn't love his mother. The displacement from the Arab victim of murder onto the mother who died of natural causes is the text's clearest signal of its own—and colonial society's—cover-up.[17]

I must add to the growing list of what I wasn't taught (I and several hundred thousand other American students)—four censored passages. The excisions occur in the 1955 American edition. Brée and Lynes fought to keep them, but they lost out to the publishers, who were worried about making the novel acceptable in American high schools.[18] The preface says that the original passages "might prove embarrassing in classroom reading." This was thirty-five years ago, but the sentences have never been put back into the Brée/Lynes edition.[19]

Three of the excisions come from the Raymond episode. Raymond, a neighbor of Meursault, rumored to be a pimp, has asked Meursault to help him by ghostwriting a letter to his ex-mistress, a "Moorish woman" on whom he wants to exact revenge. Recounting a conversation he'd had with his mistress, Raymond explains: "Et puis, je lui ai dit ses vérités. Je lui ai dit que tout ce qu'elle voulait, c'était s'amuser avec sa chose. Comme je lui ai dit, vous comprenez, monsieur Meursault." The sentence "Je lui ai dit que tout ce qu'elle voulait, c'était s'amuser avec sa chose" gets excised from the United States edition, and what's left is: "Et puis, je lui ai dit ses vérités. Comme je lui ai dit, vous comprenez, Monsieur Meursault."

The American edition doesn't censor the portrait of Raymond as a pimp, or the description of his mistress as a woman who lives off men. But when it comes to her desire for sex, it cuts out her own bodily pleasure, her "chose." This word in English obviously means "thing," but in this context, "thing" stands for the female site of sexual pleasure, the clitoris.

Raymond's desire for his mistress is tampered with in this second passage: "Raymond a continué. Ce qui l'ennuyait, 'c'est qu'il avait encore un sentiment pour son coït.' Mais il voulait la punir." All that is left is: "Raymond a continué. Mais il voulait la punir." His desire for revenge is no longer qualified by simple physical desire. Once again, it's the genitals, however indirectly, that get omitted.

The third instance of censorship is consistent with the first two. Here, Meursault is recounting Raymond's revenge fantasy, using Raymond's own words: "Après, quand elle reviendrait, il [Raymond] coucherait avec elle et 'juste au moment de finir' il lui cracherait à la figure et il la mettrait dehors." What remains in the American edition is: "Après, quand elle reviendrait, il lui cracherait à la figure et il la mettrait dehors." In this version of the revenge, Raymond spits in his mistress's face standing up, not lying down. Physically, spatially, emotionally, the whole meaning of the Raymond episode has been severely altered.

The last instance of censorship comes from the second part of the novel, when Meursault is in prison. He is discussing women with a prison guard—how hard it is being in prison where there aren't any women. The guard says, "Oui, vous comprenez les choses, vous. Les autres non. Mais ils finissent par se soulager eux-mêmes." The prisoners' "soulagement," a reference to masturbation, is cut, leaving only: "Oui, vous comprenez les choses, vous. Les autres non."

In each case, the American publisher has violated the truth of the novel by leaving out details that show a mixture of lust and cruelty, emotions and desires that are "imperfect" ones (sometimes they are actually expressed in the imperfect tense: "elle voulait s'amuser," etc.)—the kind of behavior that makes these characters human. And the reason the censored material would, indeed, prove "embarrassing" in the classroom is that they are so vital, especially to adolescent readers who are discovering their sexuality. What does it mean to say that a woman likes to "s'amuser avec sa chose?"[20] And what constitutes a "soulagement" when you're trapped in prison? Nor does Camus name sexuality straight on. "Chose," "soulagement," "finir": these common words, part of any second-year French vocabulary, are already metaphors for the physical, anatomical world. Even though they are simpler than the words they stand for, it takes some work of interpretation to understand them. I have seen native metropolitan speakers of French marvel at the oddity of these sentences—"s'amuser avec sa chose" (to play with her thing) is unheard of in regular conversational French; "avoir un sentiment pour son coït" (have a feeling for her coitus . . . or for coitus with her?) sounds bizarrely formal to the modern ear. The passage reads as though Camus is playing consciously with registers of language. The thug Raymond speaks with the intonation of street French—*pataouète*—but uses almost classical dic-

Table 1. Variations on Four Passages from *L'Etranger*

Gallimard, Pléiade edition, 1962	Appleton-Century-Crofts (now Prentice Hall), Brée/Lynes edition, 1955
J'ai bien vu qu'il y avait de la tromperie. Alors, je l'ai quittée. Mais d'abord, je l'ai tapée. Et puis, je lui ai dit ses vérités. Je lui ai dit que tout ce qu'elle voulait, c'était s'amuser avec sa chose. Comme je lui ai dit, vous comprenez, monsieur Meursault: "Tu ne vois pas que le monde il est jaloux du bonheur que je te donne. Tu connaîtras plus tard le bonheur que tu avais" (1147).	J'ai bien vu qu'il y avait de la tromperie. Alors, je l'ai quittée. Mais d'abord, je l'ai tapée. Et puis, je lui ai dit ses vérités. Comme je lui ai dit, vous comprenez, Monsieur Meursault: "Tu ne vois pas que le monde il est jaloux du bonheur que je te donne. Tu connaîtras plus tard le bonheur que tu avais" (50).
Raymond a continué. Ce qui l'ennuyait, "c'est qu'il avait encore un sentiment pour son coït." Mais il voulait la punir (1147).	Raymond a continué. Il voulait la punir (50).
Après, quand elle reviendrait, il couche-rait avec elle et "juste au moment de finir" il lui cracherait à la figure et il la mettrait dehors (1148).	Après, quand elle reviendrait, il lui cracherait à la figure et il la mettrait dehors (51).
"Oui, vous comprenez les choses, vous. Les autres non. Mais ils finissent par se soulager eux-mêmes." Le gardien est parti ensuite. *Et le jour après j'ai fait comme les autres.*[*] Il y a eu aussi les cigarettes (1181). [*]This italicized sentence appeared in the first 1942 edition of *L'Etranger*, on which Gilbert based his translation. It was removed from subsequent editions.	"Oui, vous comprenez les choses, vous. Les autres non." Il y a eu aussi les cigarettes (97).

Table 1. Continued

Knopf, Gilbert translation, 1946	Vintage Books, Ward translation, 1988
So I knew there was dirty work going on, and I told her I'd have nothing more to do with her. But, first, I gave her a good hiding, and I told her some home truths. I said that there was only one thing interested her and that was getting into bed with men whenever she'd the chance. And I warned her straight, "You'll be sorry one day, my girl, and wish you'd got me back. All the girls in the street, they're jealous of your luck in having me to keep you" (38).	It was clear that she was cheating on me. So I left her. But first I smacked her around. And then I told her exactly what I thought of her. I told her that all she was interested in was getting into the sack. You see, Monsieur Meursault, it's like I told her: "You don't realize that everybody's jealous of how good you have it with me. Someday you'll know just how good it was" (30–31).
Raymond went on talking. What bored him was that he had "a sort of lech on her" as he called it. But he was quite determined to teach her a lesson (39).	Raymond went on. What bothered him was that he "still had sexual feelings for her." But he wanted to punish her (31).
Then, when she came back, he'd go to bed with her and, just when she was "properly primed up," he'd spit in her face and throw her out of the room (40).	Then, when she came running back, he'd go to bed with her and "right at the last minute" he'd spit in her face and throw her out (32).
"Yes, you're different, you can use your brains. The others can't. Still, those fellows find a way out; they do it by themselves." With which remark the jailer left my cell. Next day I did like the others. The lack of cigarettes, too, was a trial (97).	"Right. You see, you understand these things. The rest of them don't. But they just end up doing it by themselves." The guard left after that. There were the cigarettes, too (78).

tion. These seemingly simple words are difficult to translate because they operate through a play on Algerian and metropolitan codes of usage. In any case they were deleted because they would make American students ask too many questions.

Table 1 contains two English translations of the four censored passages. Whatever sexism or puritanism is inherent in the censorship seems to have been rendered right out loud by the translators. Again, the most striking aspect of mistranslation is the total failure to render "s'amuser avec sa chose." Raymond's Moorish mistress doesn't get a chance to "s'amuser avec sa chose" either in the Stuart Gilbert translation of 1946 or the Matthew Ward translation of 1988.[21]

Gilbert does this with the mistress's "chose": "I said that there was only one thing that interested her and that was getting into bed with men whenever she'd the chance." No desire of her own here. Just the desire for men.

Ward doesn't do much better: "I told her that all she was interested in was getting into the sack." "The sack"—vaguely popular in tone, but even more disembodied.

As for Raymond's conflicting desires, Gilbert renders them as: "What bored him was that he had 'a sort of lech on her' as he called it. But he was quite determined to teach her a lesson." "Ennuyait" becomes "bored" instead of bothered—which, while not impossible as a translation of "ennuyait," is grossly insensitive in this context—and Raymond's rather formal word "coït" becomes "a lech."[22] The need to punish is rendered as a need to teach her a lesson—an added touch of pedagogical sadism that strikes me as coming from British public schools. The translation by Ward makes "coït" into "sexual feelings"—a feeble euphemism from the American language of therapy, without the archaic, Old Testament force of "coït."

In the third, revenge fantasy instance the offending phrase "juste au moment de finir" becomes in Gilbert's hands "just when she was properly primed up" (sounds like an engine). Ward is better but less active: the verb "finir" becomes the noun phrase "right at the last moment."

As for the "soulagement" of the prisoners, neither Gilbert ("they do it by themselves") nor Ward ("they just end up doing it by themselves") is able to render the sense of physical relief in Camus's reflexive verb.

Missing body parts, missing desires, missing body politics—a city that is "inexplicably" part European and part Arabic. The reader cannot see the bodily pleasure of Raymond's mistress; cannot imagine the sexual component of Raymond's revenge, nor the bodily relief of the prisoners. Raymond's mistress, Raymond, and the prisoners are disconnected from their bodies, not unlike Meursault. They are more indifferent; therefore he is less strange. And with only a picturesque Algiers as introduction, the reader of the American edition of *L'Etranger* cannot understand that the Moorish mistress, the silent Arab brother, the crude garrulous Raymond, and the scribe Meursault all participate in a larger set of relations, dictated, in 1942, from the French metropolis.[23]

What do we still not know? For all that we can now know and say about colonialism and displaced crime and censored sentences, there is still another *oubli*, and that is Raymond's Moorish mistress. She is the distant cause of Meursault's distress. Her body is slighted in censorship and in translation; her ethnicity is exoticized in the novel. She is called "Mauresque" (Moorish)—the word has an archaic, religious connotation; while her brother is simply an "Arab." [24]

The question of women in the novel has not been adequately explored, and it is as important as the censored sentences.[25] How does his attitude toward women fuel the demise of Meursault? It's not his indifference toward his mother, as the prosecution insists, but Meursault's support of Raymond's revenge on his mistress that counts—for Raymond is the mediator of Meursault's crime. As we saw in the censored passages, Raymond tells the dirty tale about his mistress; Meursault listens and helps Raymond get back at her. It is a homoerotic complicity, based on a man's description of sex to another man, with the woman herself absent.

Even the climatic incident in the novel relies on a little-remarked-upon detail. Why does Meursault wander back on the beach, after Raymond is wounded? Why doesn't he return to Masson's cabana?

> Je l'ai accompagné jusqu'au cabanon et, pendant qu'il gravissait l'escalier de bois, je suis resté devant la première marche, la tête retentissante de soleil, découragé devant l'effort qu'il fallait faire pour monter l'étage de bois et aborder encore les femmes.
>
> (I accompanied him to the cabana and while he climbed the wooden stair, I stayed in front of the first step, my head full of sun, discouraged by the effort that would be necessary to climb the wooden stair and encounter the women again.) [26]

In as close as he will come to explanation, Meursault cites the effort it would take to go back to the women. In his fatigue with the feminine, in his dread of the domestic, isn't Meursault—my favorite stranger—behaving in a familiar misogynist way? Think of the thousands of women readers (women, the majority population in most American French classes) who have learned to lionize the Meursault who plans vengeance on Raymond's mistress; the Meursault who consents to marry Marie—but only because she wants to; the Meursault who wanders on the beach with a gun, and kills, because he cannot bear the effort it would take to join the company of women. Women are taught that this Meursault is unconventional—and avant-garde.[27]

At one point I abandoned Meursault altogether, in a seminar on the Algerian war.[28] L'Etranger didn't fit in that course: it has none of the dialectical power of Memmi's Portrait du colonisé précédé de portrait du colonisateur (1957); none of the horror and transcendent solidarity of Henri Alleg's torture narrative in La question (1958); neither the psychological acuity of the case histories of Fanon's Les damnés de la terre (1966) nor the political acuity of the portraits in Assia Djebar's Les enfants du nouveau monde (1962).

So what's left? Do I even want Meursault to survive into the 1990s? Where does he belong within a new agenda of "race, class, and gender" studies? How does he challenge the agenda? And wouldn't I rather teach the passionate texts of national liberation—Alleg, Djebar, Fanon, Memmi—than L'Etranger, where all I have to work with is the absent presence of the Arabs, the absent presence of colonialism, the absent presence of women?

What do I still like about this book?

I still like the writing. I cannot stop liking the writing, and I cannot stop finding something in it of the value I assign to literature. Why? Why am I so passionate about the language of Meursault's indifference? I come back again and again, in my thinking about L'Etranger, to a statement Camus gave to Carl Viggiani, who was interviewing him for a future biography: "Personne autour de moi ne savait lire: mesurez bien cela" ("No one around me knew how to read. Think about it—mark my words").[29]

No one around Camus knew how to read. French wasn't his mother tongue in a literal sense—his mother was deaf and illiterate—and unlike colonized Africans, he had no alternate indigenous language he spoke at home. He was neither a native, nor a nonnative speaker of French. His street language was one kind of French, and his school language another. The two registers are united through the plot of L'Etranger—the smooth, literate Meursault, a Cyrano of hate, writes a letter for the unschooled thug Raymond.[30] His French came from his teachers, first Louis Germain, who pushed him to take the exams to get into lycée (and to whom he would dedicate his Nobel Prize speech of 1957), then Jean Grenier, his philosophy professor. He was the kid who made it through school, the one poor kid picked out of the classroom who made it to the metropolis.

And therein lies the deep connection to the remarkable success of L'Etranger among American students of French. Camus has furnished students of French with the book that bridges the gap between language and literature. Our literacy text. But also the thrill of reading a sentence, the literacy thrill. The feeling of understanding for the first time—the thrill, in language classes, of knowing how to say something before you understand what it means, and then gradually coming to know what it means. This is the faith of language teaching: to inspire an awe about what isn't known. And the pleasure of having learned a foreign language is to know something but still remember the fragile not knowing.

American French professors teach students who aren't native speakers, who have neither metropolitan nor colonial training. And so we try to provide some sort of history and culture as well as phonetics and grammar, to bring the students up to speed. But in our attempt to make them "catch up," the danger is always that we will mythologize everything that is French simply because we don't live it—and get conned. Camus, on the other hand, was always trying—at least poetically—to get away from France. The *New Yorker*, describing Camus in a "Talk of the Town" column on the eve of his first visit to New York, claimed that what bothered the writer most about France (and French culture) was the oversupply of historical and literary association.[31]

Camus practiced thin description. He wanted to strip his text of all extraneous associations, and he produced a clean and elegant language. This sounds fine from the point of view of a working writer, wanting to emulate another writer. But how could an *undersupply* of historical and literary association be an advantage to a student reading French, wanting to learn about literature? In the course of interviewing readers of L'Etranger, I spoke to a graduate student in French, who explained to me that when she first read L'Etranger in a high-school French class, she didn't understand that the Arab had died. Instead she remembered something surreal: Meursault had knocked at someone's door, even though he was outside on the beach. This was her understanding of the dramatic conclusion to part I of L'Etranger, written in a surprising dreamlike imparfait: "Et c'était comme quatre coups befs que je frappais sur la porte du malheur" ("And it was like four quick knocks that I was knocking on the door of unhappiness"— my translation).

Like this student, people who work in languages that are not their own are always in danger of mistaking a tired cliché for a brilliant new figure of speech, or a figure of speech for a statement of fact—because we don't know the difference between an old cliché and a new figure. But this also means that we have access to more poetry than do jaded readers. We see Meursault out on the beach, knocking at the door of fate before we figure out that the knock is a metaphor for the gun shot.[32] Another graduate student in French at Duke described taking a literature course taught in English, with English language texts: "The sentences just don't have the density that they do when the language is foreign to me," she said. Because ordinary understanding resists her in French, because she isn't part of France, she believes that she can see its ideology, its prejudices, its banalities, represented in the literature—both in tiny details and big structures. Whereas in English the scaffolding of ideology seems to disappear, is too familiar to her.

But haven't I just contradicted myself? I began by arguing that we aren't taught enough about the history and the politics of Algeria and that our textbook has censored out body parts and desire, so we have read L'Etranger indifferently—we have colluded with Meursault. Now I'm saying we get something out of not knowing, out of being foreigners. How can knowing (being historical), and not knowing (being foreign), each take place in the process of reading?

For many years I have thought of history as a prize to catch, context as my goal. My students would know the independence day of Algeria, and no detail in the text would escape some larger understanding. I have worked hard, trying to erase my own ignorance with a search for every allusion, literary and historical. But in the attempt to master context, to make the text fit into its times, there is a risk of doing away with the strangeness, doing away with what we don't understand—which is also a strength. Do we want to kill the alienation that we bring to our reading, the critical edge that foreigners—whoever they are, wherever they are—bring to a host culture?

What we may fail to see when we try to read Camus historically is his thrill just in knowing how to write, which is both repressed *and* comes through in every word he wrote. The thrill of writing, in the case of Camus, and in the case of Americans reading Camus, is not ahistorical, because it has to do with school and family and linguistic community. It doesn't yield immediately to the pressure of the archive because it is not signaled by description. It has to be gleaned through the pleasure of the sentences themselves. When Camus tells his biographer to "mark" the fact that no one in his family could read, he is marking his ascension to reading. He is astonished at his place in literary history, his arrival. His family was illiterate; Camus was a foreigner to French literature. And at the same time he had always known he was a Frenchman. His success was the triumph of a colonial school system that excluded non-Europeans. In his social and linguistic complexity, Camus urges me to try and re-unite the kind of knowledge that language learning demands—grammar, sounds, tenses—with historical, political knowledge: the two kinds of knowledge I have demanded from *L'Etranger* at two different phases of my education.

The relationship between literature and history is always an imperfect one, a process, like the pedagogical memory of tenses I began with. In the big picture—on the chalk line—Camus is one of a whole series of authors favored in American French departments, all of whom use French at a distance: Duras, daughter of the colonial schoolteacher; Sarraute, learning French as a white Russian; Ionesco, whose plays are parodies of language methods that we transpose back into language methods; and Camus, the good student, the textbook example. They are favored not always because they are "easy" syntactically—in fact their language is often deformed and unconventional—but because these authors speak to us of those moments when language is still raw, thrilled with itself. Of course, language that is thrilled with itself is a *lieu commun* of twentieth-century French prose in a tradition including writers as diverse as Sartre, Leiris, and Roussel. Twentieth-century French literature is, in some important sense, *about language*. And since part of the "civilizing mission" of French colonizers was to inculcate subjects with this metropolitan respect for language in and of itself, readers of colonial French texts cannot ignore style, even as they analyze power. Style can be a defense or a revenge, or—as in the case of Camus—an instrument of mobility. Style and power are not strangers.

Notes

1 A first draft of this essay was written for the conference called "French Studies in the 1990s" held at the University of California at Berkeley in April 1990. I am grateful to Howard Bloch for his invitation to that event. Subsequent versions of the paper were given at Washington University and the University of Wisconsin, Madison, in September 1990 and February 1991. My thanks to Jane Burns, R. W. B. Lewis, Kristin Ross, and Naomi Schor, to Cathy Davidson, Marianna Torgovnick, and Jane Tompkins, and to Linda Orr for their helpful comments at various stages, and to Toril Moi for calling my attention to variants in the French editions of L'Etranger.

2 Maurice Grevisse's venerable Le bon usage (Paris, 1980), the most complete French grammar manual, refers to the imperfect as a "process line."

3 Verb tense has also been a theme in critical writing about L'Etranger. For the idea that Camus favored the passé composé over the imparfait, see Jean-Paul Sartre, "Explication de L'Etranger," in Situations I (Paris, 1947); and Emile Benveniste, "Les relations de temps dans le verbe français," in Problèmes de linguistique générale (Paris, 1966), 237–50; for a polemic against Sartre's "Explication," see Renée Balibar, "La rédaction fictive dans L'Etranger d'Albert Camus," in Les Français fictifs: Le rapport des styles littéraires au français national (Paris, 1974), 231–90. Harald Weinrich, Le Temps (Paris, 1973), 308–14, treats Camus's passé composé as a "judiciary tense."

4 My source was an editor at Prentice Hall/Simon and Schuster, the company that now owns Appleton-Century-Crofts.

5 Germaine Brée, letter to author, 9 February 1990.

6 The Cure, "Killing an Arab" (London, 1979). The cassette is sold with a black label on the wrapper which reads as follows: "The song Killing an Arab has absolutely no racist overtones whatsoever. It is a song which decries the existence of all prejudice and consequent violence. The Cure condemns its use in furthering anti-Arab feeling."

7 Albert Camus, L'Etranger, in Théâtre récits nouvelles, ed. Roger Quilliot (Paris: Gallimard, Bibliothèque de la Pléiade, 1962), 1205.

8 "I could tell you knew about these things" (translation of a verb in the imparfait); "I worked hard all week" (translation of a verb in the passé composé) (Albert Camus, The Stranger, trans. Matthew Ward [New York, 1988], 33–34).

9 The context evoked by Brée and Lynes is that of an intellectual movement —existentialism—and an *esprit du temps* created by the French national experience of the German occupation (Albert Camus, *L'Etranger*, ed. Germaine Brée and Carlos Lynes, Jr. [New York, 1955]). For the history of the novel's first appearance during the Occupation, and the role played by Gallimard in obtaining the support of German cultural ambassador Gerhard Heller, see Herbert R. Lottman, *Albert Camus: A Biography* (Garden City, N.Y., 1979), 248–51; and Pierre Assouline, *Gaston Gallimard: A Half-Century of French Publishing*, trans. Harold Salemson (New York, 1987).

10 Consult, especially, "Un homme, une ville: Albert Camus à Alger, avec Jules Roy," a series of radio interviews by France Culture available in audiocassette from Cassettes Radio France (1978).

11 Julia Kristeva, *Etrangers à nous-mêmes* (Paris, 1988).

12 See Roland Bacri, *Le roro: Dictionnaire pataouète de langue pied-noir* (Paris, 1969).

13 Jules Roy claims Camus's primary school class was one-third Arab ("Un homme, une ville"); Lottman's research refutes him (*Albert Camus*, 32). The statistic on primary schools is from Mahfoud Bennoune, *The Making of Contemporary Algeria 1830–1987* (Cambridge, 1988). According to Bennoune, the illiteracy rate for the total Algerian population was 85 percent as of 1954; the female illiteracy rate was 95 to 98 percent (68).

14 Lottman, *Albert Camus*, 618.

15 Albert Memmi, *Portrait du colonisé précédé de portrait du colonisateur* (Paris, 1985).

16 Frantz Fanon, *Les damnés de la terre* (Paris, 1966):

> Why did he kill? He doesn't answer the question, but asks me if I've ever seen a European in prison. Has there ever been a European in prison, arrested after murdering an Algerian. I answer him that, in effect, I have never seen any Europeans in prison.
>
> "And yet, there are Algerians killed every day, no?"
>
> "Yes."
>
> "So, why are there only Algerians in prison? Can you explain it to me?"
>
> "No, but tell me why you killed this boy who was your friend?" (206; my translation)

17 Criticism of *L'Etranger* since 1960 seems to have approached and then retreated from the question of racial violence in the novel. In 1961, Pierre Nora makes what is generally acknowledged as the first critical intervention linking *L'Etranger* to colonialism—he surmises that the guilty conscience of French "colons" toward Arabs has something to do with the plot of the book (*Les Français d'Algérie* [Paris, 1961]). Conor Cruise O'Brien reads this guilt as bad faith: a Frenchman would not even have gone to trial for murdering an Arab in 1942 (*Albert Camus of Europe and Africa* [New York, 1970]). O'Brien's own passion

in engaging Camus's novel marks a high point of Camus's importance on the American scene. Twenty years later, in an era of postcolonial criticism, the question of Camus is no longer burning. Edward Said, in a tone equally critical yet dismissive in comparison to O'Brien's, describes the Arabs in L'Etranger as "nameless beings used as background for the portentous European metaphysics explored by Camus" ("Representing the Colonized: Anthropology's Interlocutors," Critical Inquiry 15 [Winter 1989]: 205–25). Camus, a pied noir intellectual who wanted to belong to the metropolis, mutes the identities of the Arabs in his novel for the same reason he is reluctant to support Algerian independence. See Mary Ann Witt, "Race and Racism in 'The Stranger' and 'Native Son,'" The Comparatist (1977): 35–47; and Louise K. Horowitz, "Of Women and Arabs: Sexual and Racial Polarization in Camus," Modern Language Studies 17 (Summer 1987): 54–61.

18 Brée, letter to author, 9 February 1990.

19 Those wishing to see the missing sentences restored should write the Prentice Hall College Book Division, Sylvan Avenue, Englewood Cliffs, N.J. 07632.

20 There is an entire corpus of feminist theory devoted to the question "What is a woman's chose?", the chosalité of a woman's desire (see, for example, Naomi Schor's now-famous "clitoral reading" of Edgar Allan Poe's The Purloined Letter, "Female Paranoia: The Case for Psychoanalytic Feminist Criticism," in Breaking the Chain: Women, Theory, and French Realist Fiction [New York, 1985], 149–62).

21 To my best knowledge, "s'amuser avec sa chose" is unheard of in metropolitan French. Pierre Guiraud's Dictionnaire historique, stylistique, rhétorique, étymologique, de la littérature érotique (Paris, 1989) reports that "la chose" in the feminine is used in the phrase "faire la chose" (meaning "to do it"—"la chose" referring to the sexual act). "Le chose" is used with reference to the penis; "la chose" with reference to the "sexe de la femme," although "le chose" can refer to either penis or vagina as instruments of sex, as distinguished from "la chose" meaning the act itself. Guiraud does not mention a clitoral "chose."

22 Albert Camus, The Stranger, trans. Stuart Gilbert (New York, 1946), 38–39; and Ward, trans., The Stranger, 31. This use of the substantive "coït" with an ambiguous possessive pronoun (his, hers, their coitus together?) is exceedingly uncommon. It is possible that both the phrases "s'amuser avec sa chose" and "avoir un sentiment pour son coït" have some relationship to North African French dialect. André Lanly insists on the increased use of reflexive pronouns (pronoms d'intérêt) among North African French speakers due to Spanish and Provençal influences (Le Français d' Afrique du Nord: Etude linguistique [Paris, 1970]).

23 Camus was in France when he finished L'Etranger, on the eve of that country's capitulation to the Nazis. The war delayed the novel's publication until 1942. A full sociohistorical analysis of the novel and its reception would, of course,

consider North Africa's highly ambiguous site in the geography of Occupied France and its uncertain status as Vichy or free territory, well after mainland France had fallen to the Germans.

24   For the social nuances of words such as "Maure," "arabe," "Algériens," "Musulman," etc., see Lanly's *Français d' Afrique du Nord*.

25   The dearth of readings of any of Camus's work informed by feminist scholarship is astonishing, but there are two notable exceptions: Louise Horowitz places *L'Etranger* in the tradition of the homoerotic fable as defined in the American context by Leslie Fiedler. She suggests in a note that the murder of the Arab by Meursault might be read closely as rape (see "Of Women and Arabs"). In sharp contrast, see Vicki Mistacco's analysis of "La femme adultère," the only Camus story in which a woman is the main character ("Nomadic Meanings: The Woman Effect in 'La femme adultère,'" in *Albert Camus' L'exil et le royaume: The Third Decade*, ed. Anthony Rizzuto [Toronto, 1988], 73–86). Mistacco is currently working on a feminist reading of *L'Etranger*. As possible homoerotic models for an analysis of the Meursault-Raymond relationship, see Judith Fetterley's *The Resisting Reader: A Feminist Approach to American Fiction* (Bloomington, 1978); and Eve Kosofsky Sedgwick's *Between Men: English Literature and Male Homosocial Desire* (New York, 1985).

26   Albert Camus, *L'Etranger*, 1166; my translation. See the Pléiade edition for a 1942 variant.

27   The glorification of misogyny by the avant-garde is not a new theme in feminist criticism; it goes back at least as far as Kate Millett. Margaret Waller, in her study of gender and the nineteenth-century "mal du siècle"—might be reexamined for its gendered aspects ("*Chercher la femme*: Male Malady and Narrative Politics in the French Romantic Novel," *PMLA* 104 [March 1989]: 141–51). *L'Etranger* would be key to such a study, both in terms of the text and its reception. O'Brien, for example, points out that although Meursault clearly deceives Raymond's mistress and lies to the police, his students nonetheless see Meursault as a "hero and martyr for the truth" and identify with him (*Albert Camus of Europe and Africa*, 20). On avant-garde misogyny in a wide range of literary texts and cultural artifacts, see Marianna Torgovnick's *Gone Primitive: Savage Intellects, Modern Lives* (Chicago, 1990).

28   The course was inspired by a course that Ann Smock developed for the civilization curriculum at University of California, Berkeley, and that Kristin Ross and I have each taught versions of, independently, at Duke University and University of California, Santa Cruz.

29   Carl A. Viggiani, "Notes pour le futur biographe d'Albert Camus," in *Albert Camus: Autour de l'Etranger*, ed. Brian T. Fitch (Paris, 1968), 206.

30   Roger Grenier, in yet another edition of *L'Etranger*, attributes to the critic Roger

Quilliot the idea that Camus transposed certain aspects of *cagayous*, a popular Algerian speech pattern, in creating Raymond's speeches and more generally in the play of the *passé composé* and *imparfait* in the text (*Oeuvres complètes d' Albert Camus*, ed. Roger Grenier [Paris, 1983], 25).

31 Lottman, *Albert Camus*, 380.

32 Gilbert's translation kills the figure by explaining too much: "And each successive shot was another loud, fateful rap on the door of my undoing" (*The Stranger*, 76).

Decades

NANCY K. MILLER

The year 1990 was Year Zero of the post-Cold War world.—Richard J. Barnet (New Yorker, 1991)

I am convinced that the politics of saving the family will be the politics of the 90's.—Gary L. Bauer (New York Times, 1991)

Meaning is in for the 90's. It's got a beat and you can dance to it.—Bob Holman (New York Times, 1990)

There's something almost irresistible about decades, about taking them as an index by which to measure social change or to identify the spirit of an age: the culture and values of a generation. The seductiveness of decades is exceptionally powerful at their turn—even more so at the end of a century, not to say a millennium. Of course it's a lot easier to name a decade when it's over, than when it's just begun. In the United States the 1980s were, everyone seems to agree, a time of greed—junk bonds, leveraged buyouts, and S&L scandals. If that's what we're coming out of, what, in the aftermath of "Desert Storm," are we heading into? A recent cartoon, which appeared in the New Yorker (3 September 1990), underlines the difficulty. Two men in hardhats are standing in a lumber yard. One says to the other: "Well, Al, the sixties was *peace*. The seventies was *sex*. The eighties was *money*. Maybe the nineties will be *lumber*." What will the 1990s be? If not lumber, what? One's guess depends on one's vantage point: let me begin with my own.

Maybe I'm attracted to decades because I was born with one, or almost. But since decades rarely follow the neatness of chronology, I don't think the difference really counts. In any event, for me, the 1960s were my twenties, the 1970s my thirties, the 1980s my forties. I feel particularly lured into thinking by decades now because we've entered a new one and because I've just turned fifty: this is a decade I cannot fail to take seriously, which is also to say personally. In what follows I reread these decades autobiographically, and at the same time through the grid of academic feminism: trying to keep alive the tension between the detail of my experience and the history of feminism in the institution, and ending with a look at the dilemmas confronting us as feminists in the 1990s. This attempt to hold the individual and the institutional together through an autobiographical narrative should be seen both as a continuation of earlier modes of feminist performance—which emerged from the empowering conviction that "the personal is the political"—and as a renewed practice within the current collective academic project to construct an *archives*: to produce a feminist retrospective.

Like most decades, mine coincide imperfectly with units of ten. I date academic feminism with the first publications that in the United States mark its beginnings—Mary Ellman's *Thinking about Women* (1968) and Kate Millett's *Sexual Politics* (1970)—but for my own part I begin before that beginning, in my unconscious struggles over issues of gender and power (those terms were *not* in my vocabulary at the time) in the early 1960s.[1]

=====

Before Feminism: 1962–1968. In the 1950s, as Rachel Brownstein remembers it, we dreamed of going to Paris:

> Ideally, one would be Simone de Beauvoir, smoking with Sartre at the Deux Magots, making an eccentric domestic arrangement that was secondary to important things and in their service. One would be poised, brilliant, equipped with a past, above the fray, beyond it, foreign not domestic. (And ideally Sartre would look like Albert Camus.)[2]

It's 1962. I've just turned twenty-one in Paris. For my birthday, my roommate at the Foyer International des Jeunes Filles has given me a copy of the *Lettres portugaises*, which she has inscribed with a message that invites me to consider how wonderful it is to be like the *religieuse portugaise*—young and passionate—and concludes: "Dis 'fuck you' à tous les garçons [she was learning English from the Americans who ate down-stairs at the Foyer's student restaurant] et aime-les." This edition of the letters, in which the typeface looks like handwriting, is illustrated by Modigliani drawings of women looking unhappy, or at least withdrawn poignantly into themselves. Modigliani is an artist whose images of elon-gated women I at the time find entrancing. I am knocked out by these letters. They are written, I think, by a real Portuguese nun, Mariana Alfo-carado, seduced and abandoned by a real, if anonymous, Frenchman, and obsessing about it. I identify completely, even though I'm of course not Portuguese (not to mention a nun). I have only begun to meet Frenchmen myself and I can tell already that I'm out of my depth.

I'm also studying for my M.A. with the Middlebury Program in Paris and taking a year-long seminar on Laclos. Antoine Adam, an authority on the early history of the novel in France, standing in front of the lectern in a huge amphitheater of the Sorbonne, produces a weekly lecture on Les liaisons dangereuses. I'm supposed to write an essay on it; the choice of topic is up to me. The program has assigned me a tutor whose task it is to over-see the writing. I'll call him M. Souilliez. He lives on a dark street in the cinquième arrondissement, on a steep incline, somewhere near the Sorbonne, maybe behind the Pantheon. It's April. A first draft of the mémoire is long overdue; I haven't begun the outline (the outline, "le plan," is at the heart of the French educational system). I have spent Christmas in Italy with an American boyfriend on a motorcycle; Easter vacation with my roommate at her home in Tunisia where I have discovered, among other things, the art of leg waxing with lemon and sugar. I don't know how I'm going to write this essay, let alone an outline for it.

In despair I go to see the répétiteur one evening in his apartment. We sit in the living room and talk about Les liaisons dangereuses; we talk, that is to say, about sex. I am inwardly panicked because I cannot come up with an essay topic, so I try to appear worldly and unconcerned, and with studied casualness hold forth on sex and love, and men and women. Suddenly, I get an idea: I'll write on the women in the novel, how each of them is betrayed by the images others have of them and that they each have of themselves. I sit at a table opposite M. Souilliez and start to make an outline. I'm inspired, excited. As I write, he gets up and walks around the room. I forget about him—I'm so happy that I at last have an idea! Then as I sit at the table, I feel a hand on my breast. M. Souilliez, standing behind my chair, has reached down and slipped his hand through my blouse around my left breast. I stop writing.

Despite the fact that I realize the moment I feel the hand feeling me that I have been chattering away about precisely these kinds of moves in the novel, it hasn't really occurred to me to make the connection between seduction (not to say sex) and M. Souilliez.[3] I am now nonplussed. I try to imagine that I'm Madame de Merteuil, not Cécile, even though I feel a lot more like a schoolgirl than a libertine (that's Cécile's problem in a nutshell, of course). I don't want to have to go to bed with M. Souilliez (he's "old" and not, I think, my type) but I also don't want a bad grade. The hand is still moving around inside the blouse. I remove the hand and sigh. "Oh monsieur," I say, pausing, and hoping for the world-weary tone of the Marquise in my best American jeune fille French, "j'ai déjà tant d'ennuis sans cela."

He goes no further, shrugs (in a Parisian gesture which seems to mean either: it's your loss or you can't blame a guy for trying), and lets me leave. I race down the stairs out into the street and up the Boulevard St-Michel to the Foyer. When I get back to my room, I begin to wonder how much harm I've done myself. I finally write the essay—"La femme et l'amour dans Les liaisons dangereuses: La trahison de l'être par l'image"—and wait for the grade. The comments in the margins alternate between, "b," bien, and "md," mal dit. In general, I seem to have more insights than argumentative force. I take too long getting to the point: "What you say is true and interesting, but what's happened to your outline?" ("Le plan.") I expect the quotations to do the work of commentary (they should play only a supporting role). And my favorite: "Never hesitate to be clear." In the light, I suppose, of these weaknesses, and despite a nice overall comment (he thinks I'm smart), I get a mediocre grade on the essay (my own fault, I tell myself, for doing it all at the last minute; it really wasn't very good, anyway).

In 1968 when, having returned to New York, I decided to apply to graduate school, I went through my box of "important papers" and discovered the M.A. essay.[4] I looked at the grade on the title page and it suddenly seemed to me—correctly, as it turned out—that the number grade (French style) was the equivalent not of the "B" on my transcript, but an "A"; the number had been mistranscribed. In 1968, it still didn't dawn on me to be angry about M. Souilliez's hand down my blouse. By then, flirting with a libertine incarnation of my own (I took the sexual revolution seriously), I congratulated myself instead, Merteuil-like, for having played the right card (didn't I get an "A"?). Recently, I ran into an old friend I knew when I was first living in Paris. I asked her if she remembered my scene with the tutor. "Oh yes," she said, "at the time we thought that sort of thing was flattering."

═══

I sometimes think that I have missed everything important to my generation: 1968 in Paris, 1968 at Columbia. The 1960s really, although I did hear the Beatles sing on (pirate) Radio Caroline, "I Want to Hold Your Hand."

═══

During Feminism: 1969–1977. I'm in graduate school at Columbia and feminism is in the streets . . . at least in a mainstream kind of way.

August 26, 1970, is the first annual nationwide "Women's Strike for Equality." Friends and I join the march down Fifth Avenue to celebrate the fiftieth anniversary of suffrage. Kate Millett publishes *Sexual Politics* and makes the cover of *Time Magazine*. At Town Hall, it's Germaine Greer et al. (*The Female Eunuch* came out in the States in 1971) vs. Norman Mailer. Mailer can't understand why women would become lesbians. After all, men can do to women what women do to each other—90 percent—and then some. Jill Johnston walks off the stage in disgust and embraces her lover in sight of the audience.[5]

There is, in general, lots of writing and talk about female orgasm, how many (multiple, preferably), and what kind.

In January 1971, after reading an article by Vivian Gornick in the *New York Times Magazine* about consciousness-raising groups, some friends and I start our own group.[6] At our first meeting, we are amazed by our commonalities. In particular, we talk about how we don't want to be like our mothers, who, we believe, did not know what they wanted. What do we want? The specifics are not clear but the project involves taking charge of one's own life. It is nothing less than a fantasy of total control: not only having what we want, but on our own terms and timetable. The point of the group as we see it is to help each other bring this about: not to be a victim.

What does this mean for graduate school? In graduate school, where the men are the teachers and the women the students, it's harder to say when things begin (certainly not in courses); it's more about things coming together—personally. One day, the man who was to be the second reader on my dissertation, an eighteenth-century specialist, a man in his sixties, takes me aside to issue a dire warning: "Don't try to be another Kate Millett"—*Sexual Politics* was originally a Columbia English department Ph.D. thesis—"she wasn't first-rate to begin with." This man, who had coedited a popular anthology on the Enlightenment, taught a course on eighteenth-century French literature (from the anthology) in which, to see whether we had done the reading, he would pull questions out of a hat and match them with some hapless student. This had something to do with why I didn't want him as my advisor. But he did tell great stories: in fact, the account he gave of Julie de L'Espinasse's life, the way a real woman (and a great letter writer) "died of love," sealed my fate: of course I was going to "be" in the eighteenth century.

In June 1972, fortified by our ongoing weekly discussions in the group, I take the plunge. I'm going to get serious about my work (no more reading; it's time; I'm thirty-one years old—old!): write the dissertation.[7] I buy an electric typewriter; second-hand filing cabinets on 23rd Street, and a door that when placed on top of them makes a desk; I declare my thesis topic (equipment first): "Gender and Genre: An Analysis of Literary Femininity in the French and English 18th-Century Novel." In those days in the Columbia French department this is also called a stylistic structural analysis. I am going to analyze nine novels according to the principles of narratology and rhetoric: Propp and Greimas, Riffaterre and Genette, Barthes and Kristeva. I am going to do this, I say, as a feminist.[8]

I had become a feminist and a structuralist together. That's a little condensed: this happened in a single temporality, though on separate tracks. Feminism meant the group, *Ms. Magazine*, feminist fiction, and a whole set of what today we might more portentously call cultural practices. It meant a revolution in relationships—between women, between women and men—and one's perception of the real—in material and symbolic terms (even if we didn't talk that way). Feminism had to do with our lives. And yet despite pockets of activity—the annual Barnard "Scholar and Feminist" conference, the occasional undergraduate offering—the academic institution was impervious to the dramatic changes occurring in social relations wrought by feminism. Despite 1968, even at Columbia. Affirmative action began officially in 1972, but its immediate effects were (and remain) almost invisible (as far as I know, the tiny number of tenured women has not changed at Columbia since the early 1970s).

In 1972, as I remember things, the phrase "feminist criticism" was not yet an acknowledged working category, at least not on the fifth floor of Philosophy Hall where formalism reigned supreme.[9] There was literary criticism and there was feminism (feminist perspectives, the phrase often went). They could illuminate each other, but they were separate: separate but equal? I liked to think that criticism and feminism worked together. After all, both are modes of critique: the one of the ideology that regulates the relations between men and women in culture and society; the other, of modes of criticism blind to their own ideology about literature and art. It's hard to see now, but in the early 1970s, structuralism, as it was understood in American universities, seemed to mean a break with a reactionary past: the men's club model of lit. crit., carried out today by people like Denis Donoghue and Helen Vendler. This "science of literature" was exciting, enabling; it provided a new language: a fantasy of total clarity. In the rupture of the continuity binding literature to the world—but whose world?—at last we could see what was going on. I can still remember the moment when in a study group I understood Saussure's model of the sign: never again would I confuse the word and the thing; sign and referent; signifier and signified (little knowing that Lacan had already turned this upside down).[10] This epiphany was on a par only with the thrill of discovering binary oppositions and how they organize cultural universes. Lévi-Strauss delivered the truth of this fact in person in the Barnard College gym in 1972 (this gives an idea of the jet lag that characterizes the intellectual traffic between France and the United States).[11] What I mainly remember from this event was the conviction (his, then rapidly mine) that binary oppositions were embedded functionally in the brain. For me, it all went together perfectly with Beauvoir's magisterial analyses of the polarizing operations that opposed man as Same to woman as Other, and even with the lowly housewife's "click" that Jane O'Reilly dissected famously in Ms. In both cases, the principles of analysis rescued you from the murk of ambiguity (not to say personal confusion) and privileged authority (the variously tweeded "I's" and "we's" of a 1950s legacy). Between the capacious categories of narratology and the stringent lines of feminist hermeneutics, there was no text we—a new "we"—couldn't crack. It was a heady moment.

Is it true that there was no problem in articulating feminism and struc-

turalism together? Yes and no. It's probably that combination of enthu-
siasms that British reviewers of the book (about French and English
eighteenth-century novels) my thesis finally became—The Heroine's Text
(1980)—found so deadly: structuralist jargon and feminist ideology. I kept
seeing the same story everywhere, they complained. Well, yes, that's the
whole point (which American academics—at least the feminist ones—
generally got). Those objections to my language and approach (plot summary, as the unkinder put it) bothered me less (even if they were insulting
and sort of true) than a certain feminist refusal of the project for "ideological" reasons. There were those who felt (1) that all formalism was
male, hence incompatible with feminist analysis, and (2) that the task of
feminism was to respond to the issues of "real" women. In that sense I
was indeed guilty as charged. Women were strikingly absent from my dissertation. When I chose the expression "literary femininity" I meant it to
mark my distance from anything real and to sound theoretically advanced
(to ward off the ambient disdain that "working on women" generated):
women in fiction, but with an emphasis on narrative; female destiny, with
an emphasis on plot. This was my way of showing my difference both
from Kate Millett (the incarnation of "strident" feminism) and from the
mode of "images of women" that had already begun to emerge in English
studies. Any historical considerations were necessarily foreclosed. On the
one hand, the historical seemed like an antiquated belief in the referent;
on the other, the invocation of the historical as the truth-value of literature, the dominant mode of eighteenth-century studies, was the very
thing I wanted most to escape from and oppose.[12]

And of course I was dealing with respected male authors, major figures
(with the exception of the bad boys Sade and Cleland, forgiven because of
outrageousness and sex), and famous books. It was the canon, although
the term wasn't bandied about at that point. And women authors? The
entire time I was a graduate student, during lectures, reading for semi-
nars, for the thesis, I never once asked myself the question of female
authorship, despite the fact that I must have read some women writers for
course work or exams: Marie de France, Louise Labé, Marie-Madeleine
de Lafayette, Germaine de Staël (the last two known then, of course,
as Mme de). Besides, by the time I started writing my dissertation, the
Author (male) was Dead, intentions a fallacy, and all I cared about was
The Text. I blamed—if I blamed—texts for the representation of women,

not authors. And not even texts: texts were prisoners of ideology just as men were prisoners of sex.

After my thesis defense it was reported to me that the sole woman on the jury (one of Columbia's classic tokens) had praised me for "sitting on my feelings." I've never been absolutely sure what that meant: that I was tautologically angry because feminist, but my writing was cool and "scientific"? Or that through the elaborate veils of my narratological tables she could tell I really cared. About what? About the logic of "female plot" that killed off heroines—exquisite cadavers as I called them in my first article—at the story's close?

What I really cared about then, I think, had as much to do with my own plot as with the fictional destiny of women in the eighteenth-century novel. At stake—if buried—in the ponderous prose of my structuralist feminism was the inscription of my plot: my own "coming to writing"— "as a woman"—to invoke the language of a feminist literary criticism that was to flower after the mid-1970s.[13] Despite the hierarchies and abuses of academic conventions, I saw writing a dissertation as something radical, but also literary: as becoming the heroine of my life. Despite the so-called feminization of the profession, my getting a Ph.D. felt like a violation of gender expectations. In 1961, having gathered my ideas about appropriate intellectual and domestic arrangements in the America of the late 1950s, it seemed natural for my college boyfriend to get a doctorate; my fate was to get an M.A. and teach high-school French, unless, of course—my mother's 1950s fantasy for me—I married well and got to be a woman of leisure who spoke French only in Europe. When, a decade later, I started writing and saw the pages pile up on my desk—a lot of the time spent at my desk involved admiring the height of the chapters—it seemed miraculous: as though someone else were responsible for producing the work. The man I lived with at the time, who had mixed emotions about my passion for the enterprise, did a drawing of me sitting with my hands thrown up in the air, as if in astonishment, watching the pages—produced by my cat pounding away at the typewriter—fly upward with a life of their own. But when my typist met me with the final version of the manuscript, I burst into uncontrollable tears on Broadway at 116th Street: I suppose that's part of what I was "sitting on" during the defense.

Part, but not the whole story. I was not, of course, merely a tearful heroine overcome by the events taking place around her. I was also the author of her destiny. I had a very clear sense of having done the work and wanting to own it. And so, in 1973, inspired by the example of Judy Chicago, I renamed myself. I had been using my ex-husband's name—I married briefly and unhappily in the mid-1960s—and the idea of seeing the signifier of my misery embossed on my diploma seemed suddenly and thoroughly unacceptable. At the same time, the idea of returning to my father's (also my "maiden") name seemed dangerously regressive. Not bold enough to go all the way and call myself Nancy New York, or to pick a name that pleased me out of the phone book, I took my mother's name, Miller. It was not lost on me that this was still to take a man's— my grandfather's—name, nor that I was taking the name of my worthiest adversary, my mother.[14] Despite these contradictions, it seemed an irresistible solution.

I will admit to a certain homesickness for the gestures of those years in feminism that now have come to seem transparent, like being called Ms. I sometimes long for the conviction we had then that changing the language counted for something.

=====

And why don't you write? Write! Writing is for you, you are for you; your body is yours, take it.—Hélène Cixous, "The Laugh of the Medusa"

Feminist Literary Criticism: 1978–1989. By the fall of 1978, after having taught my first course—a graduate seminar—on (French) women authors, I wrote "Emphasis Added" (the second of my essays on women's writing). I had both regressed to and returned from the Portuguese nun. I had fully lived out Simone de Beauvoir's analysis of the *grande amoureuse*—the woman hopelessly and desperately in love—and changed literatures. I wrote this essay, which takes its examples from Lafayette's *La Princesse de Clèves* and Eliot's *The Mill on the Floss*, in total solitude, in the aftermath of a story with a Frenchman that had turned out badly (let's just say that I had renunciation thrust upon me). When I discovered—by teaching the letters in a course on women writers—that the Portuguese nun was really a man (a literary hack) in drag, I was more embarrassed at my ignorance, I think, than disappointed. Besides, I didn't need her anymore: I didn't need to be in love to write. That was half of the story; the other half was falling in love with the Princess of Clèves: the heroine and the novel.

When I say that I fell in love I mean both that this book swept me away and that it took me somewhere. Working on "Emphasis Added" six years after starting to write my dissertation was like a second coming to writing. The dissertation was still sitting on my desk waiting to be revised, transformed (one hoped) into the tenure book. It seemed to me that I needed to do another kind of writing in order to talk about women writers; but the old task demanded its due and the two projects were at odds with each other. As it turned out, it was writing the new essay that allowed me to finish the old book, to finish off a certain past with the flourish of an epilogue. Those few pages are the only part of that book I can still bear to read.

I wrote the epilogue to *The Heroine's Text* in a single sitting, in rage against an anonymous and extremely hostile (female) reader's report. I wish—or I think I wish—I still had a copy of the report. As I recollect it, the reader complained—among other things—that I didn't seem to realize that the novels I analyzed were written by men. This felt at the time an outrageous objection to make to me, of all people! Still, I had to ponder the remark and it led me to make the point explicitly at the close of the book: that these novels were written by men for men through the double fiction of the female reader and her heroine (male bonding before homosociality). It also led me to think about my complete failure to consider what difference women's fictions would have made to my argument about the limited arrangements of closure that I called the heroine's text. That was a point less easily fixed. It seems to me now that a lot of the energy that fueled my writing after the epilogue came from a desire for reparation: How could I not have taken female authorship into account from the beginning?

The move to working on women's writing had a double effect on my career and on my sense of myself as a feminist critic. Once I started working on women writers and on feminist criticism as literary theory, I felt myself to be instantly losing status: not within the feminist community at large, of course, but within the little world of French departments that I was used to. (I'm still not sure whether this is true, or just what I worried about.) No doubt this anxiety was bound up with the fact that at the same time (before coming up for tenure) I began to "leave the century"—what would it mean not to "have" a period? But that is the matter of another reflection about the organization of literary studies.[15]

At one point, a feminist critic brought me up against this anxiety of authority as we were returning from a conference in which I had given a paper on women's autobiography: "You've always worked on women, haven't you?" she asked. Panic-stricken, I cringed inside myself: she was right. Male authors, but women all the same. I never would be taken seriously. Not for me all the stories of the first, "real" tenure book "for them," and how one then saw the light: and worked on women. This was not, it turned out, what she was getting at, but it fueled my paranoia. If I had always been a feminist in my work on male writers, "working on women" seemed to make me into a different (read "lower") order of feminist: soft instead of hard, marginal instead of central.

Nonetheless, that was where I was going; nor was I alone. Despite, or perhaps because of the excitement, even the scandal, of *Sexual Politics* and the success of Judith Fetterley's *The Resisting Reader* in 1978, the trend in feminist literary studies was moving massively toward the study of women's writing. With the publication in 1976 of *Literary Women*, in 1977 of *A Literature of Their Own*, and in 1979 of *Madwoman in the Attic* the turn had been taken. A first step in splitting the field in two was Elaine Showalter's almost generic distinction between feminist "critique" (to describe work on male literature) and "criticism" (for work on women's), and the valorization of the latter; the distinction was consolidated with the baptism in 1979 of the study of women's writing as "gynocritics." Although since the publication of Eve Kosofsky Sedgwick's *Between Men* (1985) the interest and value of studying "gender" and men's writing have now been rethought, for many years the consequences of the split meant that feminist criticism (the good kind) came to imply working solely on women's writing.[16]

For me to have resisted the turn to women's writing would perhaps have required greater explanation than my involvement with it. And again I am struck with the difficulty and strangeness of evoking a time when just *saying* "women's writing" had a radical edge to it. When I began to "work on women" in the late 1970s, I had no idea of what that was going to mean for me and more generally for developments in feminist theory. My immediate reaction was a new sense of self-authorization that changed my relation to all of the issues in the profession—especially to "theory"—and changed my identity within it.[17] This is because in North American feminist criticism, by an interesting process of slippage, authorial subjectivity (itself implicitly constructed on the model of the heroine) became a homologue for female agency. Through these effects of substitution, it became possible for me, a reader of novels (alternately, a critical heroine), to cast myself (at least in my own eyes) as a feminist theorist. Or so it seemed at the time. By the early 1980s, the metaphorization of feminist theory had been accomplished. This process, which can be tracked, if a little too neatly, by two titles that seem to echo each other—*Madwoman in the Attic* (1979) and *Honey-Mad Women* (1988)—was emblematic of the decade's intellectual style.[18] Although differences of position separate these two powerful works that I'm placing here as bookends of an extraordinarily productive period in literary studies, Sandra Gilbert and Susan Gubar, on the one hand, and Patricia Yaeger, on the other, rely importantly on metaphors of female experience and identity to make their cases.

The 1980s saw the widespread formalization of Women's Studies programs, many of which had come into being in the late 1970s, throughout the United States. In 1981, when I moved across the street from Columbia to Barnard as the director of their fledgling Women's Studies program, it seemed to me (and this was part of what allowed me to take an administrative job that I was otherwise unprepared for) that the rise of feminist scholarship as an institutional force derived at least in part from the sense of self-, but finally, collective-authorization that "working on women" provided. From my office with the decorator-purple (we hoped subversive) walls, I wrote a book-length collection of memos, characterized by the rhetorical turns of feminist righteousness, demanding courses and prose in a style a colleague from political science taught me, called "bullets" (you take aim at your interlocutor with pellets of information; my memo style, she explained, was too narrative).

By 1985, however, that interlocking sense of personal conviction and political solidarity—speaking "as a feminist" for all women—had begun to erode within the feminist community. (Put another way, this was the moment when mainstream feminists finally began to pay attention to internal divisions that had been there from the beginning.) By 1985, the date I assign somewhat arbitrarily to this crisis in representativity, women of color refused a definition of feminism that by the whiteness of its universal subject did not include them, and post-structuralist critics looked suspiciously upon a binary account of gender with referential claims; did we really want to posit a *female* experience as the ground of women's identity?[19] Not to be left out, mainstream academics (male and female), who saw themselves as upholders of literary standards, trounced feminist critics for confusing aesthetics and sociology. Couldn't we tell art from women? This last position, which has continued to thrive in the 1990s (I'm thinking of Helen Vendler's recent attack on the excesses and failures of feminist criticism in "Feminism and Literature"), in many ways announces the colors of the 1990s to date: a return to a 1950s Cold War ideology that takes the form of an intertwined belief in Art and the Individual.[20]

=====

Bob Dylan is clearly the first rock-and-roller to reach 50 as a meaningful artist.—Dave Marsh (New York Times, 1991)

After Feminism? 1990–. I became a feminist critic along with a certain history: as it was being made around me. By this I mean that my decades of intellectual formation coincided with those of another chronology, a chronology of social revolution. I said earlier that I had missed 1968. That's true if we think of 1968 as a single apocalyptic event, or even as a network of events with specific locales: the Sorbonne, Berkeley, Columbia. But 1968, we know, can also be seen as a trope: the figure of diffuse political movements, including feminism, that came to restructure the social imaginary. In this sense 1968 didn't miss me.

Teresa de Lauretis has argued famously that feminism's unique method was what in the United States we referred to as "consciousness raising" and what she prefers to call, through translation back from Italian, the practice of "self-consciousness."[21] And certainly it was in the space of this group work that I began for the first time to make sense of my life as a good daughter of the patriarchy. What flowered from those moments and flashes of insight were the elements of an analysis—a reading—that would make a larger kind of sense when articulated collectively. The decades of the 1970s and 1980s saw the invention of new social subjects, critics and readers who, in the cultural aftermath of 1968, created the feminism we now look back on.[22] Whether one calls this the institutionalization or, as I prefer, the textualization of feminism, what matters is the fact of that construction: the library of feminism's literatures.

But, you may say, this sounds so elegiac, as though what matters to you were solely the invention of feminism's noble past, or worse, its future anterior: what feminism will have been. It's true. At fifty, like Lot's wife, I seem rigidly turned toward the past. What have I left behind? Despite the fashion look-alikes, it's not the 1960s and I don't have to worry about M. Souilliez's hand down my blouse. It's not the 1970s and I don't have to hide my rage in writing from my judges. It's not the 1980s and I'm not running a Women's Studies program. Still, you point out, sexual harassment is an ever-present feature of academic life for students, and they, like our younger colleagues, continue to undergo Lucy Snowe's command performances. You're just giving us a personal narrative of escape from certain penalties of youth and more vulnerable professional location. What is it exactly that you miss?

I confess: I look back wishfully to the 1970s and the extraordinary conjunction of structuralism and feminism that fed both my writing and my life. But, most of all, I miss the passion of community (what we took for community), and our belief that things would change. In *Conflicts in Feminism*, Evelyn Fox Keller comments on her attachment to this period: "If I were to name one feature of femininist theorizing in the seventies for which I am openly nostalgic, it is the conviction then widely held that there was important work to be done—work that could be supported in the name of feminism not because all feminists held the same priorities, but because that work had a radical thrust from which, we believed, feminists—and women—would generally gain some benefit." [23] The loss to contemporary feminism of the energy that emerged from that conviction cannot be underestimated, even if the reasons for it are important. Keller adds: "We have learned well the lesson that differences can be suppressed; I suggest we need also to learn that commonalities can be as facilely denied as they were once assumed."

Perhaps this is what lumber for contemporary feminism will entail: a rebuilding of alliances on new grounds. Reconstruction after our civil wars.

Having arrived at this point, I should now adopt a more confident, visionary tone and scan the cultural firmament for signs of things to come: portents for feminism in the 1990s. But that would require that I feel either prepared to speak for feminism, or willing, as I had been so often in the past, to predict what its next moves might and should be. I seem instead to be more at ease reviewing (even teaching) the history of a

feminist past than imagining its future; waiting, as the decade unfolds, to
see what the critical subjects we have created in our students will bring
about. The 1990s, in this sense, are theirs, and lumber what they make
of it.

=====

That would have been a graceful way to end, and because not altogether
unpredictable, rhetorically satisfying: a return to the pedagogical relations with which I began, only with me no longer the student—not me
as the object of a botched "seduction," or sitting at the master's feet. Me
as the teacher. Yes, but a little disingenuous too. As if the matter of generations and the transmission of feminism's body of knowledge were an easy
matter; as if I had forgotten the painful ironies of the feminist classroom
in which female authority is regularly contested.[24]

The ending I want here will have to deal with what links a singular and
a collective destiny, the tangled figures of representativity: what is and
isn't unique in the construction of a subjectivity.

I have been personally identified with academic feminism over two
decades, emotionally and intellectually attached to the crises of its development. The intensity of that cathexis may explain why I cannot see
clearly where "we" are going. To some extent my uncertainty is an effect
of feminism's historicity: its self-critical movement into middle age, the
pondered doubt of retrospection. But it would be more honest to admit
that the failure of vision I experience emerges from the panic of my own
aging. The panic, which occasionally assumes the shape of impatience
(notably with our official pieties), has a lot to do with the ways in which
feminism and its history have irrevocably shaped the plot of my life—the
trajectory and detours of my own story.[25] But it also has to do with the
infrequent stories of women's lives after fifty.[26] Is there life for a female
academic after the feminist plot of tenure and promotion?

I can't see from here how that life-writing is going to turn out. For the
time being, however, I find myself needing to resist the lure of feminism's
self-authorization. This has meant, among other things, the experiment
of an explicitly autobiographical criticism: an attempt to free myself from
the compulsion to represent feminism (feminism's founding gesture) as
though I had no differences from its positions. I'm not saying that I no
longer believe "as a feminist" in our interventions; nor have I stopped

"working on women." Rather that for me this work now requires another language and another set of conventions for performing it.

Notes

1 The books that electrified me then were Doris Lessing's *The Golden Notebook* and Simone de Beauvoir's *Memoirs of a Dutiful Daughter*. They gave me clues to other ways of being a woman, but I wasn't ready to do anything about it.
2 Rachel M. Brownstein, *Becoming a Heroine* (New York, 1982), 18.
3 In a recent book on Simone de Beauvoir that a friend gave me for my fiftieth birthday, Judity Okely, a British anthropologist who is exactly my age, describes her encounters with Frenchmen in Paris circa 1961, which seemed eerily familiar. I was struck by her account of spending the night—without losing her virginity—with a man who, "over breakfast" asked her "to read aloud the seduction scene from Laclos's *Les Liaisons Dangereuses* . . ." (Judith Okely, *Simone de Beauvoir* [New York, 1986], 13).
4 I talk about this decision, which I saw at the time primarily as leading to a way of earning a living teaching French less awful than high-school teaching, in "The French Mistake," in *Getting Personal: Feminist Occasions and Other Autobiographical Acts* (New York, 1991).
5 *Ms. Magazine* includes this event in its time line for 1971.
6 Four of us—myself, Hester Eisenstein, Bethany Ladimer, and Naomi Schor—subsequently became feminist scholars; one, Ellen Sweet, became an editor at *Ms. Magazine*; another, Elizabeth Silk, became a therapist committed to women's issues.
7 Actually, writing the dissertation seemed a solitary undertaking of such enormous moment that I withdrew from the group and indeed from therapy in order to "work." (I returned to both after "finishing.") Holed up in a tiny room in a ground-floor tenement in the Village, I wrote cut off from the pleasure of the support that had gotten me there in the first place. I guess that was my idea of being a scholar (though I did watch daytime TV for relief).
8 Rereading this after having seen a three-hour profile on Richard M. Nixon on public television, I try to think about what it might mean to have been writing a dissertation during the Vietnam War and Watergate. I learn that on June 23, 1972, as I was, perhaps, drafting an introduction to "Gender and Genre," Richard Nixon was having a conversation with H. R. Haldeman about diverting the FBI. I easily remember spending hours watching the Watergate proceedings on TV in total fascination and indignation, but I can make no connections between the privacy of the desk and the public scenes.

9   My memory here turns out to be slightly at odds with the history of feminist
     criticism in English studies, where the Chicago MLA meeting of 1970 is the
     scene of feminist criticism's originary event: a session sponsored by the Com-
     mission on the Status of Women in the Profession (formed in 1969) at which
     Adrienne Rich read "When We Dead Awaken." Fraya Katz-Stoker published
     "The Other Criticism: Feminism vs. Formalism" in 1972, in Susan Koppelman
     Cornillon's pioneering anthology, *Images of Women in Fiction: Feminist Perspectives*
     (Bowling Green, 1972). Carolyn Heilbrun and Catharine Stimpson's "Theories
     of Feminist Criticism: A Dialogue" took place in 1973 and was published in
     1975 in Josephine Donovan's now classic *Feminist Literary Criticism: Explorations
     in Theory* (Lexington, 1975). If datable, as we look back, that 1972 emerges as
     the beginning of feminist criticism's published history (this is the date with
     which Jane Gallop begins her new history of feminist criticsm, *Around 1981*,
     forthcoming), it still remains true, I think, as Elaine Showalter describes that
     moment in "Women's Time, Women's Space: Writing the History of Feminist
     Criticism," that in its origins "feminist criticism derived more from feminism
     than from criticism" (*Feminist Issues in Literary Scholarship*, ed. Shari Benstock
     [Bloomington, 1987], 36).
10   We have to keep in mind that there is always a time lag in these things; post-
     structuralism, with a whole new set of emphases, had already unsettled struc-
     turalism in France. Colonials necessarily live according to belated cadences.
11   I was amused to see that Marianna Torgovnick, whom I did not know at the
     time, also remembers this moment as having the aura of truth (see her *Gone
     Primitive: Savage Intellects, Modern Lives* [Chicago, 1990], 210–11).
12   A colleague of mine used to do a wonderful imitation of a former teacher
     who, in teaching Montesquieu's *Persian Letters*, would intone in a singsong
     (complete with full-blown American accent): "Dans chaque lettre il y a une
     idée, et l'idée c'est la liberté."
13   Hélène Cixous's "The Laugh of the Medusa" appeared in an issue of the jour-
     nal *L'Arc* devoted to Simone de Beauvoir in 1975. An extraordinary manifesto
     of what was to become known as "French feminism," it was here that Cixous
     invoked the wonders of "écriture féminine" with all the contradictions and
     ambiguities we have since pondered. I found its cadences almost mesmeriz-
     ing at the time. Jane Gallop has a succinct account of this moment in "1975:
     French Feminism," in *A New History of French Literature*, ed. Denis Hollier (Cam-
     bridge, Mass., 1989).
14   Not my grandfather's real name either, which may have been Middlarsky, but
     the Ellis Island rendition of an immigrant's desire to be a "Yankee": from
     Pinchas to William.
        I kept Kipnis as my legal middle name and made the initial K. part of my

new signature. My father, who was a lawyer, took care of the change for me and never said how he felt about it. My thesis advisor, however, who took the conventions of the patriarchy very seriously, was, to my great amusement, shocked. The woman typing the dissertation, a student at General Studies, who was rapidly changing her life, also changed her name (a lot more creatively), and I felt quite pleased to have inspired her to do it.

15 At a departmental party recently I was deep in conversation with a female colleague. We were interrupted by a male colleague, who asked what we were talking about. When we foolishly revealed the truth about the subject of our absorption—our haircuts (we go to the same haircutter)—he was jubilant: "Oh," he said, "I always wondered what women talked about when they were alone." I guess I didn't look at him as witheringly as I had hoped since he went on to pursue his interruption. Did I, he wanted to know, have a period? Being what is called "peri-menopausal," I had to work hard not to answer in terms of my newly haywire cycle. I censored my "sometimes" and said no, since he was merely looking, as it turned out, for someone to serve on an orals committee. But it's true that not having a period can be a problem.

16 This focus on women's writing meant not noticing a lot of very interesting work, like Nancy Vickers's on the Renaissance and Naomi Schor's on French nineteenth-century literature, to cite two well-known examples. Showalter herself maps the shifting currents of women's writing/men's writing in the history of feminist literary studies, and the turn to "gender" in the introduction to Speaking of Gender (New York, 1989).

17 The publication of Cixous's "Le rire de la Méduse" (1975), along with Irigaray's Speculum de l'autre femme (1974) and Ce sexe qui n'en est pas un (1977), profoundly stirred those of us working in French, on the margins of mainstream American feminism, because these texts (which, with the exception of the Cixous essay, were not to have their full impact in the States until they were translated in the 1980s) took as their subject the very ground of 1970s theory—language, sexual difference, writing, power—and made it women's. To be sure, what was to become known as "French feminism" was not directly concerned with women's writing as a historical, or even social, phenomenon. But it did create a theoretical context for posing the question of women's relation to cultural practices that diffusely found its way into so-called Anglo/American projects.

18 My book Subject to Change (1988) clearly belongs to this project (and in this sense already seems dated to me). I think that the prestige of feminist literary theory, or at least the appeal of its metaphors, will continue to wane in the 1990s, to be replaced by feminist theories emerging from philosophy (this is already implicit in some 1980s work, even in Yaeger's), science (Donna Har-

away's cyborgs, for instance), and psychoanalysis. This change also has to do, on the one hand, with the shift toward gender and "gender bending," redefinitions of lesbian configurations, and, on the other, away from the attempt to identify female specificities altogether.

19 This view was most famously summarized by Jonathan Culler's conversion of Peggy Kamuf's "writing like a woman" to "reading as a woman" which "deconstructed" the experience model, recasting it as a trope. It is less frequently noticed that Culler at this point (his On Deconstruction was published in 1982) was dealing uniquely with the feminist criticism of men's writing.

20 Helen Vendler's "Feminism and Literature" appeared in the 30 May 1990 issue of the New York Review of Books.

21 See Teresa de Lauretis, Introduction, in Feminist Studies/Critical Studies (Bloomington, 1986), 8.

22 Teresa de Lauretis brilliantly analyzes the implications of this process in "The Technology of Gender," in Technologies of Gender (London, 1987).

23 Conflicts in Feminism, ed. Evelyn Fox Keller and Marianne Hirsch (New York, 1990), 384.

24 I'm thinking here of the questions rehearsed so cogently in the introductory essay of Gendered Subjects: The Dynamics of Feminist Teaching, "The Politics of Nurturance," co-authored by Margo Culley, Arlyn Diamond, Lee Edwards, Sara Lennox, and Catherine Portuges (New York, 1985).

Most recently, I found myself unable to answer personally—without taking an absolutely querulous tone—questions on this very subject put to me as part of a discussion on feminism and the institution by a group of graduate students. See "Conference Call," differences 2 (Fall 1990): 52–108.

Part of the problem has to do as well with the Bildungsroman of the feminist critic: Can she accede to cultural authority when the role of the female intellectual seems to require disassociation from feminist causes—Susan Sontag, for instance, and most recently her grotesque, self-appointed rival, the media-created antifeminist Camille Paglia?

25 Probably the most important piece of this fallout involves my not having had a child—not, as it turned out, entirely by choice. This had everything to do with feminism in the 1970s. Deborah Rosenfelt and Judith Stacey comment sharply: "The reaction to the fifties' cloying cult of motherhood freed millions of women like us to consider motherhood a choice rather than an unavoidable obligation, but it may also have encouraged many to deny, or to defer dangerously long, our own desires for domesticity and maternity. One of the ironic effects of this history is the current obsession with maternity and children that seems to pervade aging feminist circles, a romanticization that occasionally rivals that of the fifties" ("Review Essay: Second Thoughts on the

Second Wave," *Feminist Studies* 13 [Summer 1987]: 351). (The key notion here for me personally is "defer dangerously long"; the romanticization they point to applies as well.) But Ann Snitow, speaking as "the child of this moment" in "A Gender Diary," underlines the fundamental contradiction of this conjuncture (the 1970s rereading the 1950s): "I don't think the feminism of this phase would have spoken so powerfully to so many without this churlish outbreak of indignation" (in Keller and Hirsch, eds., *Conflicts in Feminism*, 31). This will have to remain the subject of another essay, and I hope an edited book, on what this double truth of liberation and deferral has meant to women and feminists of my generation: the 1990s rereading the 1970s.

26 This is a central piece of Carolyn Heilbrun's *Writing a Woman's Life* (New York, 1988).

The Duplicity of the Southern Story:

Reflections on Reynolds Price's *The Surface of*

Earth and Eudora Welty's "The Wide Net"

LINDA ORR

"A story? No. No stories, never again."—Maurice Blanchot

I t is no accident that I prefer an overtly self-conscious literature that produces a permanent suspicion of story. Moreover, I have converted this aesthetic preference into a critical position that defines my professional life and career. Or maybe it happened the other way around: the position I have taken as a critic of French literature and history has retrospectively informed the intuitions I had, without knowing it, growing up in the South. I am exploring here that dialectic between my autobiography, my "subjectivity" (or "subject position," as we say in a more critical language), and the way in which I read and interpret literature.

The "southern story" stands in tradition, legend, and literary history for the South's special patrimony. It is both cliché and serious birthright just as other regional and ethnic literatures put claims on their own corner of a national and international literary heritage. The South is famous for its "natural" storytellers. The blurb on the Bantam anthology (1978) of *Stories of the Modern South* describes the contents as "glowing with the rich storytelling tradition of the American South."[1] One breathes stories in the air down here like the scent, rarer these days, of tobacco warehouses. The southerner supposedly has stories in her or his blood.

But the good ole story, especially when it's southern, makes me nervous. I automatically ask what is going on between the lines that both is and can't be said—scary stories, schizogenic, dangerous and manipulative. To be suspicious of the story is to put into question the foundation of southern culture, if not the function of cultural foundations in general.

Story (the way I define it) and history have a close rhetorical relation, besides the nice pun by which "story" is literally found embedded in the word "history." That pun reminds us of the serious double entendre in Romance languages like French, where *histoire* means both story and history.[2] The two rhetorical forms share the same Aristotelian tradition. They specialize in beginnings, middles, and ends, origins and teleologies, and suggest, because of this basic organization, cause and effect, explanation: call it logic or plot. Story and history depend upon strategies of *mimesis*, which come from Greek tragedy, especially the use of dialogue. Story, in the sense of realistic fiction, and historiography further enhance their imitation of reality by effacing the signs of narrative process, by diverting attention away from the rhetoric they are in the act of exploiting.[3] Story and history that develop, at their most extreme, what can be called a "master narrative" may be highly self-conscious but do not call attention to it. That illusion of guilelessness in southern culture and writing especially fascinates, aggravates me. The guile that looks guileless comes close to duplicity. Southerners have to seem simple, or rather "just folks," when they're razor-sharp and tricky.

Neither story nor history exists outside of a specific context, and the combination in the context of southern culture and history is extremely potent: perhaps the most powerful example of the fit necessary for a total cultural system to succeed for generations. Something apparently "unspeakable" circulates in southern history (read as both history and story). Yet you can't get a good handle on it, and it isn't really acknowledged because everyone seems to know it already. Maybe this description can be generalized to other societies, but I will stick to this specific instance of cultural complicity. Slavery, part of the South's specificity, may well be what its writers and historians are trying not to name—or the way women and the working class were conned into holding up the overall system—but I want to try to look more closely at the process as much as at the content of what makes southern history work and not work.

This means that I do not consider story to be an innocent form, an empty vehicle for the use of good or bad agendas—or even an inherently evil form. It is a highly effective cultural form whose use entails taking serious responsibility for it. Anything that comes into being as a story assumes in that act the air of rightness and automatic legitimacy. And with the authority of the Bible behind it, its own authority is almost unquestionable. I'm not asking for some (impossible) overthrow of story. What I'd like to see more of in the southern story along with its ingenious plots and "real-life" talk is a thoroughgoing disclaimer of what drives it: its reliance on and use of story. Then the narrator, especially when "omniscient," would not be able to hide behind the authority of the good ole story. Instead, the form of the narration itself would throw its own shady practices into relief.

Storytelling can provide a force of political subversion for groups out of power (contemporary African-American women writers, for example) but maybe not with impunity—these groups too are looking to shake up the forms. Others may think they cleanse and renew storytelling of its implicit violence and historical repressions, but I cannot separate my own collective and subjective experience from my reactions as a profoundly ambivalent reader. When that story starts to flow sweet poison in my ears (or pen), I say to myself here comes trouble.

That is why I applauded with a perverse glee when I came upon the conclusion, which is not of course a conclusion, in French writer Maurice Blanchot's The Madness of the Day (1973): "A story? No. No stories, never again."[4] I realize that I am simplifying by setting up French literature in opposition to the literature of the American South. But French cultural references serve as my outside from which to look back on the South and myself as a southerner. I have made a countertradition of self-reflective writing, like the works of Diderot or especially Flaubert. The latter wanted Madame Bovary to be more than a realistic story about characters in a particular society; he aspired, above all, to write a "book about nothing."[5] Then came Flaubert's progeny: the wily, disarming Nathalie Sarraute and the deliciously perverse Maurice Blanchot. Faulkner, like Flaubert, has a double fictional legacy in which one line appears iconoclastic, experimental and the other is traditional, realistic. But Faulkner's legacy is more frightening to me. Besides initiating conflicting modernist points of view, his work also managed to construct a monolithic monument of this exportable cultural object, the South.

The works of Reynolds Price and Eudora Welty are a challenge to my hypotheses and instincts as a reader—especially Price's The Surface of Earth, whose opening passage I will examine, and Welty's famous story "The Wide Net." An overall impression emerges from their fiction (their language, although different in each case, reinforces this impression) that, despite whatever has gone on, all will be or remains well in the end. This reconciliation is not exactly a happy ending, but somehow the tensions, conflicts, and hidden violence smooth over and allow nothing structurally to shift, especially the underlying notion of story itself.

In both *The Surface of Earth* and "The Wide Net," the isolated moments of narrative self-consciousness (those moments when the story is commenting upon itself) do not add up, or I'm not sure that they do and am left hanging with my own suspicions (of duplicity?), wishing that my instincts would be confirmed or at least acknowledged. In the end, a kind of conformity results whereby underlying authority seems to be reconfirmed. Price and Welty get away with murder in their fiction and come out smelling like roses. If I let myself be swept along with the riveting obsessions of *The Surface of Earth* or pleasantly guided through "The Wide Net" I'm fine, but if I listen to my uneasiness and try to articulate it, I realize that reading a certain southern literature is a potentially crazy-making experience that reminds me of how I felt growing up in the South.

If someone asked me what was my native tongue, I would answer irony. Behind all the sweetness and light of a southern childhood and education, something was wrong. I knew that. And I think I knew that very early, almost from the beginning of language (a black "nanny," a white mother). I denied that intuitive knowledge for a long time because the prevailing truth (1950s and on) reinforced the opinion that we were all gentle, loving people, gracious, law-abiding, moral, and religious, and that our social system corresponded to those principles. So a double grew within me, deep-seated and irreparable; I learned to smile and say everything was fine, when I suspected that underneath it was not. Or there were the times when I could no longer take the pressure of the double and began to wonder if I was crazy. I thought my perceptions of the undercurrents were off; I was "the only one" to feel estranged in my own land, in my own literature—even when that literature offered me crazies with whom I could identify, proving to me, ironically, that I wasn't the "only one." In some ways, these loony characters kept me from being the analytical self, capable of calling into question the "prevailing truth," which I needed to go elsewhere ("France") to find.

I cannot, with confidence, place myself outside these southern texts I identify with, both intimately and autobiographically through history (the Orrs were a prominent slave-holding political family in South Carolina). Despite my own disclaimers, my strategies often resemble the ones I criticize in Price and Welty. But such is the "space" I would like to create in this essay, that midspace of self and cultural critique, acknowledging uneasiness, demanding a more open dialogue with the text, which pushes my capacities as a reader. I would like to think along with the narrator whether she or he is absent or not.

======

Price opens his long novel published in 1975 with a scene that serves as an allegory for the southern story. The scene has to take place on the front porch of a white frame house at dusk, and the storyteller has to talk in hushed tones from his rocking chair (southern throne) to the children gathered around. The storyteller might be weaving folktales from the mountains (my favorites: Richard Chase's *Grandfather Tales*) or ghost stories from the Dismal Swamp. But usually he mesmerizes the listeners, because his tale dictates the conditions of their intimacy, by recounting the family's past, oral history, family ghost stories.

This rich vein of southern literature continues to this day. Lee Smith has most precisely named that space in her titles (*Oral History, Family Linen*). An interview in the *Wall Street Journal* (1985) explains that "Ms. Smith was also exposed to the storytelling abilities of people whose forums were front porches and backyards." Smith responds: "If you ask a simple question in my family or of almost anyone in the South you get a long complicated answer."[6] And the myth is continually reinforced. The *New York Times* reviewer of Allan Gurganus's *White People* (1991) starts out talking about how "the author loves to tell stories. . . . [H]e loves storytellers and the art and craft of storytelling, too."[7] The identity of southern literature and storytelling is so interconnected that they mutually define each other. They are practically inseparable.

In *The Surface of Earth*, the father around whom the children assemble appears loving and concerned, wise and given to foresight. At the same time he is manipulating his listeners, not just superficially for that evening, but for the long term. He manipulates the way they will see and live their lives, initiating them into the exercise of family and cultural power. In this way, the opening scene of Price's novel shows how the southern story operates more generally with its innuendos and warnings. In the opening sentences of the novel, the reader is treated like a member of the family, entering midconversation into the group, but (also like the children who listen?), the reader scrambles to figure out what exactly is going on, and, at the very least, gets the sense of forboding mystery.

> "Who told Thad she was dead?" Rena asked.
>
> "Thad killed her," Eva said. "He already knew."
>
> Their father—from his rocker, almost dark in the evening—said, "Hush your voices down. Your mother's on the way. And never call him *Thad*. He was her dear father, your own grandfather; and of course he never killed her."
>
> Kennerly said, "He gave her the baby. The baby killed her. So I think he did justice, killing himself."
>
> "Shame," their father said. He drew at his cigar.
>
> "I hope none of you lives to face such a choice." Another draw. "But one of you will. Then remember tonight—the cruelty you've talked against the helpless dead."[8]

It is important that we get the children's feistiness up front. The general, if not omniscient, third-person narration will shift points of view, but is here almost neutral—unless it draws the reader's sympathy toward the children. Both reader and children have to be prepared and primed for the story, rallied or even frightened into order—so that the official family story as about to be told by the father takes effect.

In the father's official version that follows, no one in the family was actually "killed." Italics heighten the drama of the dialogue ("But never say *killed*"). There were only deaths, no blame, no crime, although that doesn't preclude an overwhelming, albeit misplaced sense of guilt on somebody's part—in this case, their mother's. When their mother was born, their grandmother died in childbirth, and her husband Thad blew out his brains and fell onto his wife's dead body. The novel does not begin with this dramatic tale of tragedy, but, instead, with a murky misdeed denied: with the question of whether there was in the beginning a crime or not.

The words "their father" emphasize his symbolic position. The father, Our Father, teaches several lessons that begin with that familiar infantilizing tactic. He corrects the children's language. They are much too familiar in the way they talk about the patriarch as *Thad*. And no family patriarch would ever have done harm, much less "kill" the one he loved.

Slow draws on the cigar . . . reinforcing the law, and the hush-hush of conspiracy give the story its tingly excitement. The story is a secret kept from the mother; her absence and ignorance give the story even greater impact. Finally, all of this buildup leads not to the paternal blessing but to a curse: you'd better watch out how you talk about the "helpless dead" because the same will happen to you someday and you won't want to be unjustly called murderer yourself. The father won't say who will come to such an end, thus leaving all his listeners vaguely implicated (for life).

We imagine the curse will land on Eva, with such a name, and thus project the shape of the novel like a prophecy: indeed, she ends up metaphorically "killing" (hurting) the most people. But the curse literally falls on her only son Rob, whose wife dies in childbirth while he is drunk from the guilt of sleeping with an old girlfriend. On this particular opening night of the novel, Eva, the falling angel, secretly departs later that very evening from the paternal roof, knowing that she is her father's favorite (of course: the wild one) and associated with his own dead mother. Eva, however, will not get far. In a year she is back, with baby, without husband, to spend the rest of her life caring for her father. Her revolt does not last long, but for this one evening, she speaks for the other children:

> Dark as it was, Eva met his eyes and waited him out. Then she said, "What's shameful, sir, in wanting the truth? We're all nearly grown. We've heard scraps of it all our lives—lies, jokes. We are asking to know. It's our own story."
> Her father nodded. "It would kill your mother to hear it."
> They were all silent.[9]

Eva, like Eve, wants knowledge, wants to hear the family history that determines her own identity (and her son's and grandson's who come after). She wants the "true story" and throws up to her father that ambiguous meaning of the word "story" which is both history and falsehood, truth and "lies, jokes." (Recall the familiar usage of "story" in the context of parent admonishing child: now don't you tell me a story, I want the truth.) "Story" in the sense of joke or funny little fiction plays as large a role in traditional southern sociability as the literary form, story, plays in southern literature. At a cocktail party everyone gathers around the one—I'm thinking of my own father—who is known for always having a good story to tell, and he often starts out as if what he is telling is true, and everyone is hooked while the tale veers off and people catch on (a real pleasure at that point) that the tale will be wild until the punch line. "Stories," like Freud's jokes, make everyone in the circle feel good, that they belong; the story reinforces dominant values, respect/disdain, and social cohesion. If my father's stories tested the bounds of the tellable, particularly on the subject of sex, my "Yankee" mother was there to censor—but the tellable also evolved as did taste and political consciousness. In *The Surface of Earth*, Eva wants more than jokes and lies, yet the ambiguity of story, which Price's novel tries to deny as it goes along, is well established in this first passage and remains constant.

The children learn as much from the father's framing of the official family story as from the story itself, just as the form of the southern literary story is often as powerful as its content. They learn that they cannot criticize the "helpless dead" with impunity, that some superstitious system is at work so that if they bad-mouth the ancestors, the same fate will befall them . . . only worse? And they also learn that stories have immense power, whether told to or kept secret from the very person who should (not) know: Double bind? Duplicity? It is no accident that the secret is kept here from the mother, although later secrets are both unveiled and kept from everyone (especially devastating in the case of the black half-brother, Grainger). Finally, the children learn that your own history can kill you. But at the same time (just like the taste of that old apple) they are inflicted from the beginning with a terrible "hunger" for their one and only story.

The introduction to *A Palpable God*, Price's translation of Bible stories, shows the importance of this driving force behind *The Surface of Earth*, the hunger for story. Price was doing these Biblical translations while writing his novel. Here is the first sentence of that introduction: "A need to tell and hear stories is essential to the species *Homo sapiens*—second in necessity apparently after nourishment and before love and shelter."[10] Price locates story as an almost physiological need and as a prelinguistic, almost unconscious need ("all healthy babies dream"). The title of that introduction, "A Single Meaning: Notes on the Origins and Life of Narrative," signals a specific definition of story in ontological terms (more than straight religious ones): "The need is not for the total consolation of narcotic fantasy . . . but for credible news that our lives proceed in order toward a pattern which, if tragic here and now, is ultimately pleasing in the mind of a god who sees a totality and *at last* enacts His will. We crave nothing less than perfect story." What Price also calls a true and sacred story, evidenced first and foremost in the Bible, implies a teleology to human existence, written as a "Divine Comedy." Whether the perfect story satisfies the "hunger for solace" is not absolutely clear: "Hunger has not precluded food."[11]

I do not argue against the need for order and reference in the constant process of making sense and community which our lives and language depend on, nor will I argue which came first, truth or deceit. "They [Biblical accounts] are plainly not deceitful," Price writes, "in some awareness of the range of objections." Notable for a "smoothness of surface," Old Testament stories (like Jacob's) were "devoid of small narrative seductions because they were certain of offering one huge seduction."[12] But Price and I differ in our definitions of story and in the role that origins and ends play within that definition. I see origins and ends as products of history and interpretation, constantly reposited and never fixed. So I define story as a literary and cultural form that has evolved over time, and not always peacefully, and that has no ontological claims to a privileged status.

It is possible to imagine that story has another history, less pure and based on usurpation, rather than on the ultimate priority of origin. Plot or story in the sense of the Greek *mythos* grew out of Aristotelian tragedy along with dialogue and took over other hybrid, less orderly forms like epic or dithyramb until it occupied the major European literary terrain as the novel. Had those other forms not been overshadowed, a whole other conceptual narrative apparatus might have emerged which we can only guess at by surviving fragments.[13] We don't even have a good word in English like the French *récit* for an imaginative prose work that is not a plot-defined novel. Those fragments of alternative forms represent writing that exceeds what Price calls the "narrative skeleton."[14] Outside of this skeleton, for instance, self-consciousness, descriptions, discursive language (whaling in *Moby-Dick*), repetitions ("genealogies," the begat sections of the Bible), all disturb the storytelling totality that tries to settle in too soon.[15]

The Surface of Earth looks like a realist narrative building toward orderly life stories, but its structure is actually based on the repetition of stories that produce a cycle of seduction and frustration. The story each character tells raises more questions and only creates hunger for more stories. Certain narrative moments, usually a funny instance of dialogue, point to this duplicitous rhetoric of storytelling. In one particularly deadpan, funny-horrifying reply, Hutch tries to keep his father Rob's story at bay, tries not to get hooked: "Do I really need to hear this? Things worry me a lot." [16]

These moments of self-consciousness do not, however, shed a critical light on the process of storytelling itself and do not warn readers to be on guard especially against the novel they are reading at the time. For this reason, the narrator, whether man or woman, is as devious and manipulative as the father was in the novel's opening section. The (omniscient) narrator of The Surface of Earth does allow me to poke fun at the father, puffing on his cigar, and, at that point, I take the side of Eva, but the two points of view, Eva's and her father's, equal out—although he reaps the long-term advantages. His daughter's anticipated rebellion is nipped in the bud, so she'll eventually take care of him instead of having her own life, and both Eva and her father (all three, including the narrator) conspire together by coding her sacrifice as fate, even Biblical fate, or as natural in that social system. [17] This dynamic of seduction and control in The Surface of Earth does not worry me as much as the way in which the novel's structure functions in southern culture. The complicity of southern literature and history, at the edges of intention and a cultural unconscious, is what disturbs me.

The double bind implicit in the structure of The Surface of Earth—hunger-inducing stories vs. the satisfying Story—raises questions concerning the novel's representation of personal and social responsibility, forgiveness, and fate. Between the horrible origin and final foregiveness lies a gap, a space that I would call history and that is missing in The Surface of Earth. By the word history, I don't just mean the larger political or social-history "story"—this kind of literal critique of history in Price is too easy. I mean a concept of undetermined history or story, which privileges nonpermanent, everyday errors, a character's particularities, and so forces her or him to take responsibility and maybe change. Ambiguous, "sweet killing" characters and situations are prime matter for fiction, but not when these characters, no matter what they've done, in the end join the untouchable category the father called the "helpless dead." Emotional harm, "crimes" in The Surface of Earth, are committed from "need not malice." [18] (In Kate

Vaiden, Kate touches in the end, almost tenderly, the cold hand of the sinister Swift who probably caused the murder of her mother and almost raped Kate herself.)

In *The Surface of Earth*, evil seems to slide and disappear into need and forgiveness. The slippery nature of evil—whom to accuse? no one is guilty—resembles too closely the burden and excuse of southern history. One cannot articulate anger at the "helpless dead" even though they continue to hold power over the living. Southern history, all history, is open to radical revision, even if such a concept did not seem thinkable in the atmosphere of former times and may not seem so now. The white women of *The Surface of Earth* are supposedly responsible because they willfully accept their fate (*amor fati*) in contrast to the irresponsible men (including Grainger, who is half-black). But a narrative angle, sharp and disruptive, could show up fate for what it is.[19] Fate is a particular form a devious history takes when it wants to appear fixed, even truthful, for all time.

The double bind that structures Price's novel, original incest vs. the sacred story, invites the leap of faith represented by his titles: *A Long and Happy Life, The Generous Man, The Source of Light, Clear Pictures*. But the cracks and tensions in Price's fiction are not allowed to split, multiply, and bring down the titles. When Price says we crave the perfect story, he makes me want to rewrite these titles imperfectly: *A Brief and Bitter Life, The Stingy Woman, The Play of Shadows, Fuzzy Pictures*. The notion of "cracks" reminds me of that sentence in *Madame Bovary*, in which Flaubert describes human language as a "cracked pot" we beat for bears to dance to when we want to move the stars to tears: "Un chaudron fêlé où nous battons des mélodies à faire danser les ours, quand on voudrait attendrir les étoiles."[20] Levels of narration surround this sentence: Flaubert's narrator is ironically defending his own language, his and Emma Bovary's passionate, empty metaphors—of which this "pot" will be a prime example. But something so moving, almost awkward from the bears yet eloquent, seeps into this bid for and horror of intimacy with the reader.

=====

Welty's "The Wide Net" is not so obviously based on the act of storytelling as *The Surface of Earth*, but story as a form of manipulation is at the center of the plot. While *The Surface of Earth* opens with the insinuation of murder, "The Wide Net" begins with the threat of suicide. William Wallace finds the suicide note his young, pregnant wife left him, when he comes

home after a night of drinking with the boys, so he rushes out to drag
the river for her body. The story "The Wide Net" is, then, already double,
maybe duplicitous, because Hazel's fragmented, mysterious story frames
what takes up the rest of the space: the male river-dragging. Hazel's story,
her gesture (a joke, or cry for help?) is more than a brief counterpart to
the main attraction of the river-dragging, but it appears at first as tan-
gential. One has to read closely. "The Wide Net" is like those Method-
ist hymns Welty talks about in *One Writer's Beginnings*: they "all sounded
happy and pleased with the world, even though the words ran quite the
other way." [21]

The river-dragging is a worthy distraction and calls for some sophisticated criticism, in spite of its incredibly smooth, shiny surface. It offers
the occasion for various interpretations. First, the boys are off on an epic
adventure, repeating all those quest myths of Western literature; second,
one can read playful and sharp social criticism; and third, the story becomes an elaborate allegory about how a story is constructed. Although
these "layers" of meaning delight the critic in me, I am even more in-
trigued by the evasive framing, "Hazel's story," and, behind that, by what
I'll call "Eudora's story." Neither Hazel nor "Eudora" ever tells her own
story directly. If they speak, they speak with other people's words. Technically, the third-person narration of "The Wide Net" starts out from
William Wallace's point of view, but, except for certain notable moments,
even his voice joins a more external (as opposed to omniscient) perspective.

At the beginning of the story, William Wallace skims his wife's suicide
note, crumples it, and rushes out to catch up with his drinking buddy
Virgil heading home in the October morning. Virgil is the tip-off: we're in
Dante, Virgil (Aeneas), Homer, Freud, and whoever after wrote morpho-
logical variations of the male adventure. To use the story's own words: "It
was the same as any chase in the end." [22] The men are ostensibly looking
for a woman or looking to get away from a woman (*Iliad, Odyssey*). They
come up with whatever "food" they need, in both a banal and deeper
sense. Thanks to the contraption of Doc's wide net, weighed down by
glittering jugs and bottles, they dredge up ladies' beads, lots of unmated
shoes (plodding of old plots), and mostly "the same old fish" everyone
enjoys fried up. The guys forget whether what's-her-name ever threw
herself into the river or not and have a great time on such "a pretty day." [23]

Each searcher finds something for himself. Two orphan brothers work out their own version of the quest for the father. Grady, the oldest, has a kind of "mirror stage" (informal use of term from Jacques Lacan) experience along the way, looks into the water, sees "the image in the river . . . his father, the drowned man," comes to terms with himself. His little brother Brucie "looked, but showed no recognition." And of course (Welty is having fun, so are we) the boys are mostly out to confront, prove their emerging masculinity; they "rassle" with an eel, an alligator, and that titillating "King of Snakes." [24] We readers, like Grady or Brucie, can read whatever we want into this epic poem or "show no recognition."

Welty also gets in some good jabs at the repressive social situation this river-dragging both alleviates and confirms. The two little black kids who are accepted into the expedition, as long as they stay little and funny, babble to give themselves courage, while everyone else is hushed by the quick outburst of a storm. Doc, who owns the net, the old wiseman and wiseguy, a "god" to Virgil and Dante, asks Robbie and Sam Bell: " 'Why do you little niggers talk so much!' 'We always talks this much,' said Sam, 'but now everybody so quiet, they hears us.' " The two black kids get their voice, their identity, on the trip, a nice cultural gift, a slit in the texture, an exception that won't last long. And the view of women is no less typical of that southern place and time (before "a war"). Hazel is smart. The guys repeat that. And her mother is big, scary, and powerful. Doc, the mock-patriarch, best shows up the culture's double standard about women: "Whatever this mysterious event will turn out to be, it has kept one woman from talking a while. However, Lady Hazel is the prettiest girl in Mississippi. . . . A golden-haired girl." Hazel's mischief can be forgiven because she's pretty, and calling her pretty strips her of her brain power, puts her back in the niche of the sweet, demure thing. Doc's comment shuts her up just as effectively as the chase itself does. Both take all the words and attention away from her, while pretending to search for her body in the first place. When the triumphant, bedraggled pack parades with their fish through the dusty town of Dover washed "like new," even the poverty "in its wood and tin, like an old tired heart" has been transformed or covered up by the "shiny mosquito-netting," by the "wavy heat" of the air, a kind of shimmering narrative haze. [25]

The title and the not-so-subtle references to "thread" (with a pin Brucie dangles), "string" (of ladies' beads), and "mosquito-netting" underline for the reader the metaphorical link between narrative and net. One

Writer's Beginnings talks about the act of writing in terms of "strands" or "threads" and exposes a related concept of history: "Writing a story or a novel is one way of discovering *sequence* in experience, of stumbling upon cause and effect in the happenings of a writer's own life." The writer learns to "find in the thick of the tangle what clear line persists." I would reformulate these statements, saying that the writer constructs the clear line, then makes it appear as if it was found, while the tangles and stumbling are hardly visible anymore. Or the writer's experience is inseparable from the old stories, so the net "so old and long-used . . . looked golden, strung and tied with golden threads." [26]

This process of story making, not just the smooth result, is revealed and hidden in "The Wide Net." Virgil tells Dante-William Wallace straight out why he's there: "I come along to keep you on the track." "What have I done the whole time but keep this river-dragging going straight and running even, without no hitches?" Welty is saying what she means to do in her story; she wants no hitches left in the clear line—but she allows this subtle "hitch," saying she wants no hitches. Her own alter ego (O. Henry? Faulkner?) in "The Wide Net" is more often Doc than Virgil: "Don't let her [net, story] get too heavy, boys"; "Things are moving in too great a rush." What Doc says almost automatically turns into an allegory of story: "The excursion is the same when you go looking for your sorrow as when you go looking for your joy." Finally, he pronounces that blasphemy everyone/we know all along—from the beginning Hazel "wasn't in there." While protecting William Wallace from Doc's candor, Virgil also explains one of the oldest strategies in literature: "It's only because we didn't find her that he wasn't looking for her." Whatever the wide net of language catches is what the story is about—not the eel or everything, the everything that is lost . . . or is the latter, the loss, the real story? Virgil looks like a postmodern semiotician when he muses early on: "Virgil gave a sigh, as if he knew that when you go looking for what is lost, everything is a sign." [27]

So Welty, like Price, appears to be writing a realist, Aristotelian story but is really writing a "narrative" with barely a story line at all. In a helpful summary of "The Wide Net," Guy Davenport comes close to describing Welty's form. After analyzing the chase as a Homeric "heroic game," he sees another displaced meaning we could also call the displacement of meaning:

Throughout the story the dialogue addresses itself neither to the drama of the suicide, nor to the problem between husband and wife that might have caused it. That life happens at all times in a context we do not understand . . . and that when we do try to be articulate we usually talk about one thing while meaning another are things we all know.[28]

Using William James's phrase, Davenport concludes that the story is about "the incoherent buzz of experience, the way we live."[29] I'll go farther and suggest that Welty (Price too in his repetitions) has written a story about everything and nothing—the nothing (in Flaubert's terms) that constantly begets (Biblical pun intended) story. As I pull more interpretations from the text, I can't say Welty via Doc didn't warn me, the reader-critic: "I'd be more careful what I took out of this net."[30]

The major hitch in the story that is not ironed out is the framing, Hazel's muffled words, and the hole or gap of Eudora's story inside that. Davenport stopped too soon and could have gone on to examine the slighted story about the couple and the contexts "we do not understand." These gaps or hitches show up for me in the beginning and ending frame with Hazel and William Wallace and in the central, most mysterious act of the story, William Wallace's deep dive into the river supposedly to find her. Those three moments are summarized by the crushed note, the spanking, and the trouble/elation.

The opening and closing of "The Wide Net" are oddly suggestive of a muted violence. A specific reference to writing opens the story: Hazel's suicide note, her "little letter." We don't get to read that actual note; we read, or rather don't read it, through William Wallace's point of view. "After one look he was scared to read the exact words, and he crushed the whole thing in his hand instantly, but what it had said was that she . . . was going to the river to drown herself." Can we believe what William Wallace thinks the letter says since he didn't read "the exact words"? His reaction is both banal and strangely violent—especially in the detail of the language: "crushed" the "whole thing" "instantly." At the end of the story, William Wallace returns and finds her sitting there pretty as can be because she had been there all the time—"so close" "you could have put out your hand and touched me." He is angry (and so is she), but playfully? He "turned her up and spanked her. 'Do you think you will do it again?' he asked.'" She says no, but when she's up again, smiling, teasing: "I will do it again if I get ready. . . . Next time will be different too." But the story does not end here, when it's as if Hazel is sticking out her tongue at him, taunting; instead, it strikes a harmonious note of dusk. She, like Dante's Beatrice or like a woman drawing her man to bed, takes his hand and leads him into the house "smiling as if she were smiling down on him."[31]

Besides being strung with strands of gold, the wide net is a trap. "That was doing something behind someone's back," William Wallace says when the suicide note appears after he comes back into the room from searching the house. From the beginning, Virgil is suspicious: "It's a woman's trick." Hazel is absent from the river-dragging yet leads it just as surely from her invisible remote control. Her husband says, "I never saw a girl to leave less signs of where she's been."[32] Hazel, that tough nut to crack, who spreads a haze around her, is not a simple character. I don't know in what context to interpret these bizarre, if not titillating moments. Spanking may well be a euphemism for abuse; there is something shocking about it, even playful. I imagine this psychodrama: the woman has to be punished for having so much fun at the men's expense. "Eudora's" story begins to emerge behind Hazel's. "The Wide Net" is "a woman's trick," lots of maneuvers are going on behind our backs. Does "Eudora" metaphorically punish herself for having all this fun? She'll do it again next time, and the next story will have a new strategy or trick.

Is Hazel's story or Eudora's a clever joke or a sign of deception? In One Writer's Beginnings, Welty talks a lot about "true meaning" and "clear line," but she also appreciates, even likes, the duplicity she finds in her own family: "It was taken entirely for granted that there wasn't any lying in our family. . . . It took me a long time to realize that these very same everyday lies, and the stratagems and jokes and tricks and dares that went with them, were in fact the basis of the scenes I so well loved to hear about."[33] It takes time, training in the South to hear the lying, recognize the tricks under the facade that insists no one is ever deceptive in this society. The river-dragging is Hazel's trick that she learned to defend herself, to have a little fun, to stave off suicide—and "The Wide Net" is Eudora's.

The murkiest moment in the story, which is supposedly the clearest—the moment of revelation—occurs when William Wallace dives to the bottom of the Pearl River, seeing there in the golden net Hazel's "shining eyes" as Dante sees "pearl on a white brow" in "limpid and still water." Here William Wallace finds his wife's secret:

Had he suspected down there, like some secret, the real, the true trouble that Hazel had fallen into, about which words in a letter could not speak . . . how (who knew?) she had been filled to the brim with that elation that they all remembered, like their own secret, the elation that comes of great hopes and changes, sometimes simply of the harvest time, that comes with a little course of its own like a tune to run in the head, and there was nothing she could do about it—they knew—and so it had turned into this?[34]

This passage is so knotty as to be a riddle. Underlying Hazel's suicide note is her "true trouble" but that trouble turns out to be an elation— or is that the way William Wallace wants to see it, since we still do not have Hazel's "exact words" or even if we did, "words in a letter" cannot speak whatever it is anyway. Just when we think we're closing in on Hazel's secret, if once-removed, that elation is immediately made collective ("they all") and links up with the cosmic season. The elation (fear, panic?) of Hazel's pregnancy parallels the earth's cycle when "everything just before it changes looks to be made of gold."[35] Finally the trouble/ elation becomes a "tune" out of her control ("they knew," "who knew?") and so it turned into this: "The Wide Net."

I think the trouble is anger at having her words (Hazel's, Eudora's) crushed and taken from her by the Docs of this world and more anger at having to cover these feelings up so as to have a clean slate, a "net" result in the end. ("Net" in this second sense does not come from the etymology "to connect," but from the root "to shine," like *net* in French: clean, neat.) I think the elation is the joy of writing, a guilty pleasure for which a woman is spanked because women aren't supposed to have that much "triumph, power, or relief"—words in the Random House dictionary definition of "elation." Using contemporary French terms, I would say that the elation is the (sexual) power of a woman writer, her *jouissance* that must, above all, be covered up—especially during that historical moment when Welty did much of her writing.

But I wish she, or Hazel, had given me a more open sign, acknowledging all this going on instead of ending in a haze of nature and reconciliation and leaving me in the same place of having to deny my own feelings and reactions. Southern seductiveness is, thus, passed on from one woman to the next. The narrator reveals intimate emotion without really revealing it and denies responsibility for it—"there was nothing she could do about it." I am not suggesting that Hazel or Welty should change her personality and sound like a 1990s feminist, but the narrator could give the reader more credit for figuring the contradictions out. I admit that this narrative gesture is a challenge in "The Wide Net" or any piece in which a character like Hazel, though smart, is not very verbal or introspective. I'm suggesting something like this character of Colette's who asks herself after scribbling a note to her lover: "Will he be able to make me out in all this untidiness? No. I am still concealed in it." [36] This kind of gesture is needed to offset the possibility that the laconic central character (Hazel), whose words are repressed, also covers over the absence of a narrative position, absence as a narrative position. [37] Welty confesses: "I wished to be, not effaced, but invisible—actually a powerful position." As a child, she was sorry to find that "books had been written by *people* . . . not natural wonders, coming up of themselves like grass." [38] Story, like "objective" history, must seem to write itself, to authenticate itself. It leaves very few traces for the search party.

"Camouflage," to use Carolyn Heilbrun's term describing Welty's autobiography, fits the fiction even more precisely. [39] "The Wide Net" frustrates me because the narrative points to a moment when the secret will be revealed and then it turns out to be another secret. "One secret is liable to be revealed in the place of another that is harder to tell, and the substitute secret when nakedly exposed is often the more appalling." [40] It's not so much that Welty wants to keep secret her anger, fear, sexual joy, and power—such a dynamic would go against all we know about her. But in the substitute secret she hides the duplicity she has to call upon in order to write: the little spanking, the tune unaccounted for. It is taken for granted that the southern story—painfully contradictory like the society it supports and that supports it—has a simple, clear meaning that grows as naturally as grass or talk. This untouchable simplicity makes me look pretty silly, even if I think I'm right and have worked hard to prove it. At the end of "The Wide Net," when Hazel smiles down on William Wallace, I have a sneaking feeling that the narrator is also smiling down on me, the reader.

=====

Despite more overt criticism and a continuous chipping away, how tenacious is the radical binary culture of the South, based on race but legitimating all kinds of oppositional distinctions. [41] A gap defines the South:

between civility and violence, public and private persona, not always or just the difference between truth and lie but between conflicting representations of history and the self. Those shocking doubles and reversals can occur in the same spaces, groups, and individuals (examples from popular culture: *Steel Magnolias, Alice Doesn't Live Here Anymore*). Those intimate with the ways of the South can always detect the unspoken, unspeakable distinctions between inside and out, accepted and unacceptable, and there is the discomfort zone of in-between where most of us are: nobody, finally, fits in. I remember when our neighbor, a successful lawyer, came out with that cliché against Vietnam War protesters at dinner while I was visiting my parents—"ought to line 'em up and shoot 'em." Who was I? On what side of the firing line?

The summary of my family history strikes me as pure southern gothic. My great-great-grandfather was the governor of South Carolina (1866–68) during the window of compromise after the Civil War, before "Radical Reconstruction" (1868–1877). He is the patriarch, and I had sympathies for him because he was caught by circumstances. He had been in Congress, had northern friends, but had to join with the South. An "upcountry" man from Anderson, he was looked upon with suspicion by the real aristocrats from Charleston. (My father, in *My Fair Lady* style, offered me money if I could pass for a native Charlestonian. . . . At that time I wanted more to pass for a Parisian.) Still, Governor Orr's postwar trickle-down theory of human rights was typical of the white landowning class, and he already had an ambiguous vision of the new industrial South. He died in 1873 because of complications from a cold he had during his first months as a diplomatic emissary to Russia (heartsick and without bourbon).

It's my great-grandfather whom I really don't like, called, of course, the "Colonel." He was the hero of my personal "original" scene of historical guilt, a scary-farcical moment in South Carolina history that signaled in 1876 the coming end of "Radical Reconstruction." Two different houses of representatives struggled for legitimacy. The Republicans (the Mackey House) were inside and represented the government in power composed of "negroes, 'Scalawags,' and 'Carpet Baggers.'"[42] The old-guard white Democrats (the Wallace House) were outside. One of the brown, chipped clippings in my family's album reads: "It was the strong shoulder of Col. Orr that pushed in the doors of the House of Representatives in Columbia when the democrats took forcible possession." That same (duplicitous) James L. Orr was said in *South Carolina During Reconstruction* to have "moved that the House adjourn" so the matter could be left up to the courts and violence would be avoided. An explosive combination of Hampton's "red shirts" (white) and the Charleston "hunkihoris" (black) was gathering outside.[43] You know who won, thanks to the courts. The Wallace House gang.

Read the "revised" Mary C. Simms Oliphant textbook (*The Simms History of South Carolina*) used in South Carolina schools from 1917 to 1985–86 to get the flavor of the kind of history I osmosed and grew up with.[44] I thought Reconstruction in the South was the equivalent of the Dark Ages in Europe:

> For the next nine years (1868–1877), South Carolina was governed by a set of thieves and plunderers. . . . More than half the legislators were negroes, many of whom could neither read nor write. . . . The legislators bought at the expense of the State liquors and cigars, furniture, women's clothes, jewelry, groceries, and so on. . . . Convicts . . . were turned out of the penitentiary. . . . With the arming of the negroes, crime increased greatly. Houses were burned in the night. White women were often insulted if they appeared alone on the streets.[45]

What a shock to find out that Reconstruction lasted only nine years. Is it any wonder that I suspect history? I am convinced that my present work on the German Occupation of France has to do with that ambiguous history of the only Occupation that took place in the United States. Surely the literary and philosophical methods of deconstruction appealed to me as an angle on Reconstruction.

After his adventures in defending white democracy, the "Colonel" set up many paternalistic, New South textile mills, became a judge, then died when his arm got gangrene after a train window fell on it. His daughter-in-law, my grandmother (who wrote essays? lost in a trunk?), was sent away to some kind of "rest home" (for nerves?). I remind my father of her: that is, of Eva in *The Surface of Earth*. And I have no siblings and am not married (like Hutch in *The Source of Light*). My aunt with the thickest drawl is named Emily (Faulkner's "A Rose for Emily"). I have to face the fact here that I can't even conceive of my own family history, my own identity, without being completely entwined in that inseparable couple, southern history and literature—which exasperates me.

Sometimes it suffocates me to tell this, or I feel like bursting out laughing. How can I claim this ludicrous and sinister history? Yet am I not proud at the same time? Isn't it exciting to have such a past (the French people I tell it to are spellbound)? I'm jealous of the writers who can make high-level provocative fun with their southern background (Lee Smith, Clyde Edgerton), but they are finally not my models. The way Christa Wolf wrote about her childhood in Nazi Germany (*Patterns of Childhood*, 1980) appeals to me more: she splits herself in the narrative. She is both "Nelly" the girl and "you" the person to whom she talks. The "narrative," a plot constantly interrupted by "discourse," takes place in the 1940s and the present day when "Christa" (unnamed) and her family (husband, brother, and daughter) go back and visit the scenes of the past. Wolf writes: "Has [memory] proven—by the act of misleading—that it's impossible to escape the mortal sin of our time: the desire not to come to grips with oneself? And the past, which can still split the first person into the second and the third—has its hegemony been broken? Will the voices be still? I don't know."[46] Wolf has found a way to embed her conflicts and tensions in the form, not arbitrarily, but just enough to keep the reader constantly aware of what the stakes are.

A simultaneous denial and acting out of pain at the core of family, self, society, and history operate in the best southern fiction.[47] That basic contradiction can be stretched to the limit and held taut there; or the narration can double a process of working through, that can be or isn't always successful. Finally, the reader needs somehow to be challenged— to make everyday judgments and decisions in the face of devious living and dead, to be thrown back, by cracks in the narrative, to her or his own history, always painfully open to criticism. Some people consider a great work of art the one that keeps the literal plot and any self-conscious allegories perfectly superimposed so no rough edges show. Then the reader can have a "good read"; if she or he wants to do a critical analysis, fine, but it's not necessary. I agree that too much self-consciousness ruins a book (postmodernism isn't the whole answer). But I like a little messiness, and I love to be engaged with the narrator (or narration) where I don't feel that I have to do all the work—peeling back the veils might make me look smart at first, but it's tiring and I'm the dupe in the end.

I prefer to dialogue openly and on equal footing with the narrator in a tandem conversation, encouraging, goading each other's intellect and emotions.[48]

If I return to Maurice Blanchot, it is in penance for having had such fun telling pieces of my family story. To summarize the metaphysical twists in a mere fifteen pages of The Madness of the Day is to fall smack into the trap Blanchot sets up. He has a terrible, painful accident (?); someone causes him to get shattered glass in his eyes; the doctors can't believe a man as intelligent as he is can't say "exactly" what happened. His resistance to their questions makes them call in a psychiatrist who only tests him further. He supposedly tells them in the end the (avoidance of) story that we have just read, with troubling, vague allusions to World War II and Auschwitz, thus returning us to the beginning.[49] The different inspectors' desire for story is a desire for control and, when resisted, turns into interrogation:

> I had to acknowledge that I was not capable of forming a story out of these events. I had lost the sense of story [history] that happens in a good many illnesses. But this explanation only made them more insistent. . . . [They] remained firmly convinced, I am sure, that a writer, a man who speaks and who reasons with distinction, is always capable of recounting facts that he remembers.
> A story? No. No stories, never again.[50]

Notes

1 Stories of the Modern South, ed. Benjamin Forkner and Patrick Samway (New York, 1978).

2 "History" also has that troublesome double meaning: history books or historical event, historia rerum gestarum or res gestae (as Hegel names them in Lectures on the Philosophy of World History). In this essay, most of the time I mean history as the text of history, although there are occasions of ambiguity; still the double entendre of the word also reminds us that events are almost always inseparable from the accounts that shape them.

3 My view of story, history, and the history of story has been influenced, in part, by Hayden White's Metahistory: The Historical Imagination in Nineteenth-Century Europe (Baltimore, 1973), and by Roland Barthes's "Historical Discourse," in Structuralism: A Reader, ed. Michael Lane (London, 1970). See in particular page 149 of Barthes's Structuralism: "At the level of discourse, objectivity, or the ab-

sence of any clues to the narrator, turns out to be a particular form of fiction, the result of what might be called the referential illusion, where the historian tries to give the impression that the referent is speaking for itself."

4   Maurice Blanchot, *The Madness of the Day*, trans. Lydia Davis (Barrytown, N.Y., 1981), 18.

5   See Flaubert's letter to Louise Colet, 16 January 1852, in *Correspondance*, ed. Jean Bruneau (Paris, 1980), 2: 29. See also Jean Rousset's "Madame Bovary et le livre sur rien," in *Flaubert*, ed. Raymonde Debray-Genette (Paris, 1970), 117–26.

6   Joanne Kaufman, "Lee Smith: Her People Will Do Anything," *Wall Street Journal*, 17 October 1985.

7   George Garret, review of *White People*, by Allan Gurganus, *New York Times*, 3 February 1991.

8   Reynolds Price, *The Surface of Earth* (New York, 1975), 3.

9   Ibid., 3.

10   Reynolds Price, *A Palpable God: Thirty Stories Translated from the Bible with an Essay on the Origins and Life of Narrative* (San Francisco, 1985), 3.

11   Ibid., 5, 14, 28, 46.

12   Ibid., 45, 35.

13   Gérard Genette suggests the devious history of the genres or modes as they have developed from Greek philosophy to European literature and criticism: see his *Introduction à l'architexte* (Paris, 1979), especially page 28, where he shows how the supposedly "pure" narrative form (dithyramb), narrative without dialogue (all "telling," no "showing," he says, using the American categories) drops out, or is repressed, and remains only a "theoretical" possibility. I am especially indebted to Dana Rudelic-Fernandez's Ph.D. dissertation which spells out this history of usurpation by Aristotelian tragedy ("De la transmodalisation: Etude des rapports entre les modalités dramatiques et narratives du texte en littérature et en psychanalyse," Duke University, 1990).

14   Price, *Palpable God*, 19.

15   Michel Foucault, in his reading of Nietzsche, opposes genealogical history to suprahistorical or Platonic history, which he defines as "a history whose function is to compose the finally reduced diversity of time into a totality fully closed upon itself; a history that always encourages subjective recognitions and attributes a form of reconciliation to all the displacements of the past. . . ." Foucault (who has his own reductive obsessions about power) constructs a "counter-memory—a transformation of history into a totally different form of time." See Michel Foucault, *Memory, Practice: Selected Essays and Interviews*, ed. Donald F. Bouchard, trans. Donald F. Bouchard and Sherry Simon (Ithaca, 1977), 152, 16.

16   Price, *Surface of Earth*, 482. When Rob goes to tell his son Hutch the family

story, Rob thinks he is partially breaking the cycle of imperfect stories, "battered scraps but true at least." However, Hutch already expects, as Eva expected, "lies, jokes," more of the same "anger and orders or the old numb apologies, pledges, amends." Also see the passing irony of Rachel's comment about her fiancé Rob's story in her letter to Alice: "When he finished his story (longer than Leviticus and he's just twenty-one) and turned to me, expecting an answer, I said, 'Is that a complaint or what?'" (Price, *Surface of Earth*, 388, 479, 177).

17 Reynolds Price's *Kate Vaiden* (New York, 1986) also uses a clever first-person feminine narrator. The book announced at the end of *Kate Vaiden* is the one (à la Proust) that the reader has just finished reading, i.e., *Kate Vaiden* ("But I'd tell my story one final time, the whole thing, in writing" [306]). So the reader is doubling for the son whose acknowledgment or even pardon Kate wants (her ultimate devious strategy). Hardly an innocent tale, the book *Kate Vaiden* is more like a final self-defense before death, argued in front of the one true judge: reader and son. I feel more at ease with the openly sneaky narrator of Camus's *La chute*, ironically named Clamence, who reveals both that he has probably committed a murder and demands the reader's absolution without the reader's agreeing to give it. See Frank K. Shelton, "The Family in Reynolds Price's *Kate Vaiden*," in *Reynolds Price: From 'A Long and Happy Life' to 'Good Hearts,'* ed. Sue Laslie Kimball and Lynn Veach Sadler: "Kate never, even at the end, . . . comes truly to face her actions and their consequences. . . . I think that this inconsistency is precisely Price's point" (88). Also see the articulate, balanced critique in Constance Rooke's *Reynolds Price* (Boston, 1983).

18 Price, *Surface of Earth*, 288, 241.

19 The black women are both angrier (Sylvie) and more abused (Della). Gracie best punctures the rhetorical universe of the novel; she's Grace overcoming Fate when she keeps leaving Grainger to go back North, as if to say, I leave you all to your craziness.

20 Gustave Flaubert, *Madame Bovary* (Paris, 1979), 219.

21 Eudora Welty, *One Writer's Beginnings* (New York, 1984), 35.

22 Eudora Welty, "The Wide Net," in *The Wide Net and Other Stories* (New York, 1984), 72.

23 Ibid., 40.

24 Ibid., 57. See Patricia S. Yaeger's "The Case of the Dangling Signifier: Phallic Imagery in Eudora Welty's 'Moon Lake,'" *Twentieth-Century Literature* 28 (1982): 431–52. Yaeger reads the various "counterplots" in "Moon Lake" that upset the dominant symbolic male (phallic) order but concludes: "The overinscription of male sexuality . . . prevents the enactment of these alternate stories" (447).

25 Welty, "Wide Net," 63, 46–47, 64.

26 Welty, *One Writer's Beginnings*, 98, 49.

27 Welty, "Wide Net," 41, 69, 51, 55, 59, 68, 54.

28 Guy Davenport, *The Geography of the Imagination* (San Francisco, 1981), 256.

29 Ibid.

30 Welty, "Wide Net," 53.

31 Ibid., 35, 72.

32 Ibid., 39–40.

33 Welty, *One Writer's Beginnings*, 31, 16.

34 Welty, "Wide Net," 56.

35 Ibid., 48.

36 Sidonie-Gabrielle Colette, *The Vagabond*, trans. Enid McLeod (New York, 1982), 192.

37 Taking the title of her essay from Jacques Derrida, Susan V. Donaldson also reads two counterdefinitions of story: one as culminating in a modernist epiphany or revelation and the other (postmodern?) as infinitely "extending and withdrawing the possibility of resolution and unity." Donaldson describes Welty's subject and form in terms of "unfulfilled longing" and a "never-consummated courtship of the imagination." For Donaldson, this technique is feminist in its rejection of resolution, whereas I talk about it in terms of seduction and southern equivocation. I am also going another step by asking what is at stake in the complicity between reader or critical method and text and what it means when a text (or method) is adjustable to opposing positions. See Susan V. Donaldson, "Meditations on Nonpresence: Re-Visioning the Short Story in Eudora Welty's *The Wide Net*," *Journal of the Short Story in English* 11 (1988): 75–91.

38 Welty, *One Writer's Beginnings*, 95, 6.

39 Carolyn G. Heilbrun, *Writing a Woman's Life* (New York, 1988), 14.

40 Welty, *One Writer's Beginnings*, 19.

41 In the fall of 1990, Mab Segrest presented her work in progress to the Duke University Women's Studies faculty seminar. Her thesis examines the way in which the Agrarians, starting in the 1920s but continuing into the later, influential movement of New Criticism, reinscribed a definition of southern identity taken from slavery apologists and based on white mastery.

42 Mary C. Simms Oliphant, *The Simms History of South Carolina* (Columbia, S.C., 1932), 246.

43 Francis Butler Simkins and Robert Hilliard Woody, *South Carolina During Reconstruction* (Chapel Hill, N.C., 1932), 526.

44 Thanks to Henry H. Orr for writing Charlie G. Williams, State Superintendent of Education, South Carolina (January 1986) for this information. The original textbook, *The History of South Carolina*, was written by William Gilmore

Simms (Charleston, 1840), revised by him in 1866 (New York), then revised by his daughter Mary C. Simms Oliphant several times after her first revision (Columbia, S.C., 1917).

45 Oliphant, *Simms History of South Carolina*, 244–45. This 1932 edition seems more virulent than either the 1917 or 1922 (Greenville, S.C.) editions, which I also consulted.

46 Christa Wolf, *Patterns of Childhood*, trans. Ursule Molinaro and Hedwig Rappolt (New York, 1980), 406.

47 I'm borrowing from Jane vonMehren's sentence in the catalog copy and on the dust jacket of Angela Davis-Gardner's novel, *Forms of Shelter* (New York, 1991): "In the tradition of Sue Miller and Josephine Humphreys, *Forms of Shelter* brilliantly explores the ways in which a family both denies and acts out the pain at its core."

48 Nathalie Sarraute writes her autobiography, *Childhood* (Paris, 1985), as a scrappy dialogue with herself, doubling as her own worst and best critic.

49 The illusion to Auschwitz is examined in Larysa Mykyta's manuscript "Expressing the Inconceivable: Deflection out of Historical Time in Blanchot's Fiction" (Paper prepared for the Third Colloquium on Twentieth-Century Literature in French, Louisiana State University, Baton Rouge, 1986).

50 Blanchot, *Madness of the Day*, 18.

Tatami Room

CATHY N. DAVIDSON

Natsukashisa

My husband Ted and I decided to settle in North Carolina in 1989, soon after our third stay in Japan, a year in which we had decided, once and for all, that we could never live there permanently.[1] Politically and personally, there was simply too much of Japan that chafed. But we found it impossible to leave Japan entirely behind. A letter from one of our Japanese friends or even something mundane, such as a story about Japan on the evening news, filled us with *natsukashisa*, a pleasant-sad feeling of loss. Our solution was both eccentric and nostalgic. We decided to build a Japanese house in rural North Carolina.

From the beginning, I was aware that building this house meant creating, in America, a highly selective fantasy of Japan. It meant putting into solid, visible form an interpretation of certain aspects of Japanese aesthetics devoid of the underlying traditions and social relations that give aesthetics meaning and function. Architecture without the social fabric. For all of the visceral appeal of living in a Japanese house, the idea filled me with intellectual anxiety. What kind of postcolonial move was this, anyway? Would I be creating a house or a theme park? What was the boundary between a house inspired by the times we'd lived in Japan and an amusement like Epcot Center, where middle-class Americans can tour the world all for one price and without ever confronting foreign languages, odd foods, or dubious sanitation systems? More to the point, for all of the positive, romanticized impulses that would go into this project, the house itself would always be a tangible admission that, ultimately, I could not embrace Japanese culture; that, actually, I had rejected it by deciding to return to the United States.

Like most forms of nostalgia, building a Japanese house in North Carolina paid homage to a place I never really knew. In Japan, Ted and I had never lived in a traditional Japanese house; like most contemporary Japanese, we rented a spanking new, ferroconcrete apartment complex, its interior prefabricated, its furnishings a mass-produced amalgam of East and West. The apartment was owned by Kansai Women's University, the university where we taught as part of a U.S.-Japanese faculty exchange program. Located in an affluent suburb of Osaka, the apartment was indistinguishable from its neighbors except for a few features obviously adapted to visiting foreigners. We had a western-style bathroom complete with a little cartoon illustration of how to use the American toilet (i.e., a stick figure showed that one sat on the seat instead of squatting on it). We also had an oversized front door, about twenty-five percent larger than the doors on apartments of the Japanese residents in our building. Since nothing else in the apartment was blown up to western size, it was hard not to suspect that the big front door was symbolic, a warning to all that gaijin (foreigners) resided within.

The rest of the apartment was more generic. There were two main rooms, each the size of six tatami mats (heavy, woven straw floor mats, each approximately two inches thick and three- by six-feet wide). The living room was furnished western-style, with two small couches and a coffee table. The other room was a spare tatami room which served as our bedroom at night, and by day, with the futons folded away, my study. There was also a genkan, entry way, where shoes were removed and stored; a tiny galley kitchen; and, between the kitchen and living room, a small area that accommodated a table and four chairs. When friends came to visit from America, they simply could not believe that this was a luxury apartment typical of the kind found all over suburban Japan. Only when we directed them to look at the imported cars filling our parking lot (Mercedes, Volvos, BMWs, a Jaguar) did they begin to readjust their own fantasies about the unfettered opulence of contemporary Japanese life.

Tatami

What became immediately obvious from living in this Japanese apartment is that the uncluttered aesthetic that we admired in Japanese architecture books is, like so many romantic western notions of Japan, more an ideal than a reality of daily life. Since the only closets in a Japanese apartment hold the unwieldy futons, homes and apartments are lined, sometimes wall to wall, with wooden or pasteboard wardrobes designed for holding clothing and other articles for which there is no built-in storage space. Buddhist temples and imperial villas, much visited by the Japanese on vacation, exemplify the austere aesthetic absent from Japanese urban life now and probably in the past as well. But Japanese culture is metonymic by design: a well-placed rock in a tiny garden becomes a mountain, a crooked little bonsai tree can be an ancient cedar, and the tatami room represents calm, unhurried space. After the futons are folded away, there remains a bare expanse of green-gold mats, a fresh straw country smell redolent of another, rural time before a tsubo of land (the equivalent of two tatami mats in size) sold for several million yen.

Because the rituals of tatami were new to me, I could barely enter a tatami room without feeling that I was doing something significant. Inevitably, I'd be out the door, heading for work, and I'd remember something in the closet in the tatami room. No matter how big the hurry, I'd untie my clumsy western shoes, walk stocking-footed across the straw mats, and find myself contemplating what this meant, this new attentiveness. I discovered the soles of my feet. I became a connoisseur of surfaces— different kinds of wood (worn cedar planking is best) and the infinite grades, qualities, and conditions of tatami.

I know awful things happen in tatami rooms as elsewhere—arguments, betrayals, acts of cruelty. But I prefer to maintain a blind faith in the salubrity of straw. For me, within tatami rooms, time slows and I find myself lowering my voice. I hear the word "tatami" and I'm transported to a mountain temple, sitting zazen, legs folded one over the other, breathing modulated. "Tatami" conjures the sound of ancient sutras, my own voice blending in a chorus with the strangers chanting around me, a communal metaphysics of separation, introspection, contemplation, nothingness, silence.

But it would be ludicrous to suggest that only I invest tatami with such significance. Even cavalier and irreverent Japanese respect tatami. New tatami draw gasps of admiration; old ones are pampered, regularly cleaned and aired. After the death of a beloved mother, one of my Japanese friends sat with me in her mother's tatami room. She pointed to various stains in the straw mats, mapping a life through vestigial remains of a child's ink stone, overturned in frustration with a homework assignment, a tea stain made during an argument so intense that no one bothered to wipe up the tea before it left its mark. "I was a very disobedient girl," my friend said, tracing the faint, greenish tea stain in the tatami, "but she never turned against me. Many years later, after I came home again, my mother said she was going to buy new tatami for this room. I asked her not to. These tatami remind me of her love."

Treated carefully, tatami last decades. But their porousness and fragility record life's carelessness, mistakes, or violence. Tatami mats are like a conscience of straw. I've even watched drunks at parties manage to crawl off the mats to be ill. My best friend in Japan, an artist who works out of her home, tried in exasperation one day to describe just how difficult it was to share a house with her father-in-law. She confided that he was the most selfish man she had ever met. After a litany of examples ("When his wife died, the first thing he asked was, 'Who will feed me and have sex with me now?' "), she ended with the clincher. He's impossible now because he was spoiled rotten as a child: "He had four maids—and his mother let him wear shoes on the tatami." Shoes on the tatami! In Japan, this amounts to sacrilege. Even I gasped in horror over that one.

When visiting another friend, an art dealer briefly at home in her mother's apartment in a bustling section of Osaka, I was shown into a 4½-mat tatami room, nine feet square, the size of the traditional tea room. I overheard Reiko-san on the telephone in the living room speaking in rapid Italian to a business associate. The living room (which I never saw) of this three-room apartment must have been strewn with clothing from Reiko-san's half-unpacked suitcases, jammed with works of art she brought back from Europe to be auctioned to collectors, next week, in Tokyo and Hong Kong. Reiko-san and I kept missing one another on this, my third extended trip to Japan. She fit in this visit during the most hectic time in her year when we realized it would be our only chance to see one another before I left Japan. Outside it was cold, there was rush-hour traffic. But as soon as Reiko-san slid the doors of the tea room closed behind her, our talk turned to tender things. Wearing a black suede shirt tucked into slim Guess jeans, Reiko-san poured green tea into cups that resembled rough, rich red earth. She served me a tiny sweet, *nama-gashi*, placed asymmetrically on a cream-colored porcelain plate shaped like a ginkgo leaf. Kneeling on the tatami, our stocking-clad feet folded primly beneath us, we sipped tea, feeling tranquil and spacious.

Could we have achieved this peaceful state amid the couches and the bric-a-brac, paintings lining the walls, in a western-style living room? Maybe, but I don't think so. Reiko-san's tea room was decorated, as is traditional, with a single scroll. We spent only two hours together in 1988, yet I remember the conversation as vividly as I remember the elegant arch of the iris in the vase beneath the scroll. On the train back to my apartment, I felt regret that I would not see her again that year, but I also felt satisfied, as if during our time together nothing else had mattered but her and me, our friendship. Most of my life, like that of my friend Reiko-san, is filled with obligations, deadlines, demands pulling me in opposite ways at once. The tatami room is not an escape from the pressures of everyday life, but it is precious *because* those pressures exist everywhere and unavoidably outside. A tatami room is the architectural equivalent of meditation. It is a place to be uncluttered.

Kuzu

Could such a tatami room be translated to Cedar Grove, North Carolina? We weren't sure. Ted and I had never owned a house during the twenty-odd years of our marriage. In fact, I had always rejected the idea of home ownership, insisting (rather grandly) that my life's ambition was to never own a lawn mower. But the move to North Carolina necessitated major life changes, the biggest being that my job editing a scholarly journal required that I be around for most of the summer. No more camping from one end of the continent to the other for three months each year. No more summers abroad. The new commitment was frightening and suddenly a tatami room seemed the only thing that would make this change in our lives feasible. It all happened fast. Anne, our realtor, found us five acres of land way out in the country, on a lake (another one of my fantasies). She took us to meet Dail Dixon, a local architect whose work, she said, had a "Japanese" feel. Although Dail had never been to Japan, he understood about simplicity and about siting a house in harmony with nature, qualities he insisted were also characteristic of indigenous North Carolina architecture. He showed us slides of his houses, including an exquisite Japanese house he had designed for a retired army couple who had grown up in North Carolina but who had lived for a time in East Asia.

We invited Dail to come out with us to see the land that Anne had found in the country between a historic little town called Hillsborough and an even smaller village named Cedar Grove.

We drove out to the lot, down a long dirt road lined with overly lush vegetation that reminded us instantly of Japan.

"Kuzu!" we exclaimed, recognizing the tangled vines winding around the trunks of trees and into the branches.

Kuzu is an arrowroot plant. It produces a starch that, Japanese cookbooks insist, is expensive because kuzu "only grows in the wild." We learned from Dail that kuzu was transplanted from Japan to the South over a century ago as a porch vine and worked well to shade against the blistering summer sun. But then, during the Depression, federal agricultural agencies decided kuzu would prevent erosion and serve as feed for cattle. It was planted all along the roadsides and in barren fields, and with disastrous effect. Now, known as kudzu, it is one of the most invasive, destructive, and pernicious weeds in the whole region.

"Is this what happens when you try to transplant something Japanese to America?" I asked anxiously.

"Only if you go overboard," Dail suggested in his calm North Carolina drawl, "and if you forget to respect the uniqueness of the place you are."

The kuzu/kudzu became our metaphor for building a Japanese house in Cedar Grove. With Dail's help, we'd work to find some balance between our Japanese dreams and this North Carolina landscape that felt as new— as exotic—as Japan once had.

By the time Anne stopped her car, the lot had become a "site." We got out and made our way through trees and underbrush so thick that, even in winter, we couldn't see more than five or ten feet in front of our eyes.

"Look! A ravine!" Dail shouted.

We followed the sound of his voice and saw him standing there, pondering a ravine that ran diagonally through the property. It was lush with Christmas ferns. Light came in slant and glowing here, illuminating an enormous, old druidic-looking tree stump from which maple saplings shot tall and limber.

The four of us followed the ravine down the sharply sloping hillside, pushing tree branches out of our way, until we came again to daylight, the shoreline. It was a quiet cove, lined with willows, with the lake winding diagonally out of sight. A gnarled redbud tree slanted out over the water.

"This could be a scene in a Japanese woodblock print!" Ted exclaimed.

On the way back to town, I drew Dail my idea of a Japanese house. I said I wanted the front of the house to be pretty private, but with small windows marching up the stairway, something I'd seen in a traditional Japanese house out in the countryside near Shiga, one of our favorite pottery villages. I described the way each small window in the Shiga house framed some specific bit of nature—a patch of tree bark or the tips of a dogwood—so that, as you walked down the stairs, you came to appreciate nature not as a huge and impersonal force but as something intimate, human, artful, framed. And Ted and I both started describing the tatami room.

"Wait! Wait!" Dail exclaimed, "You're way ahead of me. What I'd like you to do is send me photographs of all your Japanese things, your art, your furniture. And send me letters, lots of letters, about your sense of what a Japanese house looks like."

"Actually, I don't really want it to *look* like a Japanese house," I said. "I want it to *feel* like one."

"That's much harder," he smiled.

Ma

Over the next few months, we sent Dail clippings from magazines, articles about Japanese design, and long letters describing why we loved certain things, certain concepts, like *ma*, one of the foremost principles of the Japanese aesthetic. *Ma* is the space or interval between objects (not the objects themselves). The closest we come in the West is with our concept of "negative space," but even that term suggests its secondary importance and lesser aesthetic status. In Japan, without *ma*, there is no beauty. *Ma* is beautiful in and of itself but it is also what creates relationships among objects such as stones in a Zen garden, twigs and sprays in a flower arrangement, characters (*kanji*) in calligraphy, even words in a haiku poem. In one sense, *ma* orders chaos, turns accident into art. A house that fails to pay attention to *ma* is a clutter, a jumble. If you do it right, the observer too is part of the relationships created by *ma*, creating a peace, openness, and harmony without anything like the western dependence on symmetry to order objects in a space.

When the blueprints finally arrived, what we saw was worth the wait. A small, simple house, as we insisted, but with an affect that was somehow Japanese without being a copy. There were gridded battens on the front of the house suggesting *inuyarai* and *komayose* (now-decorative wooden fences) on the front of Japanese houses but also in keeping with North Carolina vernacular architecture where battens are often employed to emphasize the clean linearity of the design. The house was set against the slope of the ravine, following the contours of the land, nestled into the hillside on one end and then suspended over the ravine on stone supports on the other. The small windows I had hoped for, like the ones at the potter's house in Shiga, marched down the ravine side of the house, making the views intimate and personal. Lots of *ma*. We called Dail, excited, and he confessed that he had been anxious, afraid we wouldn't like it. Obviously, sending a client plans is the architect's equivalent of a writer sending off a manuscript.

"But you realize this is just the beginning," Dail warned, once we all had expressed our delight. "There's a big difference between blueprints and a house. Now's when the work really begins."

For the next several months, the process of building took over our lives. I found myself obsessed by faucets or towel bars. Day and night, I'd pore over hardware catalogues, finding exactly the right drawer pulls and, from a different catalogue, the right contrasting washers. My purse filled up with paint sample cards with names like "Silver Fox," "Old Parchment," "Cloudy Day," "Paris Nights." There wasn't a detail in the house that I hadn't discussed with Dail and either approved or rejected. Still, as Ted pointed out, only half-jokingly, I'd begun referring to it as "my house," not "our house," and the switch to the singular pronoun disturbed him. It took me a while to realize that my new possessiveness about the house was not directed against him, but against *them*, an army of other people who were crowding into our lives, each with some kind of claim on this house: the architect, the builders, contractors and subcontractors, all of the people who were becoming invested in the creation of this product, the Japanese house in Cedar Grove.

Shikiri

One day "they" are Dail and Sam, the principal architect and a landscape architect.

"It's the worst possible place for the entry," Sam says matter-of-factly, turning toward Dail.

A small smile plays at the corners of Sam's eyes, but the line of his lips is as taut and straight as a carpenter's level. This is a challenge. Dail looks at him, expressionless, and doesn't say a word.

I have no place in this conversation. These men are planning the site for my house. Mine. But it belongs to me just now only in some intangible way that has to do with mortgages, family, dreams, a fantasy of escape, solitude, privacy, and calm being recreated in a house in Cedar Grove, North Carolina. Standing in the forest on a sultry July morning with the architect and the landscape architect, such things don't count for much.

This is their argument, it is their house. Dail's blueprints for the house lie on the moist ground, anchored by a large flinty-blue Carolina rock. We stand on a knoll which will someday be the beginning of a covered walkway from the garage to the front door. We face the ravine, the lake to our left. I feel as extraneous to this conversation as one of the dogwoods.

Entry. They argue over entry. These are strong-willed, quick-witted men, Dail highly verbal, Sam more cautious with the words he spends. They are both natives of the region and Dail loves to lace his usual sophisticated articulations with colorful down-home colloquialisms. At his office a colleague complimented him on the beautiful shirt he was wearing and Dail responded, "When I found it in the store, in the sale bin, I was so excited I almost made an outloud noise." A few days later I warned him that I'm thinking about writing a book about Japan, a book in which our Japanese house and its architect might have a role. "Make sure to put a little meat on my bones!" he admonished. Dail glides effortlessly from tall-tale hyperbole to dry understatement in a way I've heard often in the six weeks since I've moved to North Carolina. He grins appreciatively at anyone else's bon mot, too, something else I've noticed. North Carolina is a place that likes language, and the humor—at once self-deprecating, slyly knowing, and a touch condescending (we're foreigners again)—reminds me very much of Japan.

But Sam's not playing the game this morning. He's resorted to quizzical expressions, the intermittent raised eyebrow. He has not stopped looking at Dail although Dail now has one knee resting on the ground. With his fingertips, Dail traces the blue lines of his architectural renderings, lines that represent a covered walkway, parallel and perfectly straight, garage to house. Dail brushes clay from his hands and looks up at Sam. Sam gazes down at him.

"Dail, you sure know houses, but landscape is my territory."

Mochi wa mochiya, I think to myself, an old Japanese proverb: If you want rice cakes, go to the rice cake maker.

"If you're going to call this a Japanese house, you can't just plot it down in any old bunch of trees," Sam says, his voice low and even. "Either a Japanese entry *means* something—or it doesn't mean anything at all."

He tells Dail the Japanese folk idea that the devil walks a straight path so the way you can keep him from your house is by making a crooked one.

"Is he right on that?" Dail asks us.

"Mmmm, hmmm," Ted nods.

We are not about to get in the middle of this scene. It's like the *shikiri* (waiting period) at the beginning of a sumo bout. There's no definite beginning to sumo. There's no bell, whistle, or gong to signal when the fight begins. Each contestant looks the other in the eye and determines when the other is ready. If you go too soon, when the other partner isn't ready enough, the referee calls you back and the *shikiri* continues. The trick to winning in sumo is to determine the unreadiness within the readiness, to find that exact moment when your opponent thinks he's ready but really isn't.

"And there's lots more to it than that," Sam adds. He talks about the whole philosophy of *feng shui*, the Chinese art of geomancy which involves siting dwellings in accordance with certain natural principles. One of the foremost is that one must not situate a house along long, straight lines in the landscape since these are unlucky. Especially the entry to a house or a garden must be curved or sinuous or angled. *Feng shui*, like many other things Chinese, was adopted by the Japanese and then adapted to the Japanese aesthetic.

"You shouldn't be able to predict where a Japanese walkway will go," Sam continues. "The whole point is you have to watch where your feet are going. It forces you to pay attention. When the walk stops, you look up and then you see what you're *supposed* to see."

Sam paces out a different pathway through the forest, one with a right-angle turn that takes him abruptly to the edge of the ravine, directly in front of the druidic-looking stump Dail found on our first visit to these woods. Sam glances back at us over his shoulder, making sure he has our attention, then strides toward an imaginary front door.

"That has the Japanese ring, doesn't it?" Dail smiles up at me and Ted, then bends over the blueprints, marking off the new entry on the sheet.

The new, angled walkway suddenly creates an interior courtyard. In the middle of this forest, Ted and I see a rock garden, a koi (carp) pond, a stone lantern, bamboo arching in the shifting light.

Maru

People who've never been to Japan often ask what is Japanese about my house.

"The salami room," I now answer.

This is a private joke between us and the builders. Bob, early on, couldn't get his mouth around the word "tatami." "T-t-t-t-t-t-atami room," he joked one day, pretending to be a child fumblingly imitating a word he'd heard for the first time. Later he forgot the word again.

"I'm just gonna call it the 'catalpa room,'" he drawled with a straight face, followed by a smirk and a wink. In a jocular way, we all accepted the eccentricities of a tatami room in Cedar Grove.

Then came the day we had to explain to the heating man just why it was that we wanted him to move the heating and air conditioning vent that leads into the tatami room. He had placed the vent in the floor of the tokonoma, a kind of alcove that is the most special place in a Japanese house. Traditional Japanese tea rooms are heated by small braziers, sometimes built into the floor. Unwilling to go quite that far, we sought a compromise between Japanese aesthetics and American comfort and decided that the central heating and air conditioning duct should be hidden away in the tatami room's closet, the place where, traditionally, the futons are stored out of sight during the day.

Mr. Chalmers, a man in his mid- to late sixties, was so surprised when I requested the change that he lost his customary Carolinian civility and just asked, "Why?" The look on his face said, unmistakably, "dingbat."

I opened my mouth to tell him and then shut it again. I was literally speechless. I realized the only way I could explain why the vent had to be moved into the closet was by describing what a tatami room is all about. I'd have to tell him how the walls are the color and texture of sand, recalling older times when the walls were made of mud (the right mud, of course, selected by an expert who knew precisely what earth tones soothe the soul). I'd have to tell him how a tea room must be circumscribed by wood, richly knotted, diversely grained, a quiet celebration of the diversity of nature. There are stories of monks who've spent years contemplating a single knot hole. And I'd have to explain to Mr. Chalmers about the tatami mats in their asymmetrical maze-like patterns, black-banded, each referring to one of the eight ancient Chinese principles of life, the small inner half-mat representing the center, maru, zero, return, emptiness, completion, the end of all striving, the goal of the contemplative life. Although I don't meditate in any formal way, I wanted the understated, unfurnished room to be my place to unwind, relax, escape from the day's cares and deadlines. A heating vent? Here? The metallic, high-tech, modern form belies everything that a tatami room stands for. My mind was reeling out philosophical explanations about mutability and the Zen ideal of the unmoving empty center, the heart of all Japanese domestic architecture, all of which I was sure I could not explain to Mr. Chalmers.

"Why don't I have my husband see what he thinks," I copped out shamelessly and went outside to find Ted.

He was talking with Bob and Greg, the contractor. Bob was up two stories, on a trestle, carefully fitting into place one of the grooved cedar boards that Greg was cutting on the electric saw set up at the side of the house. I explained the problem with the vent and how I had done the fearless feminist thing and relegated the decision to my husband.

"What are you going to tell him?" I asked.

"Easy," Ted said. "I'll just say, 'Chalmers, you know there can't be a heating vent in a tokonoma.'" Bob and Greg thought that was pretty funny.

I don't know what Ted actually told Mr. Chalmers but it worked. He agreed to do what we wanted, as long as we knew it wasn't going to be very efficient come winter and summer.

"So he bought the explanation?" Ted asked Greg the next day when we came by and saw that the duct system had been rerouted and the offending vent removed.

"Naw—he thinks you're nuts."

"Well," Ted noted, "at least we saved the tatami room."

"By the way, that's not what Chalmers calls it," Bob smiled. "He re-named it the 'salami room.'"

The name stuck. After that, when any of the subcontractors or delivery men who came onto the project happened to inquire about the funny little room out on pillars over the ravine, it was described, solemnly, as the Davidsons' Japanese Salami Room. Over time, this explanation came to seem Zen.

Genkan

The tatami room is the one feature of the house that is a direct translation from Japan, but almost everything in the house is inspired by something that we have come to think of as "very Japanese." The house is not so much a representation of Japanese architecture as an appreciation of Japanese space, an attempt to capture some of the basic principles of Japanese aesthetics.

The first principle is mediation. In Japan, everything is entered in stages, slant. There is always some middle ground, between indoors and outdoors, from room to room. Porches, gardens, hallways, foyers: in Japan, the process of entry is all-important and every entry leads to another entry. You never see anything directly but, always, framed; nothing singly, but always in relationship.

This is evident the moment you walk in the front door. Every Japanese dwelling, even the smallest apartment, has a genkan, an entryway that mediates and makes visible the difference between the outside world and the inside. To step from the genkan entry into the house itself (often literally a change of levels) symbolizes the transition from outside to in, from the hectic workaday world to the calmer intimacy of home. It demarcates, too, the difference between the social self and the private person and even, metaphysically, the escape from a hostile unknowable cosmos to the finite, the known. Here is where, in Japan, you would pause, remove your street shoes, and replace them with slippers, a ritual symbolizing the passage from public to private space.

Ted and I have different ideas about the rituals of footwear in our home. Neither of us wears shoes inside the house (we can barely stand to wear shoes inside any house after the time we've spent in Japan). But Ted wants to ask people to remove their shoes when they visit us; ours is, after all, a Japanese house. I'm not comfortable with this. We live in North Carolina, not Japan, and it seems pretentious to make people take off their shoes before coming into the house. Yes, it's true that I won't wear shoes inside the house but explaining this to colleagues and friends is about as difficult as explaining heating vents to Chalmers. Besides, I remind him, if we're going to be *really* Japanese we would have to insist on the other footwear rituals, too. The Japanese change their footwear a second time before they enter a bathroom. This time they change from the cloth house slippers into special plastic bathroom slippers, always at the ready at the entrance to any bathroom in Japan. Do we inflict bathroom slippers on all guests too?

Ted admits that this would be carrying things a little too far but then he asks me, "Are *your* friends going to wear their shoes in the tatami room?" He watches my shocked reaction, then delivers the clincher: "What about high heels? You'd let people wear high heels on the tatami?"

No, I admit, I would never, never allow anyone to wear shoes of any kind on the straw mats. But tatami rooms are one thing; ordinary American wood floors are another. I'm still uncomfortable having all my American visitors take off their shoes in the rest of my house. When I think about this a while, I realize it is partly because, for me, removing shoes in America means something different than it means in Japan. Here it implies a certain intimacy, an almost familial closeness, and there are some acquaintances I prefer to keep shod.

Our quandary about removing shoes reminds us of another basic feature of Japanese homes that we have not yet resolved for ourselves. In Japan, one hardly ever entertains at home. Most Japanese enjoy a rich social life but it is almost always conducted at restaurants, coffee shops, or bars. Several of my colleagues in Japan have never been to one another's homes—despite having taught together and been friends for decades. One rarely entertains as couples and seldom meets the spouse or family of a business associate. Rather, a man has his friends and a woman has her own. Seldom do those different sets of acquaintances ever meet. A home is about privacy; it is the place where one will not be interrupted, where one can be "oneself," and where one can remember what that self is when not subdivided into the whole constellation of obligations and categories demanded by public life. In the West, we call this (pejoratively) "compartmentalizing," but I find the Japanese way of structuring public and personal life extremely appealing—although I haven't quite figured out a way to pull this off back in America.

For the time being, Ted and I leave the matter of shoes and visitors undecided. But these are the kinds of issues that remind us that, for all our appreciation of certain features of Japanese culture, neither of us remotely possesses the rule-generating tendencies of the orthodox Buddhist nor the Confucian reverence for order. We opt for relativity. We will invite some friends to our house and ask some of them to remove their shoes some of the time.

Katsu

We do not need to debate the rituals of entering a tatami room. You remove your footwear (shoes or slippers), then step up into the tatami room. Sensualists, the Japanese luxuriate in the textures of wood and straw against the soles of unclad feet.

The new tatami are pale yellow-green, straw-scented, immaculate. In one part of the room is the *tokonoma* that contains the only decoration in the room—the *ikebana* flower arrangement and a scroll done in bold calligraphy. *Katsu*, it says, the thunderclap of enlightenment in Rinzei Buddhism, the instant that turns a life around. ("Oh, we know all about that in the South," Dail jokes, the first time we tell him what the scroll means. "Here, we shout 'hallelujah!'")

The tatami room defines its own space and shapes the space around it, the way a thunderclap defines silence. *Katsu*. No phone, television, stereo, word processor, fax machine, nor even a heating vent: a still place in a crowded life. It is an illusion, like its Japanese prototypes, but an enticing one. The traditional tea room is the supreme Japanese fiction: a vision of order, peace, and grace in a crowded world. Like everything in Buddhism, it makes no pretense of stopping that world. That would be both arrogant and futile and, besides, without the world, the tea room would not need to exist, it would have no existence. A still, calm center requires a whirlwind.

Ryokan

We had our first Japanese houseguest about six months after we moved in. My friend Kazue-san called from New York to say that she was traveling around the States on an open-ended airline ticket and I immediately invited her to visit us in North Carolina. I told her we had plenty of room and would love to see her again.

What I did not say is that she would be our first Japanese guest in our new house. This was a test. Kazue-san could certify whether the house worked or whether it was just a stage set for homesick tourists, a construction of false memory and displaced desire. Her visit would foreground all of the anxieties that plagued us as we built this house—about imitation and authenticity, translation and appropriation, travel and colonization, homage and rip-off.

Kazue-san was the exact person to perform this reflective task. Instinctively kind, with a delicate and nuanced sensibility. I've seen her, in a single sentence, run the gamut of emotions the way certain musical voices move up and down the scale. As I wait for her at the airport, I remember back to 1980, the first time we met, at a gathering of feminist activists, mostly Japanese but some other westerners too. It struck me then as curious but perfectly understandable that Kazue-san could be a social activist, working for civil rights for women and for minority groups in Japan, but could also be versed in traditional Japanese culture, in particular tea ceremony and calligraphy. She is a strong woman who has mastered delicate arts.

Her plane comes in around six. We go for a quiet dinner and then, well after dark, make the long drive on winding North Carolina backcountry roads to the house. Outdoor lights illuminate the Japanese garden. The colorful koi rise to the surface of the small pond when they hear our footsteps on the wooden walkway. A frog even obliges by jumping in.

"Oh, yes, we must have a frog!" Kazue-san laughs. "It's a requirement."

She enters the house, automatically removing her shoes in the genkan, entryway. I pull Japanese slippers from the bottom drawer of the tansu (chest) and she slips her feet into them. I feel a rush of nostalgia as Kazue-san walks across the floor: the swish of backless slippers sliding against smooth wood. A Japanese sound, I think to myself.

She walks around the house, appraising.

I wait for her to deliver a verdict.

"It's more Japanese than Japan!" my first Japanese houseguest exclaims, clapping her hands with delight.

While she unpacks, I make us sencha, a kind of Japanese green tea, and serve it in the tatami room.

"Itadakimasu," we both say automatically, the ritual utterance before one partakes of food or drink in Japan. We bow to one another and sip our sencha. We are kneeling close together in the tatami room. The room is

4½ mats, the size of a tea ceremony room, and we observe the traditional rules for host and guest: Kazue-san sits with her back to the tokonoma alcove. Looking at her, I also see the scroll, vase, and ikebana flower arrangement behind her in the tokonoma. I once read a poignant explanation of why Japanese sit this way, with the honored guest facing away from the most beautiful part of the room: it's so that the guest actually becomes part of the room's beauty. After she leaves, Kazue-san's image will linger there in my mind every time I look at the tokonoma. This is the essence of Japanese art, not only what's there but what's not, not just the object but its relationship to the people who have admired it.

"Oishikatta!" Kazue-san says after she finishes her tea, that was delicious. We bow again, "gochisō sama deshita," the formal ending of any meal or refreshment.

I give Kazue-san a fresh yukata, a cotton robe. While she bathes in our deep Japanese-style tub, I clear away the tea things and take the futon out of the closet in the tatami room to make up her bed for the night.

I've done the same before for American houseguests but this time it seems different. False. Alone now in this room, I keep thinking about her phrase "more Japanese than Japan." She said it with joy and, at first, I felt delighted too. But now I'm wondering just what it means, trying to preserve one highly selective, romanticized image of another culture as a buffer against the pressures of one's own culture. Smoothing out the futons, arranging the pillow case around the hard, beany little Japanese pillow, I feel like a character in some schlocky play, an American actress in a geisha wig, pancake makeup, and thick liquid eyeliner designed to make the eyes go slant.

I remember, with discomfort, a man I once saw at a flea market and antique sale held outdoors at Tōji Temple in Kyoto. He was a western man wearing traditional Japanese clothes, the full regalia: a man's haori jacket, hakama culottes, and even the high, wooden geta sandals of another era. Well over six feet tall, he loomed imperiously, his blue eyes resolutely refusing to make contact with any westerners who looked as if they threatened to approach or even address him.

He fascinated me. I watched him slowly bend and pick up a delicate jade snuff bottle. He examined it carefully, turning it in his long, pale fingers, then he addressed the antique dealer in an elaborately refined and polite Japanese.

"Hyheehhh?" the antique man exclaimed in alarm.

When the *gaijin* (foreigner) started up again in his elegant Japanese, the merchant waved his hands in front of his face, "No Engrish, no Engrish," he said frantically.

The westerner carefully set down the snuff bottle, pulled himself up to his full height, and strode past me, determined and long-legged, unmistakably American male: Gary Cooper in *geta*.

At the time, the *gaijin* in his traditional Japanese costume seemed comical to me. I enjoyed telling the story of seeing him to various Japanese and western friends.

Now, waiting for Kazue-san to finish her bath, I find myself trying to understand that western stranger in Japanese garb, trying to guess what his motivation might have been. What did it mean? Did he enjoy dressing like that or was he on the lam, hiding from some other self? What would drive a person to such a relentless quest for self-transformation (or was it self-erasure)? What are the rewards and costs of leaving one life to find another? What happens when the thrill of cultural cross-dressing fades and you look in the mirror one day and realize that it's all just Halloween, that the elaborate costume has done nothing to keep the ghosts at bay?

Of course, I'm not just thinking about the man at the temple sale but also about Ted and me.

Fresh from her bath, Kazue-san's face is pink and glowing.

"You look sad, Cathy-san," she says.

I tell her about the guy at the temple sale and how I can't stop thinking about her phrase, "more Japanese than Japan." I tell her I'm feeling like an imposter.

"In Japan, I hardly ever take time to appreciate my own culture—yet I call myself Japanese," she answers thoughtfully. "Maybe it's a delusion, for us to think we are citizens of any country. Maybe it's too easy. Maybe that's what foreigners are for."

When we bow "*Oyasuminasai!*" to one another, the nighttime farewell like "pleasant dreams," Kazue-san starts to giggle.

She says my house makes her feel joy. Here, she's a child again. She tells me it's been years since she's slept in a tatami room, on the floor, snuggled between futon.

"What about at a *ryokan*?" I ask. Surely she's slept on tatami at a traditional Japanese inn.

"Yes," she nods thoughtfully. "But a *ryokan* is a kind of make-believe. That's the point. We stay in a *ryokan* and it makes us feel good about our serene and beautiful Japanese life. But how many people really live like that any more? We live in apartments, cement boxes, in cities that are noisy and huge."

Removing her slippers, she steps up into the tatami room, and sighs, "Natsukashii!" My house makes her feel nostalgia, homesickness, the pleasant-sad feeling for something that existed once before, one of the most complex and valued emotions in Japan.

"Natsukashii!" I agree.

This fantasy of Japan is no less real here than it would be amid the crazy, everyday life in Japan. And no more real. That's what I'm learning from my friend's visit. Authenticating an ersatz Japanese house isn't the issue. It's something more interior, about accepting the hybridity of our lives.

"Yes, this is an imitation," Kazue-san reassures me. "But maybe it's better for you than Japan. It happens sometimes—that the imitation is better than the original." She laughs again, "We know all about that in Japan."

I try to explain to Kazue-san about our ambivalence about both Japan and America. Wherever I am, I seem to be aware of the things that don't quite fit. There are things I like in both places but I also find myself profoundly critical of aspects of both countries; whichever one I'm in, the other one runs like a counterargument in my head, in a way that always makes me, somehow, fidgety. That's the word. My connection with Japan makes me always anxious for the place I'm not.

Kazue-san and I hold hands, something women friends do in Japan, and I realize how much I miss those contrary rituals of touching and not-touching, so different from our own. I tell her how sometimes my yearning for Japan is so intense I can hardly stand it. I thought building a Japanese house would quell some of this desire, but it has had the opposite effect. Always, just beneath the surface of cognition, there's a longing for return.

"Of course," she says simply. "Anyone could have told you that. It's like the widow who keeps her husband's photograph on the piano. It's not there because she wants to forget him."

I hear a tenderness in her voice.

"I know," she adds softly, "because I also yearn for such a Japan."

Note

1   Portions of this essay have been excerpted from *Thirty-Six Views of Mt. Fuji: On Finding Myself in Japan* (Dutton, forthcoming), a memoir based on the two years I taught in Japan (in 1980–81 and 1987–88) and on two additional, extended visits (in 1983 and 1990). Japanese names—of people and institutions—have been altered to preserve privacy.

Saving Our Lives: *Dances with Wolves*, Iron John, and the Search for a New Masculinity

JANE TOMPKINS

So we move from St. George toward the dragon.—Robert Bly, Iron John

I recently attended a meeting sponsored by the women's studies program at my university that left me puzzled and angry. It was a largely hostile discussion of the men's movement, centered on Robert Bly's Iron John. Only two of the thirty-odd people present spoke sympathetically of men: a male graduate student who had had experience counseling men who batter their wives, and a female psychotherapist in early middle age who told of her experience with male patients. Successful men, she quietly observed, are not necessarily happy. At the time I hadn't read Iron John, so I said nothing.

This essay attempts to make up for my silence on that occasion: its thesis is that books like the best-selling Iron John and movies like the academy award-winning *Dances with Wolves* are new myths for men to live by. They deserve our attention and respect because they offer men in our society ways to heal their unacknowledged suffering and to satisfy their hunger for intimacy, for belonging, and for some kind of spiritual life.

Having said that, let me admit straightway that there are cogent objections to be made to both works, many of which I share. *Dances with Wolves*, for example, marginalizes women completely. The fact that the female lead (played by Mary McDonnell) is named Stands with a Fist makes a pathetic gesture in the direction of recognizing "women's strength" that only highlights the film's refusal to take women seriously. The Mary McDonnell role represents the reappearance of a standard female character—I call her "the girl from Sarah Lawrence"—who began to appear in Westerns sometime in the late 1960s. You know her because she doesn't belong in the century, the social class, or the part of the country the other characters are in; she seems to be a character from another movie who wandered onto the wrong set. In a movie where the hero is supposed to become completely Indianized, she's especially out of place because she's white (no miscegenation, please), and wears her hair like a 1990s starlet. Arguably, her very presence in the story is a concession to homosexual panic since the strongest feelings in the movie are between men.

Dances with Wolves, moreover, is full of gratuitous violence. In addition to scenes of murder and mutilation that involve both humans and animals, the plot goes out of its way to legitimize war by having the hero discover who he truly is only after a fight with the Pawnee. Because it never explores alternatives to violence, the film powerfully reinforces two of the Western's most tightly held assumptions: (1) that violence is the only way to solve certain problems, and (2) that some people (in this case, the Pawnee and some white soldiers) are so bad that violence against them is desirable.

Still, to condemn Costner's movie on these grounds would be to miss its point completely. Though.it continues some of the Western's hoariest conventions, it does so in the course of making a fundamental break with the code of masculinity the Western traditionally purveys. Instead of a story that ends with two men putting bullets in each other's bodies, instead of a hero who proves his courage through hardness and isolation, *Dances with Wolves* is a myth of personal transfiguration through membership in a new community. It promises salvation to the suffering spirit through intimacy with other human beings. The utopian nature of the project, which some commentators on the film have criticized, is its most essential feature. It offers its audience a vision of happiness and fulfillment in idealized, symbolic terms, the way religious parables do. Rather than commenting dourly on the corrupt and incorrigible human condition, while celebrating the hero who embodies that condition (as Clint Eastwood's *Unforgiven* does), this film wants to move its audience toward the better world it envisions.

Dances with Wolves begins with death and rebirth. The hero, Lieutenant John J. Dunbar, is about to have his foot sawed off by some inept battlefield surgeons. In a scene of horrifying physical pain, he struggles into his boots, mounts his horse, and rides in front of the enemy lines, his arms open wide in a gesture of total surrender. Miraculously, he survives.

The incident stands as a rejection of the army, the society that spawned

it, its butchery and listlessness (the surgeons who were supposed to operate on him had left to "coffee up")—and it symbolizes the protagonist's
spiritual renewal. The lieutenant's journey to his new post, recorded in
his journal in words and pictures, is punctuated by incidents that in-
dicate he is on the path to a new life. The suicide of the senile, loony
post commander who uses archaic language ("yon peasant," "grant you
this boon") signals the utter bankruptcy of the imperialist fantasies the
U.S. military presence on the frontier represents. And the scalping of the
drunken, foul-mouthed wagoneer who acts as Dunbar's driver suggests
the sloughing off of some baseness or soddenness in the culture, its habit
of anesthetizing itself against pain. The mule driver also acts as a kind
of spirit guide back to the body and the earth. Rising from the campfire
one night on his way to bed, he farts in the lieutenant's face and, without
missing a beat, says: "Put that in your book."

The film deliberately symbolizes Dunbar's return to nature—he is constantly falling over on his back, he walks around naked, he makes friends
and cavorts with a wolf (hence his Indian name). Leaving the sick society
of civil war behind, he cleanses himself in the wilderness landscape, and
finally advances to membership in an ideal society, represented by a band
of Lakota Sioux.

He finds himself among people his own culture has stigmatized: "Nothing I have been told about these people [he writes in his journal] is correct. They are not the beggars and thieves they have been made out to be.
On the contrary, they are polite guests and have a familiar humor that I
enjoy." And later, when he has been invited into the tribe: "I had never
known a people so eager to laugh, so dedicated to family, so devoted to
one another." Throughout you feel, as he does, that the Lakota people
enjoy being together. Their interchanges are fond, humorous. They both
know and like each other. This is the way life was meant to be.

Lt. Dunbar completes his transformation through the experiences of
buffalo hunting, fighting with the Pawnee, and making love—he falls in
love with and marries Stands with a Fist. In one scene he tells his friend,
the medicine man, Kicking Bird, that he is trying to have children. In an
enchanting pastoral setting of sunset, prairie, water, horses, and birds, the
two friends amble along. Kicking Bird says, summing things up: "I was
just thinking that of all the trails in this life, there is one that matters most.
It is the trail of a true human being. I think you are on this trail, and it is

good to see." There is music, soft focus, sunset, and Kicking Bird's parting remark: "We call you the Busy Bee."

The earnest idealization of this scene with its gentle joke at the end is a quality shared by other scenes in the movie, which makes time to create such spells as well as devoting itself to the usual cut-and-thrust, bang-bang-bang, arrow-in-the-chest, thunk, aaargh, plop business we are so familiar with.

There is a way, the film is saying, there is a way to be happy, and this man has found it. He went to the furthest frontier and discovered it there, among the wild men. It's somewhere in nature, it's mixed up with horses and dogs and buffalo and the landscape and the star-filled sky at night. And its essence is the family and the tribe. People who like being together, who stick by one another, people who are your friends forever. The trail of the true human being, the one that matters most, is to be found among them.

This sense of the film's destination is confirmed by a series of extraordinary moments that come at the very end. In the first, Dances with Wolves and the old chief, Ten Bears, sit meditatively by the fire, in the silence that precedes speech—one of several such moments in the movie—a silence intimate and shared, exquisitely open and invitational yet without the least touch of urgency, a silence into which any word might be spoken with safety. Ten Bears speaks. "Dances with Wolves is quiet these days. Is his heart bad?" The tenderness of this question, its directness and its tact, are irresistible. Dances with Wolves confides his worries to Ten Bears, as, given such an opportunity, who would not. They disagree on the proper course of action, but all is well between them. Soon after, Dances with Wolves decides to leave. He says good-bye to Kicking Bird, his closest friend, who has been distraught at the decision, though now all is calm. They exchange the gifts they have prepared for one another—Dances with Wolves has carved a pipe—and their words are:

Kicking Bird—"We've come far, you and me."

Dances with Wolves—"I will not forget you."

But the moment is portrayed chiefly through the expressions on their faces, or rather, not on their faces. For Kicking Bird (played by Graham Green, whose performance is unbelievably powerful in this regard) communicates the intensest love without, as it were, showing it at all. It is as if all the long history of male impassivity, inability to express feeling, stunted emotional life, and factitious toughness were overturned in this one scene. Here, astonishingly, the same qualities that one had thought prevented closeness and depth of feeling between human beings have suddenly been made to express the most undeniable intimacy and strength of emotion.

At this, Dances with Wolves turns to take leave of another, younger friend, Smiles a Lot, whose face is streaked with tears. And then, as if this were not enough, as he and his wife are about to depart, a voice is heard calling from high up. The camera moves, and there, astride his horse on an outcropping of rock, is the brave who had initially opposed welcoming Dunbar into the tribe, but who had subsequently exchanged gifts with him and, in nonverbal ways, signaled his acceptance. The voice cries out in the Lakota language—and we see the words translated into English on the screen as the voice repeats them: "Dances with Wolves, Dances with Wolves, I am Wind in His Hair. Do you see that I am your friend? Can you see that you will always be my friend?" On and on it goes.

Great as the moment with Kicking Bird was, this one is even greater. Here is a model of heroism one might die for. Here is courage. Here is generosity. Wind in His Hair has taken the precious treasure that the movie has been saving up and striving for, the treasure of friendship between people of different races and cultures, the treasure of love between men, and literally shouts it from the mountaintop. There is no shame in this love and, equally amazing, there is no end to it either. "Can you see that you will always be my friend?"

As Wind in His Hair shouts these words over and over, it is as if he is proclaiming a long-awaited gospel. You will never be alone, you will be loved forever.

In the last moment of *Dances with Wolves*, everything is taken away. On the exquisite winter woods are superimposed the words of history:

> Thirteen years later, their homes destroyed, their buffalo gone, the last band of the free Sioux submitted to white authority at Fort Robinson, Nebraska. The great horse culture of the plains was gone and the American frontier was soon to pass into history.

Lt. Dunbar's story is a movement from loss to recovery, and then from recovery to loss. As if only through the lens of grief could we be brought to open ourselves to the beauty and value of our heart's desires. The ending of *Dances with Wolves* resembles nothing so much as the ending of *The Last of the Mohicans*, published 175 years earlier. There the lone white hero, Natty Bumppo, says good-bye to his Indian comrade, Chingachgook, and their hot tears, symbol of their love and their grief at parting, fall down on their clasped hands. And then the old chief Tamenund, in exactly the same elegiac tones that conclude Costner's movie, announces the death of his civilization. Once again, a white man has found his true self by leaving his own society behind, venturing bravely into the woods, being befriended by the natives and participating in the wars that will eventually destroy them.

But there is a difference. Natty Bumppo never becomes an Indian. He never marries, never belongs to any family, and his identity is one with his solitariness. His symbol is the long rifle. "The American soul is hard, isolate, stoic, a killer," wrote D. H. Lawrence, "it never yet has melted." This is precisely the form of male identity that *Dances with Wolves* is trying to undo. Dances with Wolves is most on the trail of being human when he trying to have a baby *and discussing it with his male friend.* The hero's salvation does not lie in the wilderness but in the bosom of the human family, conceived not as a racial family, or an ethnic or cultural family, or as a family defined by blood relations, but as a network of affectional bonds. Friendship is the metaphor for being together in a human way. Friendship between men.

Here is the link between *Dances with Wolves* and *Iron John.*

Like *Dances with Wolves, Iron John,* as its subtitle says, is A Book About Men. About men being together not casually or accidentally, but deliberately and self-consciously. Like *Dances with Wolves,* it imagines a scene in which a man makes contact with the deepest part of himself through the agency of other men. Bly says men need to do this because they live in a society that provides them with no rituals or markers by which to know themselves and because they have lost touch with their fathers. Fathers, who by their simple presence could have taught their sons how to be men, have been missing from the home since the industrial revolution. Cut off from their deepest passions and from their highest aspirations, men, according to Bly, need to reconnect with both their animal and their spiritual selves.

Both these lost dimensions of manhood are represented in Bly's book by the mythic figure of the Wild Man, Iron John, who lies at the bottom of a pond in a German folk tale. Bly organizes his thoughts on the male life cycle around segments of the Iron John story, explicating the legend by referring to every sort of myth, folktale, and religious parable, as well as to his experiences as a leader of men's groups, and occasionally to his own emotional life.

There are a lot of things in this book that I can't stomach: its apparent misogyny, for one thing. Bly characteristically absolves himself of responsibility for dealing with women's experience by declaring that women have their own life stages about which he "wouldn't know." Worried, apparently, that his readers will somehow mistake him for a woman—a well-founded fear, since his book deals centrally with the need for men to express emotion—Bly is constantly issuing disclaimers of one sort or another. Most of what's troubling about Iron John may be the result of Bly's fear, conscious or unconscious, of being labeled gay. At least that's how I read the lengths to which he goes to reinforce gender stereotypes, denigrating "passivity," praising "boisterousness," and reinvoking the whole moldy apparatus of patriarchy, with its swords and warriors and castles and kings. Sometimes, reading the book is like spending time in a huge, dark attic where rusty spears and rotten suits of armor rattle around together making a kind of hollow noise.

Ironically, the real direction of the work is away from the very attitudes and behaviors this patriarchal rhetoric represents. The swords and warriors function, for Bly, as a kind of legitimating facade, providing a misleading sense of continuity with the images of masculinity that his book wants to shatter and re-form. With a kind of brilliant perversity, its title, "Iron John," evokes qualities of hardness and inflexibility that are the very reverse of those Bly wants men to cultivate. This paradox, I suspect, is one reason for the book's enormous success.

Bly is superconscious of the terrible price men have had to pay for the heroic code our society has offered them. The isolated, frozen quality D. H. Lawrence saw in the American soul, which expressed itself in the leathery, impassive faces of countless heroes who rode into the sunset at the end of Western films, the deadening of emotion in the lives of men who emulate these heroes, with the self-alienation and social isolation that result—these are the main targets of Bly's book. He writes of himself:

> When I was two or three years old, I went to my father and asked
> him for protection. But he was an intense man, and being with him

felt more dangerous than being out on the street. I then went to my mother, and asked her for protection. At the instant she said yes, I went numb from my neck down to my lower belly. (67)[1]

Bly glosses this personal fable as follows: "It's . . . possible I knew, or thought I knew, that if I accepted my mother's protection, I would have to learn to feel as a woman feels. But I was a man, and so I decided to have no feelings at all" (67). He continues: "Some women feel hurt when a man will not 'express his feelings,' and they conclude that he is holding back, or 'telling them something' by such withholding; but it's more likely that when such a man asks a question of his chest, he gets no answer at all" (68).

The chapter in which these remarks appear is the one that spoke most powerfully to me. Entitled "The Road of Ashes, Descent, and Grief," it deals with the part of the Iron John legend where the young hero is wounded, leaves home, and goes to work in a kitchen. It's what Bly calls "going down," or *katabasis*, a process especially necessary for men in this century who, Bly says, "characteristically fail to notice their own suffering." The going down is a descent into pain and grief, "the rat's hole, the 'dark way,' the one that Williams or Haverford doesn't prepare one for" (70).

> One has the sense that some power in the psyche arranges a severe katabasis if the man does not know enough to go down on his own. Depression is a small katabasis, and something other than us arranges it. Depression usually surprises us by its arrival and its departure. In depression, we refuse to go down, and so a hand comes up and pulls him down. In grief we choose to go down. (75)

In passages like this I feel Bly knows what he's talking about, and what he's talking about are things that men I know could stand to hear. Not just men, either. The reason I like these places in Bly's book is that they correspond to my own experience. I've done a lot of "going down," in Bly's sense, in the past year or so, and what Bly says about the relationship between depression and grief rings true. You have to choose to acknowledge the pain that you feel, and doing so is a humbling experience. The metaphor of ashes and working in the kitchen fits.

But, as he writes, "with initiators gone from our culture, we do not receive instruction on how to go down on our own" (75). The Wild Man in Bly's legend lies at the bottom of a pond. The man who finds him in the story gets to him by emptying the pond bucket by bucket. I think of the pond as a pool full of tears. One gets to the Wild Man, the deepest part of the self, through tears. That is why Bly is afraid of being labeled a homosexual. His understanding of the way to full adulthood requires that he break down and cry. In the Western mythos tears belong to women and babies. Tears are the ultimate humiliation for the hero, what he must avoid at all costs. Bly is offering men a definition of themselves that is antithetical to what they've been taught a man should be. No wonder he masks this with an armory of military metaphors; at heart his myth is subversive of the warrior image of the male our culture still reveres.

This is what makes his book good. This is what makes men want to distance themselves from it like mad, and this is what makes it so easy, for men and women alike, to put it down. The women who spoke at the meeting I attended were adopting the same "reality is all a matter of power politics" attitudes that men in our culture have used to compete against each other and to sideline women. Hardened by their experience of injustice, the women had bought into the ideology of toughness, too, and were perpetuating it. In their insistence on looking only at political and economic conditions and not at psychological ones, they were also perpetuating, without realizing it, another salient feature of the Western hero's code, namely, a determined rejection of spirituality in all its institutional forms, and especially of any language referring to emotional or spiritual life.

One of Iron John's principal unspoken aims is to create an image of manhood that will embrace poetry and visionary experience, restoring to men the roles of prophet, dreamer, magician, and soothsayer which the twentieth century's emphasis on the enforcer/terminator model of masculinity has effaced. In writing Iron John, Bly implicitly models and claims these roles for himself.

Iron John is not merely reporting on an ancient fairy tale; like Dances with Wolves, it is itself a myth. When one realizes this, passages that seem maddening at first become somewhat more comprehensible. For example, when Bly talks about men who are constantly disappointed by the women they fall in love with, he says they're really in search of a mythical being, "The Woman with Golden Hair," whose "glory" drifts down onto pretty blondes who are only ordinary persons underneath. Then comes the maddening sentence: "During the twelfth and thirteenth centuries all this was understood" (137).

Wait a minute. All *what* was understood? By whom? Under what circumstances? Bly goes on to generalize about "the troubador poet" and "the wives of the lords" and by the next paragraph he's back in the ancient world talking about the Greeks and "Zeus energy." Skating across the ages as if they were ice on a lake, plundering mythographies from China to Peru, happily interposing remembered conversations with friends and sly observations on daily life ("a person who discreetly farts in an elevator is not a divine being and a man needs to know this"), Bly acts as if these things were all of a piece. Which from his perspective they are.

These fragments are being fitted together into a piece of mythopoeic bricolage. "The twelfth and thirteenth centuries" has no more weight as factual evidence than does the heroine's golden hair—in fact, considerably less. For the claim about the centuries is thrown at us like a dare, a piece of "evidence" from a form of discourse—rational argumentation—whose rules have long since been suspended. Iron John, a text that often brings forward quotations from the author's own poems as argumentative clinchers, can hardly take "the twelfth and thirteenth centuries" seriously.

What we have here is tapestry, texture, hues, threads running through, and sudden spots of color—a discourse that rides on its own momentum. As a prose writer, Bly taps into energy sources that are their own authority: he speaks from wisdom, from experience, out of his own shamanic powers. Widely read and carrying a great deal of knowledge around inside his head, he treats facts casually because he knows it is the spirit and form of an utterance, as much as the facts it deploys, that give it weight. The book has the force of parable or myth in the same way Costner's film does.

Like *Dances with Wolves*, *Iron John* tries to help men cut off from their emotional lives to access their feelings in a safe atmosphere, and to make it possible for them to understand their experience as part of an overarching pattern or plan. Bly writes: "Understanding that we and our fathers exist in some great story lifts us out of our private trance, and lets us feel that the suffering is not personal to us" (117). This is the way he concludes:

I once heard Marie-Louise von Franz lecture on the Wild Man, and she chose a historical wild man in medieval Switzerland, who went into the forest for many years and whose advice was much sought by both rulers and common people. She remarked that she has noticed in dreams of both men and women in recent decades a figure who is spiritual but also covered with hair, a sort of hairy Christ. She believes that what the psyche is asking for now is a new figure, a religious figure but a hairy one, in touch with God and sexuality, with spirit and earth. (249)

So we move from St. George toward the dragon. From rationality to mystery, from the cavalry to the Indians, from Lt. John Dunbar to Dances with Wolves. The move transgresses the boundary between body and spirit, sexuality and the sacred, that Western culture has traditionally patrolled. The dragon defies our commonsense modes of understanding, a creature out of childhood fairy tales, connected to a pre-industrial past and to fantasies of the future.

The dragons I remember from childhood were irritable, petulant, greedy for gold, and endowed with a sort of cranky charm. They were frightening, but the interest went out of the plot after they were killed. Those were the old dragons. What the new ones will look like, one can only imagine. But perhaps they will be less like Fafnir and the dragon in *Beowulf* than like characters that have appeared in science fiction movies in the past twenty years—characters like Yoda and E.T.—young-old, gender-less, lizardlike creatures from another galaxy, neither animal nor human, to whom we can turn for the wisdom that will save us—and for the love.

Note

1   All quotations from *Iron John* are from the Addison-Wesley edition (Reading, Mass., 1990).

Pursuing Authenticity: The Vernacular Moment in Contemporary American Art

HENRY M. SAYRE

n the late 1960s, a young Washington Heights teenager named Deme-
trius began writing his nickname, Taki, together with his street number,
183, on walls, public monuments, and subway stations all over Manhat-
tan.[1] Others quickly followed his lead. At first, it was just a question of
getting one's name—or "tag," as it was called—"up," and seen as often
as possible. But soon, in order to distinguish one's tag from the mass of
others, it became necessary to develop a certain distinctive style, size,
and color in one's work. Finally, in 1972, a writer by the name of Super
Kool entered the 221st Street train yard and painted his name in yellow
the length of a subway car. It was an immediate sensation, and very soon a
sort of "style wars" began to obliterate what sometimes seemed to be the
entire New York City subway system. In art critic Suzi Gablik's words, for
some this new wave of subculture graffiti came to "represent the destructive excesses of individualism gone haywire," while others saw it, and her
language is telling, as "an authentic new form of community art."[2]

Gablik's uncritical use of the word "authentic" is, in part, what I want
to consider here. It is a word laden with cultural values and assumptions,
but they remain largely unexamined, and Gablik is by no means the only
contemporary critic to use the word so sloppily. In the catalog to their
recent exhibition *High & Low: Modern Art and Popular Culture*, Kirk Varnedoe
and Adam Gopnik have this to say about graffiti: "The insistence on the
artist's privileged place, on his self-definition through his participation
in a restless, competitive struggle for innovation, and on his right to in-
convenience a bourgeois audience in his search for authenticity—those
beliefs, taken up without irony or cynicism, were what made subway art

different from all other graffiti that had preceded it."[3] That is, for Varnedoe and Gopnik, the expressionism of graffiti was explicitly modernist in orientation. Donald Kuspit concluded an essay for a 1983 exhibition of neo-expressionist German painters with the same sense of its connection to tradition: "I understood them now in terms of modern traditionalism and the search for an authentic identity in a world which seems to allow for none. . . . With this understanding came the recognition that the new German expressionism is a true home for radical art today."[4] What, one is inclined to ask, is an "authentic identity"? (I, for one, am reminded of my own generation's endless indulgence in what we called "identity crises"—that is, crises that resulted from the more or less periodic realization that our own identities were in fact inauthentic.) And what, one may ask, is this desire to find a "true home" for radical art, as if radical art itself were wandering the globe, marginalized but not wanting to be, something like the art-world equivalent of the Palestinians? In my own book, The Object of Performance, I am guilty of the same thing. I did not take the word "authenticity" seriously enough, for instance, to get it into the index, but I was capable of writing, in this case about paintings by Roy Lichtenstein and Andy Warhol that mocked abstract expressionist brushwork: "By the mid-sixties, the splash and the drip, the broad sweeping uncontrolled brushstroke . . . had become a rhetorical mode . . . to Pop artists such as Warhol and Lichtenstein [for whom] these gestures reeked of the fashionable, not the authentic."[5] I was, essentially, writing in agreement with Hal Foster, who argued in his 1985 book Recodings that such gestures are so "inauthentic, ironic, [and] mediated," such "simulations of authenticity and originality," that "in this fraudulence . . . [they are] in some sense 'authentic' as a symptom of our historical moment."[6] It is as if, of course, we have some standard of authenticity to measure our sense of inauthenticity against. For Foster, expressionism was, "in its era (when subjective revolt was not yet absorbed)," authentic, but now it is "ideological."[7] I am sure Foster does not mean to privilege the expressionism of, say, Kandinsky or Pollock at the expense of contemporary art. He is not nostalgic. The expressionist gestures of modernism are not a prelapsarian condition from which, in a postmodern world, we have fallen. But if we can no longer be authentic, what can we be? That is, other than inauthentic or—as Varnedoe and Gopnik imply about the position of the graffiti painters—naive? This is no easy question. What I am really asking is how can we trust, how can we believe in what we see? Or are we doomed, in a postmodern world, to cynicism and irony?

Most of the graffiti writers themselves clearly believed in the authenticity of their work, at least initially. Let me quote at some length from an oral narrative by Lee Quinones, describing the day after he and four other graffiti writers—Slave, Mono, Slug, and Doc—"bombed" a ten-car train with Merry Christmas murals twelve feet high and five hundred feet long, nicknaming themselves in the process, "The Fabulous Five":

> It was a cold day. It was two weeks before Christmas. And we were at Intervale on the 5 and 2 waiting for that train [we painted] to arrive. There were these two fine girls waiting at the train station. And then the train was coming. And I said, "look at that train." Like you could see barely on the side of it, all the colors flashing out toward the sun. The sun was right on them. And I said, "There it goes!" I got out my camera and it was coming closer and I said, "THERE IT GOES!" And it's coming closer with the cars swinging. And I said, "It's coming! It's coming!" And the girls are saying, "What's coming? What's coming?" And I said, "Look," and they said, "Oh my God!" . . . And I was going so crazy I forgot to take pictures. And Devil who was with me said, "The pictures!" So I started taking pictures but I only grabbed like four cars. And then the train was pulling out so then I jumped on. And I looked back at the girls, and they were just standing there with their mouths open. . . . We took it to 42nd. . . . At every station, it was a train stopper, a show stopper. At 14th Street, people were yelling and cheering, but 42nd Street was the biggest. . . . At 59th, the people saw it, at 86th there wasn't a big crowd, but at 125th, wow! . . . The station was packed and people were walking into the pieces with their eyes open like wow, man. It was bad. It was nice to have it pull up right in front of you and then get inside of it with windows all painted. They probably didn't know it was graffiti; they probably thought the city was doing something good for a change. They probably thought they paid some muralist to do it. . . . And then we got to Baychester. . . . I'd actually climbed out a little on the side and before the train stopped I jumped out onto the rocks and got to the other side, no matter what, cops or not, and took pictures. And then I heard the train go "whoosh" and it stopped and I knew they pulled the emergency. And

then I saw all the Fab Five jumping out of the train shouting, "Yaah, take pictures!" And everybody's there with their 35s, clicking. It was a nice sunny day.[8]

There is much of interest in this story, not least of all the urge to document the work photographically, which I will develop later, and also Quinones's sense of this train as both a cooperative effort and a positive contribution to the community. But most of all, his sense of it as a genuine and authentic work of art is unmistakable.

In part, it is the immediacy of the moment, the sense of being there that Quinones's narrative inspires, as if you can see the work passing before your very eyes, that creates the sense of authenticity elicited here. Graffiti seemed to many completely unmediated. As early as 1973, Joffrey Ballet choreographer Twyla Tharp offered a group of graffiti writers the job of painting the sets for a dance production. Roger Ricklefs described the event in the *Wall Street Journal*: "While the dancers performed to pop music, [the graffiti writers] sprayed their names and other embellishments to create a flamboyant and fascinating backdrop. As the graffiti writers took their bows, waving their cans of spray paint, the trendy, avant-garde Joffrey audience responded with loud applause and numerous enthusiastic bravos. 'They're so real!' one young spectator exclaimed to his date."[9]

By June 1980, with the famous Times Square Show in New York, and a second exhibition called "Events" later that same year at a South Bronx storefront gallery called Fashion Moda, many artists like Quinones began to enter the mainstream New York art scene, though the mood was initially very much against assimilation into the market structure of the art world. In an interview at the time with a writer from the alternative press publication *East Village Eye*, one of Fashion Moda's directors, Joe Lewis, put it this way: "There has never been a time when galleries haven't choked off younger artists. Galleries play it safe, go for the sure thing. And that stops growth. They turn art into capitalism." His fellow director, Stefan Eins, chimed in: "This is a totally non-money conscious show."[10] Yet as early as 1982, at the Documenta exhibition in Kassel, Germany, Fashion Moda organized the sale of graffiti t-shirts, buttons, multiples, and posters. As Hal Foster puts it: "[T]he specific, ambivalent content of an expression (e.g., graffiti) is first abstracted as a general, equivalent style (graffiti art) and then circulated as so many commodity-signs (graffiti boutiques)."[11]

======

The fate of individual artists, like Jean-Michel Basquiat, is even more telling. In 1980, when he was still only twenty years old, Basquiat was famous throughout New York for his graffiti messages all signed SAMO (a name most likely referencing the phrase "same ol' shit") together with a roughly drawn crown, at once an image of power (both king and champion) and martyrdom (as in *Crown of Thorns*, the name of a 1983 painting). His early graffiti was self-consciously "in the public interest." Almost ubiquitous— and he repeated it often in his later painting—was the phrase "TAR TAR TAR," evoking not only the cigarette industry's destruction of the public health, but racism (as in "tar baby"), violence ("tar and feathers," which he would entitle a painting in 1982), and, furthermore, both by association (oil is the base of both tar and oil painting) and through the anagram, the "art" world as well. Work such as this very much set his graffiti apart from others—it was neither territorial nor self-aggrandizing. It *was* political.

In early 1981, at a show organized by Diego Cortez at P.S. 1, Basquiat's work drew the attention of Swiss dealer Bruno Bischofberger, Italian dealer Emilio Mazzioli, and Henry Geldzahler, formerly curator of contemporary art at the Metropolitan and, at the time, New York City cultural commissioner. Geldzahler bought a collage for $2,000. It immediately became apparent to the dealer Anna Nosei that Basquiat would be good business: she set him up in her basement and got him to painting on canvas, included him in a group show at her SoHo gallery in 1981, and then gave him a one-person show in 1982. She would often sell the work before it was done. Basquiat suddenly found himself earning about $4,000 per week off his work, and things kept getting better, financially at least.

His painting was immediately recognized as expressionist, but genuinely so, not "neo," not fraudulent; rooted in lived, as opposed to learned, experience; direct, not mediated (or, in Fredric Jameson's word, "mediatized").[12] Like all expressionism, Basquiat's painting was, as artist Ross Bleckner has put it, "a map of mental activity," but it was not wholly subjective like Pollock's or Kandinsky's. Basquiat's mental activity, as Bleckner says, "was defined by his relationship to culture, which was problematic."[13] Basquiat felt himself to be just another example of those black musicians, athletes, and stars who have continually been exploited and colonized by the white establishment. In a painting called *Discography II* (1983), for instance, Basquiat reproduces, in the rough, quick, capital letters that characterize all his work, the cover of a Charlie Parker record jacket. It reads:

CHARLIE PARKER REBOPPERS
MILES DAVIS: TRUMPET CHARLIE PARKER ALTO SAX DIZZY GIL-
LESPIE,/TRUMPET (KOKO) ONLY, PIANO SADIK HAKIM, PIANO
THRIVING ON A RIFF, KOKO ONLY CURLY RUSSELL, -BASS- MAX
ROACH, DRUMS—
RECORDED IN NEW YORK WOR STUDIOS—
NOV. 26 1945
"BILLIES BOUNCE"
"BILLIES BOUNCE"
"BILLIES BOUNCE"
WARMING UP A RIFF
"BILLIES BOUNCE"
BILLIES BOUNCE
NOWS THE TIME
NOWS THE TIME   SIDE A
NOWS THE TIME   SIDE B
NOWS THE TIME   SIDE C
THRIVING ON A RIFF   SIDE D
THRIVING ON A RIFF
MEANDERING
KOKO
KOKO [14]

This text, printed white on black, is all there is to the painting, but it marks the reification of the blues to the second degree, not only Charlie Parker's exploitation by the recording industry, of the black world by the white "copy," but also the reissue of Parker's "original" material, a rerecording. Not Charlie Parker, the bebopper—not the being himself, not the authentic and original blues performance. But Charlie Parker reboppers, reproductions, everything in this painting (recording) repeated, removed from the original, so much so that the sound, even the music, is silenced. The painting is just the record jacket—all surface, all presentation, all representation.

Money and success become for Basquiat a "crown of thorns." In the painting of that name, the word "corpus," both the body itself and the body of work, is *copyrighted*, as if to protect the self and its production from exploitation, copying. And yet the motive for copyright, Basquiat makes clear, is purely economic. The "liberty" of the liberty dime, an image itself repeated twice in the painting, speaks to how deeply everything—the "corpus" in particular—is in fact actually not free at all, but tied up in money. Money, so they say, is freedom. A rough "diagram of the heart pumping blood" suggests that our whole system circulates in commerce.

At the age of twenty-four, at any rate, Basquiat became the first black artist to grace the cover of the *New York Times Magazine*. He started hanging out with Andy Warhol, developed a severe drug dependency, which, according to whom you want to believe, Andy either promoted or discouraged. In 1988, Basquiat died of a heroin overdose, at age twenty-seven. His paintings were selling for about $30,000 each at the time of his death. Later in the year, Christie's auctioned a 1981 canvas for $110,000. As one obituary put it, "There's no artist like a dead artist, some dealers are fond of saying." [15]

Basquiat's story is a sort of parable of the colonization of vernacular creativity by SoHovian commerce. It transpires at a place that Houston Baker has called the "blues matrix," the place where individual creativity and the forces of the marketplace come together, and not with any necessary ease. Baker sees the "blues matrix" as a "vernacular trope for American cultural explanation in general." [16] In other words, what occurs at the blues matrix is the fate of all vernacular expression, not just the blues. I like to call this intersection, this point of collision, the *vernacular moment*. Noting that the word "vernacular" means, first, a slave who is born on his master's estate—that is, home-born—and, second, an art form native or peculiar to a particular country or locality, Baker goes on to define the blues matrix as follows:

> As a force, the blues matrix defines itself as a network mediating poverty and abundance in much the same manner that it reconciles the durative and the kinetic. [Baker illustrates this point with a photograph of three men sitting on the steps of the T&P Railway Station, New Roads, Louisiana, 1938, where one train passes each day, a kind

of emblem of duration set against a backdrop of movement and possibility.] Many instances of the blues performance contain lyrical inscriptions of both lack and commercial possibility. The performance that sings of abysmal poverty and deprivation [Howling Wolf singing, "Well I'm a po' boy, long way from home / I'm a po' boy, long way from home / No spendin' money in my pocket, no spare meat on my bone"] may be recompensed by sumptuous food and stimulating beverage at a country picnic, amorous favors from an attentive listener, enhanced Afro-American communality, or Yankee dollars from representatives of record companies traveling the South in search of blues as commodifiable entertainment. The performance, therefore, mediates one of the most prevalent of all antinomies in cultural investigation—creativity and commerce.[17]

There are at least two important ideas about the vernacular moment that Baker sets out here. The first, largely unexamined by him, is that the vernacular must be performed (or performed upon). I will return to that in a moment. The second is that the vernacular moment mediates between the aesthetic object (the blues itself) and its social ground—that is, the economics of slavery, a subject not surprisingly examined by Basquiat in a work entitled Slaveships, and then, parenthetically but crucially in (Tobacco). Baker's reading of the Narrative of the Life of Frederick Douglass, An American Slave. Written by Himself (1845), for instance, demonstrates that, as Douglass himself became, in England, a black, abolitionist spokesman, selling copies of his book for profit, earning lecture fees, and arousing "sufficient sympathy and financial support to purchase his freedom with solid currency," so, in a gesture that defines the blues matrix itself, he "publicly sells his voice in order to secure private ownership of his voice-person," the very tension explored by Basquiat in the phrase "This note is legal tender for all debts, public and private." This, for Baker, is the inevitable "commercial dimension" of all African-American discourse.[18] It is signaled, perhaps most strikingly for Baker, by the moment at the end of Ralph Ellison's novel Invisible Man, when the narrator hears a blaring blues on the street outside a record shop, stops, and asks himself: "Was this all that would be recorded? Was this the only true history of the times, a mood blared by trumpets, trombones, saxophones, and drums, a song with turgid, inadequate words?" For Baker, the fact that this is a recorded blues—"one designed for commercial duplication and sale," as he says—

speaks directly to the complication of the very history it records. For whatever vernacular reality the blues possesses, that reality is expressed in and through a "modern, technological era of multinational corporations, mass markets, and advertised commodities."[19] If this is "the black artist's dilemma," as Baker posits it, it is also the dilemma of all vernaculars.

Basquiat's "copyright," which occurs again and again throughout his painting, is the embodiment of just this dilemma. A copyright "protects" an image from illicit copying, restricts its reproduction. It posits the image, in addition, as the "original" work of its author or creator. It recognizes that "human intelligence, imagination, and labor . . . [are] legible in the work, meaning that such work . . . [can be] seen, a little more crudely, to contain the reflection of the author's personality."[20] What Basquiat copyrights is hardly original—in the painting *The Price of Gasoline in the Third World*, he copyrights the word "clitoris"—except insofar as we *ignore* literal content and understand that what is being copyrighted here is *style*, not the word or phrase especially, but the raw *quality* of the script, its purposefully offensive intrusion into the space of painting—like graffiti's intrusion into the subway system—and, most of all, the congruence of economic and sexual exploitation that the copyright mark itself announces.

Signature style is, of course, the sine qua non of all the New York subway graffiti "style wars" of the 1970s and early 1980s. In Basquiat's 1982 work *Quality Meats for the Public* (Figure 1), there is no authentic or original content, there is only style, marketing. This is painting as advertising: Quality Art for Public Consumption. All surface, no substance. Copyright it. Whatever Basquiat's personal reality, his style, it is expressed in and through this commercial frame. There is, at the vernacular moment, a sort of double movement, between desire and destruction, financial reward and aesthetic impoverishment. In the crudeness of his gestures, in his willful abnegation of traditional measures of artistic "quality," Basquiat seems to embrace this impoverishment, only to realize greater profit. The irony never escaped him. One can never be certain, looking at his work, whether it is the product of a genius or a fraud, whether one is *taken with* it, or *taken in* by it—and he apparently came to like it that way. It was, for one thing, a source of power, one way, at least, that he could maintain control.

Basquiat's "style" seemed, nevertheless, at least for a while in the early

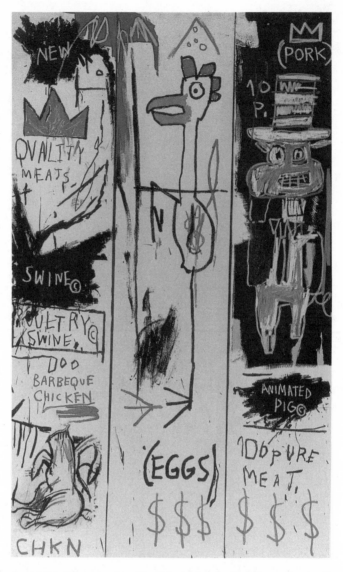

Figure 1. Jean-Michel Basquiat, Quality Meats for the Public, 1982. Acrylic and oil on canvas, 84 × 48½ in. Courtesy Gagosian Gallery, New York.

1980s, genuinely authentic, while other kinds of expressionist gesture seemed at the same time rhetorical, fashionable, inauthentic—simulations of authenticity rather than instances of the real thing. In fact, Basquiat's reputation suffered in the mid-1980s as people learned that he was not the poor Haitian ghetto kid he pretended to be but the upper-middle-class son of an accountant from Brooklyn. Nevertheless, on one level at least, Basquiat's painting seemed authentic because it was raw and untrained, not only anti-aesthetic, but a-aesthetic, as if it had come into being outside the institutions of art. This *marginality* is central to the construction of the vernacular moment, for another way to articulate the exchange between personal expression and commercial exploitation that I have been outlining here is to see it as the inevitable colonization of the marginal by the dominant discourses of culture. From this point of view, Basquiat *was* authentic, until the likes of Anna Nosei and Andy Warhol got hold of him. Speaking self-critically, it would probably be fair to say that what I am doing here to Basquiat—submitting him to theory—is itself just such an operation. But to leave authenticity at the margins—and to watch its inevitable, destructive fall into culture—would be, I think, a mistake. There is more to it than that.

===

Let me return to Lee Quinones's story of "bombing" the subway. Quinones's urge to photodocument the train he and the rest of the Fab Five had painted is a reflection of his desire to record—and hence authenticate—his work, which he knew would soon be erased, painted over by the authorities. That is, despite the thrust of Basquiat's work, his more or less Platonic sense that a loss of authenticity is the inevitable result of reproduction, there is a way to look at reproduction in a more positive light. One can see, in Basquiat's work, a certain documentary drift, as if these paintings testify to the very dilemma of the vernacular moment. Likewise, at the end of *Camera Lucida*, Roland Barthes describes the attraction he feels for the so-called "Winter Garden" photograph of his mother not so much as a function of its capturing any sense of her "unique being," but rather as a result of the fact that it "possesses an evidential force," the incontestable testimony that she was there, "*on that day.*" [21] This evidential force—the traces of an anterior moment, that *remainder*—is, I think, where we must turn our attention. After the fall, after culture has absorbed the margin, erased the original, what is *left over*, I want to argue, is the authentic.

To insist on the authenticating function of photography is to go against the grain, I realize, of contemporary critical theory, most particularly against the argument of Walter Benjamin's 1936 essay "The Work of Art in the Age of Mechanical Reproduction," which still holds almost hegemonic authority in photography discourse. For Benjamin,

> the presence of the original is the prerequisite to the concept of authenticity. . . . The authenticity of a thing is the essence of all that is transmissible from its beginning, ranging from its substantive duration [that is, its actual existence as a physical object in time] to its testimony to the history which it has experienced [the history, for instance, of its reception as well as its literal physical deterioration]. . . . What is really jeopardized when the historical testimony is affected is the authority of the object. One might subsume the eliminated element in the term "aura" and go on to say: that which withers away in the mechanical age of reproduction is the aura of the work of art. . . . [T]he technique of reproduction detaches the reproduced object from the domain of tradition. By making many reproductions it substitutes a plurality of copies for a unique existence.[22]

The attractions of this argument to postmodernist theory should by now be clear. As Abigail Solomon-Godeau has put it in an article entitled "Photography After Art Photography": "In contrast to modernist art photography's claims in regard to the self-containment of the image and the palpable presence of the author, works such as those by Robert Rauschenberg et alia emphasized in every way possible their dependency on already-existing and highly conventionalized imagery drawn from the mass media."[23] In a world of reproduction, representation's idea of the original image is lost. There is only the possibility, as I have already said, and as Rauschenberg was quick to realize, of style.

Still, Benjamin recognized in photography, if not the aura of the original, the presence of the evidentiary force of which I spoke a moment ago. He discovered, in some photographs at least, a "tiny spark of chance, of the here and now, with which reality has, as it were, seared the character of the picture."[24] He recognized such imprints in the work of "Atget, who, around 1900, took photographs of deserted Paris streets. It has quite justly been said of him that he photographed them like scenes of crime. The scene of a crime, too, is deserted; it is photographed for the purpose of establishing evidence. With Atget, photographs become standard evidence for historical occurrences. . . . They demand a specific kind of approach; free-floating [aesthetic] contemplation is not appropriate to them."[25] They demand, in other words, that they be understood historically, that the narrative of history (of the crime of history, even) be constructed around them. In the mid-1930s, in fact, Benjamin began to collect photographs for inclusion in his never-completed *Passagen-Werk*, his study of the Arcades of nineteenth-century Paris. He thought of these photographs, as he put it in a letter of 1935, as "the most important illustrative documents." They were evidentiary in force, "small, particular moments," in which "the total historical event" of nineteenth-century French social life was embedded.[26] As Susan Buck-Morss has put it in her seminal study of the *Passagen-Werk*: "Like dream images, urban objects, relics of the last century, were hieroglyphic clues to a forgotten past. Benjamin's goal was to interpret for his own generation these dream fetishes in which, in fossilized form, history's traces had survived."[27]

With this in mind, I would like to reread a continuing series of family photographs taken by Nicholas Nixon of his wife and her three sisters (Figure 2), one photograph a year, each year since 1975, photographs I have considered before in the first chapter of *The Object of Performance*. Just as Nixon has seemed intent on revising, each year, his view of his wife and sisters-in-law, or has enjoyed, however self-consciously, revisiting the scene of his annual crime against the idea of photography-as-art by creating, of all things, family photographs—the very lifeblood of untalented, local, commercial photographers everywhere—so I have been drawn back to the work, to the scene of my own earlier crime against it. The second reading of this body of work represents a revision of the first, literally a re-presentation, a revision or second seeing, forced upon me by a certain shift in the contextual trappings of the work itself. Though at first radically different from the first reading, and apparently contradicting it, this second reading actually subsumes and expands the former.

I first saw Nixon's photographs of his wife and her three sisters at the Museum of Modern Art in 1978, in an exhibition by John Szarkowski entitled "Mirrors and Windows." They constituted for me a "rhetoric of the pose." They were authentic—that is, part and parcel of our postmodern

Figure 2. Nicholas Nixon, The Brown Sisters, 1984. Copyright © Nicholas Nixon. Courtesy Fraenkel Gallery, San Francisco.

times—in their apparently conscious inauthenticity. As Roland Barthes has put it: "In front of the lens, I am at the same time: the one I think I am, the one I want others to think I am, the one the photographer thinks I am, the one he makes use of to exhibit his art."[28] (Notice, for instance, Nixon's "mark" upon the Brown sisters photograph, the shadow he and his camera cast across the group.) Like all family portraits, Nixon's institutionalize a version of the family that has no real or necessary relation to fact or feeling; they are the construction of a more or less ideal family, signified not only by their obvious well-being but most fully by the very fact of their "coming together," in the photograph and for the occasion of the photograph, each year, to make a family, to represent themselves as a family, whatever fragmentation, dissolution, distance, and difference might actually lie between and among them. Everyone has done it. We've all gone home, for the holidays or whatever, and we've played a role, we've decided to bury whatever "real" feelings we might have for the sake of the occasion. There is nothing particularly awful about this, but it is not, let me say, either sincere or authentic behavior. In fact, what family get-togethers remind us of most completely—and certainly this is one of the hardest lessons of *Hamlet*—is that there is really very little place in the world of the family for displays of sincerity and authenticity. They only lead to trouble. What Nixon's work revealed to me, then, is that the photograph is always—at least potentially, and thus, in effect, always— other than what it represents. It is fundamentally duplicitous. It posits its object as always in excess of what is presented to us within the frame, and it affirms the polysemy of representation. What we witness in Nixon's portraits is an "acting out" of the "idea" of the family, not the embodiment of the family per se, but its performance. These women ask us to contemplate whether the family is merely a simulacrum—a simulacrum of the very idea of community. The photograph is, in essence, the totem of our inauthentic and hollow age. It represents a self that can speak only through masks, a self that, in Baudrillard's words, is "only a pure screen, a switching center for all the networks of influence" that comprise it.

———

No sooner had I constructed this version of Nixon's work, and seen it to press, than I found myself wanting to revise it. In an exhibition entitled "Pictures of People," first seen at the Museum of Modern Art in New York, 15 September–13 November 1988, Nixon recontextualized the entire series of photographs of his wife and her sisters by locating them in the larger scheme of his work as a whole, work of which I had been more or less aware, but which, until the exhibition, had remained individual instances, more or less autonomous, without any necessary connection. "Pictures of People" consisted of five parts.[29] The first was called "People, 1978–82." Many of these portraits of people are family photographs, though not ones so compromised by the rhetoric of the pose as Nixon's portraits of his wife and her three sisters. One of his major themes seems to be continuity. One senses it in the family likenesses that seem to preoccupy him. If the children seem different from their parents, the implicit theme is that they will end up the same. What this continuity amounts to is a narrative both broadly historical, as depictions of American social reality, and narrowly familial, insofar as children are seen here as the inevitable bearers of their parents' social stamp.

There are three other series in the exhibition, besides his portraits of his wife and sisters-in-law: a group called "At Home" that depicts Nixon's

Figure 3. Nicholas Nixon, M. A. E., Boston, 1985. Copyright © Nicholas Nixon.
Courtesy Fraenkel Gallery, San Francisco.

wife, the second from the right in all the pictures of the sisters, and
his children; a group called simply "Old People," photographed at an
old people's home where Nixon has volunteered his services since the
mid-1970s (Figure 3); and a group of photographs depicting people with
AIDS (Figure 4). The photographs of his wife and small children contrast
sharply and purposefully with his portraits of old people, the series that
he was completing as he initiated the former. He presents us with both
extremes of age. But just as he is implicated, obviously, in the reproduction of his own children, he also implicates himself in the pictures of old
people. His entire torso and camera are literally reflected in the eyes of
the woman whose initials are M. A. E.

These photographs verge on exploitation. Indeed they have generally
been so received. Writing in *Artforum* magazine, Charles Hagen summed
up the critical response:

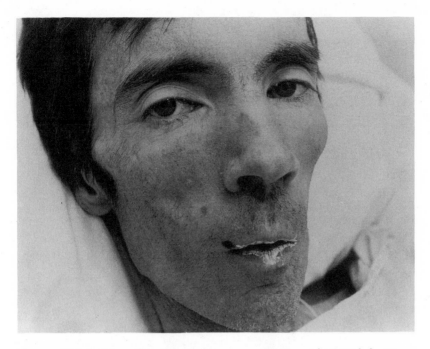

Figure 4. Nicholas Nixon, Tom Moran, January 1988. Copyright © Nicholas Nixon. Courtesy Fraenkel Gallery, San Francisco.

> We are free . . . to notice, for example, that the skin of very old people can resemble (in a photograph) the crispy, translucent skin of a roast turkey; that fine wisps of white hair can look like corn silk. The photograph allows us to form these similes only while simultaneously repelling attempts to discover deeper meanings. As patterns of tones within photographs, these people are denatured, reduced to shadows. They don't talk, move, smell, think.[30]

The problem with Hagen's reading is that he wants to take these works out of context. He insists on approaching them each individually, as individual works of art. By themselves, individually, they are exploitative, just as the photo of Nixon's two children, Clementine and Sam, revealing the genitals of both, could be read, in isolation, as an instance of child pornography. But as part of a larger narrative—let's say that it is a narrative on aging—they are something else. We become implicated in them, just as surely as Nixon is himself reflected in the otherwise vacant eyes of the woman. That they don't talk, move, or even possibly think is the point. And their dissolution is our own.

Sander Gilman, in his book *Disease and Representation: Images of Illness from Madness to AIDS*, argues that

> it is the fear of collapse, the sense of dissolution, which contaminates the Western image of all diseases. . . . But the fear we have of our collapse does not remain internalized. Rather, we project this fear onto the world in order to localize it and indeed, to domesticate it. For once we locate it, the fear of our own dissolution is removed. Then it is not we who totter on the brink of collapse, but rather the Other.[31]

The history of our representation of AIDS is of course a prime example of just such a practice. AIDS victims are Other than us—drug addicts, needle sharers (that is, not upper-class drug addicts), and also (I am quoting Susan Sontag who, one trusts, is speaking ironically, adopting the "mainstream" point of view) "promiscuous homosexual men practicing their vehement sexual customs."[32]

People with AIDS age fast, right before your eyes. Nixon's portrait of Tom Moran, taken in January 1988, just before he died is startlingly close to his portraits of the old people. In this context one begins to sense what is at stake in Hagen's insistence that Nixon should be obliged to discover "deeper meaning" or reveal the personality of his old people. Hagen wants them to have identities so that he can assure himself that they are individuals, separate from himself, their dissolution *other* than his own. "The construction of the image of the patient," Gilman explains, "is always a playing out of the desire for a demarcation between ourselves and the chaos represented in culture by disease." But what happens, Gilman asks, when we are forced to recognize that "we are all at risk— we will all be ill, will fail, will die? What happens . . . when our sense of ourselves as 'the patient,' of ourselves as existing on the wrong side of the margin between the healthy and the diseased, becomes alien to our definition of self?"[33] In the face of "Portraits of People," even Hagen was, like me, forced to revise his reading of Nixon's work. "Nixon's photographs [of AIDS victims]," he wrote in his review of the MoMA exhibition, "bring us sad news, but do so with an honesty and passion that force us to recognize the pain as, at least in part, our own."[34]

It seems to me, in fact, that this is Nixon's project: he wants us to realize that we are, have always already been, "the patient." We are the Other we seek to marginalize. In the context of this work—the families on the porches, the babies at home, old people, and people dying of AIDS—Nixon's photographs of his wife and her three sisters become an essay in themselves on aging. They assert, much more dramatically than any sense of being merely "staged" or "performed," their status as documents. They trace, that is, the history of these women, year by year, and the supposition is that they will continue to trace this history in years to come. They amount to a sort of ongoing visual record that will arrive, one day, at scenes not unlike the photo of Tom Moran. As acts of witness—testimonies—these works, like Basquiat's paintings, exist as traces after the fact, after the vernacular moment. The act of creation, of personal expression, is no longer an *originary* act—that is, a first instance; it is, rather, *exemplary*—*worth* saving, *worth* repeating. It has the authority of evidence. It is, finally, in the full sense of the word, *telling*.

For what is "left over" in these works is a story, a narrative. In an essay called "The Storyteller," written in the same year as "The Work of Art in the Age of Mechanical Reproduction," Benjamin bemoaned the fact that the art of storytelling, like so many things, seemed to be coming to an end. "Was it not noticeable," he writes, "at the end of the war that men returned from the battlefield silent—not richer, but poorer in communicable experience? . . . And there was nothing remarkable about that. For never has experience been contradicted more thoroughly than strategic experience by tactical warfare, economic experience by inflation, bodily experience by mechanical warfare, moral experience by those in power."[35] For Benjamin, the earliest avatar of this dissolution was the book and its progeny the novel, a form removed from the oral tradition like no other, removed from storytelling, removed from social life. "The birthplace of the novel," he says, "is the solitary individual." The storyteller, on the other hand, engages us in a performance, draws us in so that we might retain what we are told, assure ourselves of "the possibility of *reproducing* the story." Storytellers, Benjamin concludes, join "the ranks of the teachers and sages." They tell a story worth repeating, worth knowing. Their gift lies in their "ability to relate . . . life. . . . This is the basis of the incomparable aura about the storyteller."[36] This, too, is the basis for the aura, the authenticity, that we discover at the vernacular moment, when the aura of originality is supplanted by the aura of the authentic, the exemplary. For it is then, at the vernacular moment, that we discover a story worth remembering, that is to say, the story of our lives.

Notes

1   The most complete history of New York graffiti is Craig Castleman's *Getting Up: Subway Graffiti in New York* (Cambridge, Mass., 1982). My brief account is indebted to this work.

2   Suzi Gablik, *Has Modernism Failed?* (New York, 1984), 103.

3   Kirk Varnedoe and Adam Gopnik, *High & Low: Modern Art and Popular Culture* (New York, 1990), 382.

4   Donald B. Kuspit, "Flak from the 'Radicals': The American Case against Current German Painting," in *Art After Modernism: Rethinking Representation*, ed. Brian Wallis (New York, 1984), 151.

5   Henry M. Sayre, *The Object of Performance: The American Avant-Garde since 1970* (Chicago, 1989), 47–48.

6   Hal Foster, *Recodings: Art, Spectacle, Cultural Politics* (Port Townsend, Wa., 1985), 76.

7   Ibid., 73.

8   Castleman, *Getting Up*, 11–13.

9   Roger Ricklefs, "Co-Co 144's Underground Art School," *Wall Street Journal*, 26 April 1973, quoted in Castleman, *Getting Up*, 119.

10   Steven Vincent, "Fashion/Moda at the New Museum," in *ABC No Rio Dinero: The Story of a Lower East Side Art Gallery*, ed. Alan Moore and Marc Miller (New York, 1985), 18.

11   Hal Foster, "Signs Taken for Wonders," in *Postmodern Perspectives: Issues in Contemporary Art*, ed. Howard Risatti (Englewood Cliffs, N.J., 1990), 157.

12   Fredric Jameson, *Postmodernism, or, The Cultural Logic of Late Capitalism* (Durham, N.C., 1991), 162.

13   Quoted in Andrew Decker, "The Price of Fame," *Artnews* 88 (January 1989): 101.

14   The painting is reproduced in Demosthenes Davvestas, "Lines, Chapters, and Verses: The Art of Jean-Michel Basquiat," *Artforum* 25 (April 1987): 119.

15   Allan Schwartzman, "Banking on Basquiat," *Arts* 63 (November 1988): 26.

16   Houston A. Baker, Jr., *Blues, Ideology, and Afro-American Literature: A Vernacular Theory* (Chicago, 1984), 14.

17   Ibid., 8–9.

18   Ibid., 49–50.

19   Ibid., 62.

20   Molly Nesbit, "What Was an Author?" *Yale French Studies* 73 (1987): 234. Nesbit's article, detailing the role of copyright law in defining the idea of the author

in modernist thought, concentrates especially on the difficulty that the law has confronted in the face of photography and film, difficulties by no means exhausted today in the face of new technologies.

21 Roland Barthes, *Camera Lucida: Reflections on Photography*, trans. Richard Howard (New York, 1981), 82, 87–88.

22 Walter Benjamin, "The Work of Art in the Mechanical Age of Reproduction," in *Illuminations*, ed. Hannah Arendt, trans. Harry Zohn (New York, 1968), 222–23.

23 Abigail Solomon-Godeau, "Photography After Art Photography," in Wallis, ed., *Art After Modernism*, 75.

24 Walter Benjamin, "A Short History of Photography," trans. Stanley Mitchell, *Screen* 13 (Spring 1972): 7.

25 Benjamin, "Work of Art," 228.

26 Quoted in Susan Buck-Morss, *The Dialectics of Seeing: Walter Benjamin and the Arcades Project* (Cambridge, Mass., 1989), 71.

27 Ibid., 39.

28 Barthes, *Camera Lucida*, 13.

29 The catalog of the exhibition is published as *Nicholas Nixon: Pictures of People* (New York, 1988).

30 Charles Hagen, "Nicholas Nixon," *Artforum* 23 (January 1985): 92.

31 Sander L. Gilman, *Disease and Representation: Images of Illness from Madness to AIDS* (Ithaca, N.Y., 1989), 1.

32 Susan Sontag, *AIDS and Its Metaphors* (New York, 1989), 26.

33 Gilman, *Disease and Representation*, 4–5.

34 Charles Hagen, "Nicholas Nixon," *Artforum* 27 (December 1988): 119.

35 Walter Benjamin, "The Storyteller," in *Illuminations*, 84.

36 Ibid., 87, 97, 108–9; emphasis mine.

Becoming America's Lens on the World:

National Geographic in the Twentieth Century

JANE COLLINS AND CATHERINE LUTZ

T he history of the National Geographic Society and *National Geographic* magazine as generally told is an epic of success: an amateur scientific organization begun by Gardiner Greene Hubbard in 1888 goes on to become the largest scientific-educational organization in the world; a publication that started out as a "slim, dull and technical" journal for gentleman scholars evolves into a glossy magazine whose circulation is the third largest in the United States. *National Geographic's* success, in these accounts, is attributed to its editors' accurate reading of the American people and "what they want to know" about the world; to its willingness to use innovative new photographic technologies; and to its ability to secure a reputation for itself as an impartial, accurate, and genteel source of information on the world and its inhabitants.[1]

A more complex reading of the emergence of the National Geographic Society is given by P. Pauly, who sees the possibility of such an organization as having been conditioned by several significant historical trends converging at the end of the nineteenth century.[2] These trends included the emergence of mass journalism, the development of photoengraving technology, scientific specialization, and the awakening of American interest in the rest of the world that came with the end of the Spanish American War and the United States acquisition of new territorial possessions. The convergence of these trends created the space for an organization that could effectively operate on the boundary between science and entertainment and whose subject matter was America's place in the world.

Many historians have described the late nineteenth century as a period

when Americans developed new confidence in their status among nations. In the words of John Higham, "the jingoism of the early and mid-
nineties culminated in an exhilarating little war with Spain. The victory,
won swiftly and in a holiday spirit, required few strains or sacrifices." Following actions in the Caribbean and the Philippines in 1898, the United
States acquired dependencies, without encountering significant opposition from other imperialist powers. According to Higham, the "summons
to take up the white man's burden, preached by a few before 1898, was
accepted in a genial, light-hearted mood. What a dazzling field for American achievement opened now among 'backward' island peoples."[3] The
early National Geographic Society touted its research in political and economic geography as an important support for the nation in an era of new
global responsibilities. It published articles on the geographic and commercial possibilities of America's new possessions, discussed the benefits
of colonialism, and assigned itself the role of arbitrator in determining the
proper spellings of the new parts of the world with which colonialism
brought the country in contact.[4]

Encounters with newly colonized peoples, as well as an increasing flow
of immigrants, required the popular American imagination to develop
some way of accounting for cultural differences. Theories of polygeny and
environmental determinism had offered the nineteenth-century public
some straightforward ways of explaining difference. But as George Stocking has pointed out, a significant paradox emerged. To the extent that the
peoples in question "remained subordinate, exploited and unfree," they
challenged the "myth that 'civilization' was associated with the triumph
of liberal principles and the equal freedom of all human individuals."[5]

According to Stocking, social evolutionary thinking provided the resolution of the paradox. Inequalities could be interpreted as residual effects
of uneven biological or cultural development. Those whose status was
unequal could be assumed to be lagging behind in the mental or moral
development on which equality should be premised, and the "metaphorical extendability" of such assumptions made it possible to apply
them to a wide range of situations—encompassing inequalities among
nations, races, genders, and classes.

The anthropology of the late nineteenth century dedicated itself to
the search for evidence of the evolutionary backwardness of subaltern
peoples—inventing a wide range of biological and sociocultural indices

for the purpose. From craniometry to the cataloging of marriage principles, the study of difference was directed toward the creation of hierarchy. By the first and second decades of the twentieth century, psy-
chologists and biologists were attempting to link evolutionary schemes to
abstract, yet unilinear, measures of development, such as IQ.[6] An emerging understanding of genetic principles, combined with social evolutionary thought, fueled the eugenics movement, efforts to limit immigration,
and restrictive racial codes.

The National Geographic Society emerged in the midst of this context, and positioned itself as a key actor in the presentation of "backward" peoples for Western perusal. The Society's brand of evolutionism
was not the pessimistic Social Darwinism of the nativist and eugenics
movements—a brand of evolutionism that worried about a presumed
tendency of lower classes and "primitive" peoples to outmultiply their
betters. Rather, they adopted what Stocking has called a more "classical"
social evolutionism: an optimistic brand of the doctrine, which focused
on the "evolutionary guarantee" of progress through the increasing triumph of rationality over instinct even as it continued to justify residual
inequalities of sex, class, and race.[7] National Geographic reinforced America's
vision of its newly ascendant place in the world by showing "how far
we've come." While its photographs detailed, and occasionally lingered
on, one or another aspect of native life, their underlying story was always
the evolutionary chronicle, with its contrastive work, its encoding of
hierarchy and power relations, and its projection of an inevitable outcome.[8]

═══

If social evolutionary thought and imperialist adventures formed a precondition for National Geographic's emergence and success, a changing view
of science formed another part of the context. By the late nineteenth
century, the full impact of positivism as an intellectual development had
been felt in the United States. The new scientists held the world—both
natural and social—to be orderly and knowable. They rejected the search
for ultimate causes as a remnant of religion and metaphysics, and instead embraced attempts to discern regularities and "laws" in the world
around them. The new science was becoming a profession, supported
and housed by universities, government, and industry. "Amateur" was a
pejorative term in this context, and the "gentleman-scholar" conversant

with a wide range of fields was seen as a quaint remnant of past eras. Concomitant with a rise in specialist fields of study, there was a decline in such eclectic and broadly defined areas as "natural history."

Geography lagged behind in this process of academic specialization. In the 1880s, geography was still a "genteel social activity." No academic graduate departments existed before 1903, and the American Geographic Society was dominated by elderly amateurs. In Pauly's words, "It seemed likely that in America the more technical geographical research might be divided up among departments of geology, anthropology, economics, and engineering, while geographical societies would turn into ineffectual adventurers' clubs without substantial links to science."[9] The formation of the National Geographic Society reflected the tensions inherent to this larger process of professionalization of science, which were played out over a number of years in interactions between board members and editorial staff.

The Society was formed in 1888 by Gardiner Green Hubbard, a lawyer, a member of a prominent Boston family, and a patron of science. The initial meetings, held at the Cosmos Club in Washington, D.C., brought together thirty-three distinguished geographers, most of whom held positions in federal bureaus such as the Geological Survey, the Coast and Geodetic Survey, and the Weather Bureau. Many of these men, including John Wesley Powell, William Morris Davis, W. J. McGee, Cleveland Abbe, Grove Karl Gilbert, C. Hart Merriam, Henry Gannett, and A. W. Greely, were prominent in efforts to define an independent subject matter for geography and to professionalize the field. While from its inception the National Geographic Society was designed to have "as broad and liberal" a membership base "as is consistent with its own well-being and the dignity of the science it represents," its original goals were both the diffusion and sponsorship of geographic research.[10]

Hubbard had a history of backing "practical science," most notably in the person of Alexander Graham Bell (who married Hubbard's daughter in 1877). He gave the National Geographic Society a great deal of autonomy in the first ten years, but with the publication of the magazine left to the scientists and professionals on the Board, the content remained technical and theoretical, accessible mainly to other professionals. Membership had increased from just over two hundred in 1888 to nearly fourteen hundred ten years later—the core of an evolving "national professional geographic society," but the Society was not yet a financial success story.[11] It was approximately $2,000 in debt at the time of Hubbard's death in 1897.

Change in the nature of the Society began to occur when Bell took over in 1898. Bell, a renowned and successful inventor, was trained as a teacher of speech, and saw his scientific work as a gentlemanly avocation. The wealth generated by his invention of the telephone insured that he could pursue his scientific interests independently. Bell seemed much more attuned to the Society's mission to disseminate geographic knowledge than to the promotion of new research, and he believed that people would read geography only if it were light and entertaining. It was Bell who hired Gilbert Hovey Grosvenor (who later became his son-in-law) to help build circulation in 1899. He encouraged Grosvenor to study popular magazines of the time, particularly *Harper's* and *Century*, in order to glean ideas for the *National Geographic* magazine. He also directed him to study "popular geographers" from Herodotus to Darwin, noting that the success of such works was due to the fact that they were "accurate, eyewitness accounts; simple and straightforward." [12]

Grosvenor's first innovations were in promotion and marketing. Membership in the Society had always been by nomination. Grosvenor began actively developing lists of individuals who could be nominated, drawing names from friends and from membership lists with other organizations. He also began rejecting articles provided by the editorial committee when he found them to be too technical or difficult. Board members who resented the new popular thrust of the magazine sought to divest Grosvenor of his position during his honeymoon in Europe in 1900, but were unsuccessful due to Bell's control over financial resources. By 1902, Grosvenor had not only regained his former control, but was appointed editor. The increasing autonomy of the organization from its professionalized roots gave it the ability to create its peculiar and powerful position as an arbiter of national culture.

Two elements were crucial in carving out this niche. The first was the recapturing and revitalization of the declining field of natural history. If natural history was defunct as an intellectual arena by the late nineteenth century, it obtained a new lease on life through the institutions of mass culture. In Bell's and Grosvenor's hands, the magazine became such an institution. Grosvenor "was extending the life of the old rubric of natural history at a time when it was rapidly being parceled up among the various specialties. . . . The *Geographic* was the direct and lively descendant of the cabinet of curiosities, a close cousin of the natural history diorama." [13]

The National Geographic Society was founded within two decades after the inauguration of the American Museum of Natural History and in a period of expansion of the Smithsonian Institution. In these contexts, photographic or material traces of the colonized world were relocated to new spaces in the industrialized West. Once appropriated and transferred, they provided the materials out of which new stories about the world could be created. As James Clifford has demonstrated, collecting and display are crucial processes of Western identity formation, and cultural description itself is a form of collecting that selectively accords "authenticity" to human groups and their institutions and practices. [14] *National Geographic*, like the great natural history museums, took images of Africa, Asia, and Latin America from their historical contexts and arranged them in ways that addressed contemporary Western preoccupations. [15] The systems of classification or explanation that were chosen provided an illusion of adequate representation, and an opportunity for certain institutions of mass culture to construct stories about otherness.

Regardless of what stories were told, the very acts of collecting and presenting were significant. They created illusions of possession, of a stable and complete "humanity," and of the possibility of ordering the exotic and the foreign. [16] As Susan Stewart has forcefully argued, in collections "desire is ordered, arranged and manipulated, not fathomless. . . . Like Noah's Ark, those great civic collections, the library and the museum, seek to represent experience within a mode of control and confinement. One cannot know everything about the world, but one can at least approach closed knowledge through the collection." The knowledge thus produced is necessarily ahistoric—the context of the collection "destroys the context of origin," and the order imposed by the collector obscures the histories of production and acquisition of the artifacts or photographs themselves. [17] *National Geographic* offered the possibility of bringing such collections to the living rooms and libraries of American families on a monthly basis.

=====

The second element of the niche *National Geographic* carved out for itself also went against the grain of the nineteenth-century positivism. This was the attempt to combine scholarly and entertainment functions in the same institution or cultural product. The *Geographic* sought, on the one hand, to be a potent force in exploration and scientific research that was independent of national scientific organizations and their ideologies of specialized research. On the other hand, it sought to obtain the interest of large masses of people. What was to be gained by successfully achieving such a combination? First, it placed the *Geographic* in the powerful position of being both a "broker" and a maker of scientific knowledge. In the prevailing atmosphere of scientific specialization, and the denigration of amateurs and lay practitioners, *National Geographic* could fill the void between academic practitioners and the public by purveying science, while also claiming to foster and practice science in its own right. The funding and conduct of research had always been marginal to the institution's main role in popularizing and glamorizing geographic and anthropological knowledge, yet it was sufficient to establish and retain its reputation as a "scientific and educational organization" (emphasis ours). This made it possible for the *Geographic* to speak with the voice of scientific authority, while remaining outside and unconstrained by the scientific community.

Second, there was a tremendous flexibility to be had by playing fast and loose with the boundaries between science and entertainment. Editors concerned with market imperatives could justify photographs that glorified the exotic and ritualistic aspects of "primitive" societies, or that sensationalized head-hunting, cannibalism, mutilation, or tattoo, on the grounds that they were picturesque, or because of their role in piquing interest. Presented in a magazine that claims to present "true facts" in a judicious manner, these images were given a scholarly veneer. And readers were given reinforcement for old prejudices. Editors tended to choose photographs based on their ability to appeal to an American audience; these were then fed back to the reading public as examples of the latest, brightest scientific knowledge. In the process, the reading public's original vision of what was interesting or aesthetically pleasing about the world outside United States borders was validated, elaborated, and heightened by its presentation as scientific fact.

When a new vision of the non-Western world was called for, *National Geographic* did not have to adhere to "scientific method" in constructing it. It did not find itself constrained by scholarly opinion, but could choose images with impunity. Editors could choose a grisly photograph of a headless Ifugao warrior based on its "scientific merit"; they could justify the absence of photographs showing poverty or hunger on grounds of presenting a "positive image"; and they could appeal to aesthetics for their use of multiple photographs of attractive young women and lush landscapes. The Society's editors were attentive to both the market and the scientific community, but they were slaves to neither. They were free to construct their own particular vision of the non-Western world.

One of the topics around which the scientific halo was (and still is) placed is sexuality. In fact, nothing more defines the *National Geographic* for most older American readers than its depiction of "naked" women, with the magazine's steady inclusion of "nudity" forming a central part of the image of the non-West that it purveys. A photo of a bare-chested woman was first included in the magazine in 1903. It was accompanied by (shameless) editorial explanation. The picture, and others like it, Gilbert H. Grosvenor later said, was included in the interest of science; to exclude it would have been to give an incomplete or misleading idea of how the people being portrayed really live. This scientific purpose for use of such photos was then and is now seen as their sole purpose, with the Society taking "vehement exception to comments about the sexual attraction or eroticism of the photographs." The breast represents both a struggle against "prudery" and the pursuit of truth rather than pleasure.[18]

The centrality of a race-gender code about whose breasts to depict cannot be denied, however. With two very recent exceptions, none of the hundreds of women whose breasts have been photographed for the magazine over the last century were white; it has been reported that one bare-breasted Polynesian woman whose picture was to be included in the magazine looked "too white" to be naked and so had her skin darkened in the production process.[19] And for all its struggle against prudery, male and female genitals have been regularly airbrushed out of the picture.

The nakedness of the *Geographic*'s subjects might be seen as continuous with the nude as a perennial theme in Western "fine arts." Some of these women are posed for surveillance ("caught in the act" of their customs) and more resemble the mug shot than the oil canvas; most are rendered (through pose, lighting, etc.) in such a way as to suggest intrinsic "artfulness." "Womanliness" can then play a central role in allowing the art of photography to exist silently beneath an explicitly "scientific" agenda and thereby increase readership and further legitimate the *Geographic*'s project as one of both beauty and truth. All of this elaborate structure of signification, however, is built on a foundation of racial and gender subordination: one must first be black and female to do this kind of symbolic labor.

This boundary shifting was not unique to the *Geographic*. Much the same phenomenon has been noted in the international fairs and expositions held in the United States from 1876 to 1916. While the main exposition areas of these fairs retained a staunchly scientific/technological mode of presentation, the midways became areas where entertainment and educational functions were brought into close proximity. The midway was the major arena for the display and exposition of non-Western cultures— a place where Americans could "study ethnography." This presentation equated the non-Western world in real and tangible ways with peep shows and "freak" shows (playing on images of the harem, the overblown sexuality of the East, and the general projection of the forbidden desires of whites onto dark-skinned peoples). It also permitted the exposition directors "to have their ethnological cake and eat it too," by affirming or denying the scientific accuracy of the exhibitions to suit their needs.[20]

The midways were invariably constructed as evolutionary ladders, where tourists could move from the "savagery" of Dahomeyan culture to the more civilized Javanese "Brownies," to the Chinese and Japanese. They played on notions of the nonwhite world as barbaric and child-like, and encouraged contrast with the scientific "progress" displayed in the main part of the exposition. Because displays involved the participation of members of the culture in question, their status as representations was overwhelmed by the concreteness and concurrence of real human bodies. The significant feature for this discussion, however, was the way that the interpenetration of science and entertainment functions fomented the construction of evolutionary and racist understanding of the United States and its relation to the rest of the world. Most displays were organized by distinguished anthropologists, including Franz Boas, Alice Fletcher, Aleš Hrdlička, Otis T. Mason, and John Wesley Powell. Their work did not necessarily play to themes of cultural evolution and racial superiority in and of itself (and they may, in other contexts, have adamantly opposed these themes). Nevertheless, the placement of the exhibits, their juxtaposition with "nonscientific" exhibits that debased nonwhite peoples, and their sensationalization in brochures and promotional materials permitted exposition directors to construct a vision of the relation between the United States and the rest of the world that played to and reinforced popular notions of racial superiority.[21]

The juxtaposition of the "West" and the "rest" was also clearly at work in the pages of National Geographic magazine. The non-Western world was never the only topic covered in an issue. Stories about wildlife and about life in the United States have always been featured prominently, as were more technical pieces on climate and geomorphology in the early years. The proximity of articles on the United States to articles on the non-Western world often facilitated the depiction of progress and cultural evolution. As Joseph Hawley, president of the United States Centennial Commission, noted in 1879: "Comparison is vital to the success of any exposition. . . . You can never discover your success or failure without comparison with other nations. . . . Comparison is essential to show the effects on the industries and arts of climate, race, geography.[22] The juxtaposition of articles on New Guinea rituals with articles on orderly farms in New England or shiny new factories in the South underscored evolutionary themes in the articles and photographs themselves.

The "progressive," rather than Social Darwinist, nature of the *Geographic*'s evolutionism was reflected in Grosvenor's unwillingness to publish overtly hostile or racist material. This policy was made explicit in his "seven principles," announced in an editorial in 1915:

1) The first principle is absolute accuracy. Nothing must be printed which is not strictly according to fact. . . .
2) Abundance of beautiful, instructive and artistic illustrations.
3) Everything printed in the Magazine must have permanent value. . . .
4) All personalities and notes of a trivial character are avoided. . . .
5) Nothing of a partisan or controversial nature is printed.
6) Only what is of a kindly nature is printed about any country or people, everything unpleasant or unduly critical being avoided.
7) The contents of each number is planned with a view of being timely.[23]

The avoidance of overtly critical material contributed to an impression of good sportsmanship in the evolutionary struggle. If formerly colonized peoples hadn't quite made it to the levels of "civilization" of the industrialized nations, they were not condemned; the rhetoric was one of slightly older school chums rooting them on while they gave it their best shot.

In *National Geographic*'s continuing efforts to locate itself on the boundary between science and entertainment, photographs became an increasingly significant tool. The first photographs were published in 1896, although board policy of the era demanded that they be subordinate to, and illustrative of, the text. Early reproductions were by steel engraving, and while they were of high quality, were slow and expensive. Photoengraving had reduced the cost significantly by the early years of this century, and Grosvenor was quick to see the potential of this new technology in contributing to his goal of popularizing the magazine. In 1905, without board approval, he published eleven full pages of photographs of Lhasa, Tibet, sent to the magazine by two Russian explorers.[24] While a number of board members were shocked and angry, public response was overwhelmingly favorable. Society membership, which stood at 3,400 at the time the photographs of the "forbidden city" were published, soared to 11,000 by the end of the year. Grosvenor's move and this response served to establish photographs as the mainstay of the magazine.

By 1915, the extensive use of photographs was one of *National Geographic*'s distinguishing features. Like the text, pictures were constrained by Grosvenor's principles of fairness, factual content, and positive outlook: they were to be "beautiful" (aesthetically pleasing), "artistic" (embodying certain conventions of highbrow forms of art), and "instructive" (realist in representation). The magazine relied on sharply focused, easily readable photographs to bolster its claim that it presented an unbiased, unmediated view of the world. The use of photographs that claimed (in captions and text) to represent a pre-photographic reality went hand-in-hand with the assertion that all written material was "accurate, balanced and fair." What writers accomplished by an insistently upbeat and uncomplicated style, the erasure of conflicting points of view, and the presentation of (often gratuitous) names, dates, and numbers, was reinforced by the codes of photographic realism. Photographs lent what Roland Barthes has called "the prestige of the denotation" to the articles they illustrated. They created the illusion that the objects presented occurred in nature in the ways they were photographed: "Nature [rather than the photographer] seems spontaneously to produce the scene represented."[25]

The acceptance of photographs as a form of evidence is the outcome of a historical process that was completed only in the second half of the nineteenth century and that was bound up with new uses for the photograph in the state's practices of social control—uses that were predicated on the adoption of realist codes that took the photograph as a direct transcription of the real.[26] "Photographs were not viewed as metaphors of experience, but rather as sections of reality itself. If photographs showed gigantic trees and awe-inspiring mountains, then all the trees were gigantic and all the mountains awe-inspiring. When photographs depicted Indians as 'savages,' Indians were confirmed as savages." [27] The *Geographic* capitalized on this notion of the photograph as evidence and established itself as a source of accurate and timely information on the colonial world.

National Geographic's adoption of realist codes must be understood in relation to the photographic trends of its period. In the early part of this century, American photography was dominated by the pictorialist school—which used techniques such as soft focus to create photographs reminiscent of painting. The *Geographic* did not adopt such a style, but relied on technically adequate, but naive, prints from travelers. The goal of the editorial staff was to print photographs that were "straightforward." As one editor put it in 1915, *National Geographic* had discovered a "new, universal language that requires no deep study . . . one that is understood as well by the jungaleer as by the courtier; by the Eskimo as by the wild man from Borneo; by the child in the playroom as by the professor in the college; and by the woman of the household as by the hurried businessman—in short, the Language of the Photograph." [28] The implication was that the photograph was a direct transcription of a reality that was timeless, classless, and outside the boundaries of language and culture. The photographer's intent, the photographic product, and the reader's experience were assumed to be one. For this reason, photographs, unlike other cultural texts, were held to be readable by even the "simplest" among us.

The *Geographic*'s adoption of "straight photography" rather than pictorialist codes was shared with a tradition of documentary photography that was also emerging during this period. Nevertheless, the magazine's photographs did not possess qualities that made them of great interest to most documentary photographers, who in the 1920s and 1930s were influenced by surrealism and cubism, and who actively played with the codes of realist representation to surprising ends. Documentary photographers attempted to capture "decisive" moments in which elements came together in ways that were moving and significant, and that went beyond the literal transcription of a scene. *National Geographic* photographers, in contrast, were asked to make literal transcription their goal. Until well into the 1970s, editors shunned photographic techniques that drew attention to themselves or that revealed too clearly a photographer's "point of view." They favored those that permitted the labors and point of view of the photographer and editor to recede into the background, and thus encouraged the reader to see his or her contact with the photographed subject as unmediated, if necessarily indirect.

For some artists whose imagination was captured by the possibilities of new realist modes, this was refreshing. The photographer Paul Strand remarked in 1923 that "compared to this so-called pictorial photography, which is nothing more than an evasion of everything truly photographic . . . a simple record in the National Geographic Magazine . . . or an aerial photographic record is an unmixed relief."[29] Strand was making a point about pictorialism—and only tangentially about Geographic photographic style; yet his willingness to concede to its photographs the status of "simple records" is telling. He emphasized their unstudied quality by comparing them to aerial photographs, which necessarily exercise little selectivity over what falls within their range. In a sense, he accepted the editor's judgment that the photos possess self-evident meanings, that can be read by anyone "without deep study."

Recent work on the realist tradition emphasizes not only its distinct stylistic features, but also how absolutely it turns on an image's consistency with, and reinforcement of, cultural expectations. When we speak of photographic realism, "we must historicize the spectator"—that is, we must consider to whom and under what conditions photographic images will appear "realistic."[30] Or as Pierre Bourdieu has noted, "if the photograph is considered to be a perfect inscription of the visible world, it is above all because the selections that it makes completely conform to [the world's] logic."[31] If the sharp focus and conventional framing of Geographic photographs marked them as "records," it was their replication of existing popular understandings of the third world that made them seem neutral in their presentations, and gave them the comforting feel of "commonsense" realities captured on film. In this way, the mass media's images "become mirrors, serving to reflect Americans' feelings, rather than windows to the complex, dynamic realities of foreign societies."[32]

The Geographic brought this realistic style to bear not only on the new territories and interests of the United States, but also on unfolding world events. When World War I broke out in July 1914, the Society included a map of the "New Balkan States and Central Europe" in its August issue.

Every subsequent issue provided war coverage and updates—full of facts, figures, and diagrams, consistently upbeat, sympathetic to the Allies, but withholding any openly supportive statements until the United States entered the war in 1917. Partly as a result of this coverage, the *Geographic* was one of only a few magazines that saw its readership increase during World War I, growing from 285,000 in 1914 to 650,000 in 1918. In addition to its reporting, the Society visibly involved itself in the war effort by printing draft notices for the government, organizing a Liberty Loan drive, and collecting socks and sweaters for service personnel.[33]

Although *National Geographic* took the war in good stride, much of the rest of the world did not. The impact of the first World War on modern consciousness has been explored, for example, by Paul Fussell, who argues that the ironic stance that dominates much of modern literature originated in the "application of mind and memory to the events of the Great War." According to Fussell, the war essentially reversed the idea of progress. Writers like Henry James struggled to understand how a supposed long age of "gradual betterment" could culminate instead in an "abyss of blood and darkness."[34] And James Clifford points out that modern ethnography, too, took its shape in a world that had been shattered by World War I and that was haunted by nihilism in its aftermath. Functionalism and other representations of cultures as ordered wholes were the product of a generation of social scientists who were "acutely aware of the possibility of disorder." In Clifford's words,

> with the breakdown of evolutionist master narratives, the relativist science of culture worked to rethink the world as a dispersed whole, composed of distinct, functioning and interrelated cultures. It reconstituted social and moral wholeness plurally. If synecdochic ethnography argued, in effect, that "cultures" hold together, it did so in response to a pervasive modern feeling, linking the Irishman Yeats to the Nigerian Achebe, that "things fall apart."[35]

The "pervasive modern feeling" did not upset the *National Geographic's* institutional mission to present order in the face of rapid change and perplexing events. The order-seeking impulses of scientific theory confirmed and enriched a *National Geographic* view of the world during the interwar period, and provided a rationale for a vision of third world locations as safe, coherent, and well-integrated.

The most significant events at National Geographic during the 1930s turned on the adoption of color photography. Hand-tinted plates had been introduced to the magazine in 1910; the first autochrome was published in 1916, and tinted photographs were used throughout the 1920s.[36] The first natural color photographs to be published in the Geographic were taken at the North Pole in 1926. Through the late 1920s and early 1930s, Society photographers experimented with several other processes, including Finlay, Dufay, and Agfacolor. Kodak's fast, portable color film in rolls became available in 1936, and while it took several years to catch on at National Geographic, quickly became the film technology of choice.[37]

Color photography inevitably changes the nature of representation. Color tends to dominate the photograph, often at the expense of line and movement. It affects the mood of the image in ways that may reinforce or contradict the shape and placement of objects. Because of its high impact, color frequently becomes a consideration in choosing an image to photograph, or selecting among images already photographed:

> Even though Kodachrome was already unnaturally bright, photographers . . . splashed the strongest possible colors in their pictures so that they would be more effective in print. One result was that the staff photographers—who were constantly being sent to colorful places to slake what was seen as the public's unquenching thirst for colorful scenes—would often find themselves needing more color to take advantage of the color film and would resort to placing the people in costume.[38]

This practice has been called the "Red Shirt School of Photography."

Color photography began to differentiate the Geographic in somewhat forseeable ways from a growing tradition of photojournalism that continued to rely on black-and-white photographs well into the 1950s. It became possible to render the exotic and picturesque in ever more riveting ways, leading editors to further emphasize these traits rather than historical significance and timeliness. Pictures in National Geographic were increasingly seen as akin to picture postcards or snapshots taken by tourists: Guimond explains that because tourism is so popular and because it is considered a particularly "reli-able" way to understand realities, it is not surprising that these maga-zines' [*Time*, *Life*, and *National Geographic*] articles and photo-essays are often, in effect, tourist trips with the editors, reporters and photog-raphers acting as tour guides. . . . Similarly, many magazines, particu-larly the *Geographic*, heavily emphasize the exotic aspects of foreign cultures, even as they also often give their readers . . . simulated, "candid" contacts with their subjects—little conversations with (and pictures of) camel drivers, village schoolteachers, and picturesque peasants—which may occur during tourist trips.[39]

The use of color photography also highlighted the magazine's affinity to museum exhibits—with their highly framed, aestheticized "tidbits" of traditional culture—rather than to starker, more information-laden news reportage or scientific documentation. Like museum exhibits (as well as catalogs and department stores), the *Geographic* laid out the wonders of the world for curious readers.[40] It selected the most important and interest-ing for their perusal, grouped them in meaningful ways, and explained their qualities and fine points in its captions. Color photographs served to highlight this sense of opulence and the *availability* of what was displayed. As John Berger has noted, color photography enhances the viewers' feel-ing that they can almost touch what is in the image, reminding them that they might, in fact, possess it.[41] Though it made all the more uneasy the already uneasy place of "science" in its mission, the *National Geographic*'s increasing appeal to the popular tastes of its consumer/reader was more than compensated by the attention that their color photographs drew and by the leadership the Society was able to establish in the use of color images.

═══

The Society fared the depression well, topping one million members in 1935, and employing over seven hundred workers by the next year. These burgeoning figures must be partly accounted for by the fact that, in keeping with official policy, the human suffering of the decade did not find a place in the pages of the magazine. Articles produced in the late 1930s, most notably those by Douglas Chandler, were openly sympathetic to national socialist agendas. These pieces proved to be an embarrass-

ment for the magazine's editors, especially after it was discovered that
Chandler was funded by the Nazi party (Chandler was dropped as a con-
tributor at this point; he was indicted for treason in 1943).[42] John Patric's
coverage of Mussolini's Italy, also from the late 1930s, shows the sinister
side of a commitment to present "only what is of a kindly nature." Even
the Society's quasi-official history represents the early coverage of World
War II as a somewhat curious overextension of tact and nonpartisanship:
"John Patric's March 1937 'Imperial Rome Reborn' celebrated Italy's new
glories, but the photographs were chilling: one of gasmasked uniformed
children was captioned 'Weird Visitors From Another World? No; School-
boys Preparing For War.' Another, of children marching, reads, 'Chins
High, Shoulders Squared, Boy Black Shirts Emulate Il Duce's Posture.' "[43]

With the advent of World War II, the Society had a tradition to uphold
—the reporting of the war for Americans at home. Coverage of World
War II was marked by the same patriotic fervor as that of the first World
War. The Society once again published detailed maps, published one
major war-related article in every issue, and established a semiofficial
status for its activities through its participation in the war effort. It provided maps (and elegant map cases) to the President of the United States,
as well as to the Navy Hydrographic Office, the United States Army Map
Service, and the Coast and Geodetic Survey, which prepared maps for the
air force. The Society's 1944 map of Japan was prepared at the sugges-
tion of the army and used in enlarged form by the army air forces for the
planning of air offensives against Japan.[44] In addition, National Geographic
spellings of geographic locations were adopted by major wire services in
the 1940s.

Just as the Society took advantage of its ambiguous status somewhere
between science and entertainment, it did so with its connections to
government. It traded on its close ties to government officials, and the
official uses to which its products were put to create an image of itself
as a "national institution"; at the same time, it retained its status as a private, tax-exempt organization that was relatively unconstrained by government. Editor Grosvenor had always cultivated close personal relationships to a number of individuals in government. William Howard Taft
was his second cousin, and he developed a warm working relationship
with Theodore Roosevelt over the years. In the 1930s, the Society established a tradition of calling upon the President of the United States to

present Gardiner Greene Hubbard medals for geographic distinction. By the 1980s, at least six presidents had contributed articles to the magazine, including Theodore Roosevelt, William Howard Taft, Calvin Coolidge, Herbert Hoover, Dwight Eisenhower, and Lyndon Johnson. Members of the board of trustees have included former First Ladies, chief justices of the United States, the chair of the Board of Governors of the Federal Reserve System, the chief of staff of the United States Air Force, an assistant secretary of the Navy, a rear admiral in the Coast and Geodetic Survey, the deputy administrator of NASA, and officials of the National Park Service. Given its nonprofit status, the Society was able to enlist the aid of government officials who could not have supported private commercial enterprises.[45] Connections to industry and finance were also cultivated by the Society. Bank presidents and industrialists have regularly had a place on its board of trustees.

After the second World War and into the 1950s the Society operated in a national context dominated by the expansion and consolidation of power. Emerging from World War II with its economy relatively unscathed, the United States was in a position to finance the reconstruction of a war-devastated Europe.[46] At the same time, it began to usurp the position of European nations in relation to their former colonies, establishing important trade relationships with the new nations of Africa, Latin America, and Asia. In the early 1950s, Congress was rechanneling foreign assistance to these newly "independent" economies. Beginning with the Food for Peace Bill in 1954, concessionary grain sales were used to create food dependency in the third world, increasing the political clout of the United States and securing supplies of strategic metals and other resources needed for industrial expansion. As of 1952, the air force had 131 bases overseas, and the navy, several dozen; American companies sold arms to countries receiving military aid from the United States; Gulf, Mobil, Texaco, and Exxon had established themselves in the Middle East; and multinationals were establishing their economic hegemony.[47]

Still, the United States public tenaciously held to a view of its presence in the "emerging" and newly independent nations as benevolent. The popular press continued to stress "kindness" and "generosity" as basic American traits. GI's in Korea were photographed giving chewing gum to children. American leaders traveled abroad with candy bars and soft drinks in their hands to distribute during photo opportunities.[48] And the

Geographic upheld this image with articles such as "The GI and the Kids of Korea: America's Fighting Men Share Their Food, Clothing and Shelter with Children of a War-torn Land" (1953); photos captioned "Uncle Sam is a Good Egg: British School Children Agree" (1943); and articles (slightly more to the point) such as "Cuba—American Sugar Bowl" (1947). United States air bases were touted in captions such as the following from 1950:

> Lunch on His Arm, a New Rug Over His Shoulder, This Smiling Okinawan Symbolizes the New Hope that Has Come to the "Doorstep to Japan." . . . Battles and typhoons have ravaged little Okinawa during the past five years, but today there is cause for cheer among the island's people. . . . Long-neglected Okinawa is undergoing a face lifting. After the transformation it will be a semi-permanent, well-equipped United States air base similar to Clark Field in the Philippines.

Despite the fact that the Cold War period saw the construction of bomb shelters, the stockpiling of nuclear weapons, and the McCarthy hearings, it remained a time of defiant innocence—of optimism, power, and a sense of invulnerability—for most of the American public. The *Geographic* contributed to "softening" the entrance to the nuclear age with articles such as "Nevada Learns to Live with the Atom" and "Man's New Servant, the Friendly Atom." In the meantime, the nonsocialist third world continued to be portrayed as simple, childlike, and friendly—in the words of one caption, as "Paradise in Search of a Future."

Publishing at *National Geographic* was characterized by some strange lacunae in coverage during the period of the Cold War. Favorable portrayals of Eastern Bloc nations would have been unpatriotic; yet dwelling on their evils was outside editorial policy. For this reason, there was no coverage whatsoever of the Soviet Union from 1945 to 1959 (when then Vice President Richard Nixon described his trips to the Soviet Union for *Geographic* readers, including his "kitchen confrontation" with Nikita Khrushchev). China's people were a popular subject before the war, with seventy articles on the country between 1900 and 1935; they were covered only seven times in the period 1950–76, however, returning to the pages of the *Geographic* with President Nixon's visit in 1975.

Increasing educational levels and a growth in average disposable wealth also characterized the 1950s. *National Geographic* benefited from both of these trends in terms of increased readership—from one million in 1935 to two million in the early 1960s. Within the class system of the postwar period, *National Geographic* magazine was both mainstream and relatively "high culture." Because of its glossy, colorful (but never gaudy) design, its semiofficial status, and its well-developed relationship to schools, it could be displayed in middle-class homes as a mark of taste and as an investment that parents could make in their children's education, akin to a set of encyclopedias, a globe, or a good dictionary.

As the United States reached the apex of its postwar power, autonomous voices from formerly colonized peoples were reaching the West in louder and more articulate forms. Independence movements and anticolonial struggles in India and Africa challenged both the philosophical basis and the on-the-ground reality of Western power. The Negritude movement in Africa and the Caribbean denied the right of the West to define third world cultural identity, and offered powerful new self-definitions. The United States was attempting to forge and solidify new economic relationships to nations of the South at a time when colonial power relations were being overturned and when evolutionist theory and its corollary—"the white man's burden"—were being contested.

The anticolonial struggles that reverberated through the social sciences—generating new forms of self-examination and challenges to extant theories—only intensified the search for order at *National Geographic*. Images of safety and stability in the third world were not abandoned. On the contrary, images of Westerners were politely removed from colonial and neocolonial contexts, thereby allowing the magazine to avoid uncomfortable questions about the nature of their presence, to obscure the contexts and difficulties of the photographic encounter, and to create a vision of the cultures in question as hermetically sealed worlds—captured only in the sense of "captured on film." Again, the analogy to collections is instructive: "The point of the collection is forgetting—starting again in such a way that a finite number of elements create, by virtue of their combination, an infinite reverie. Whose labor made [the collection] is not the question: the question is what is inside."[49] In the heyday of colonial culture, the inclusion of Westerners in the photographs of the colonized served to establish a sort of authenticity—to demonstrate that the photographer was "really there." By the late 1960s, however, the colonial and postcolonial relationships that permitted *National Geographic* to photograph the world had become a site of struggle, and reference to them was studiously avoided.

It was also becoming evident that "home" was not exempt from the anticolonial, antiracist struggles that had been emerging in the third world. The contradictions beneath the peaceful, postwar veneer of the 1950s were revealed by the emergence of civil rights struggles. With the increasing radicalization of the movement after 1964, race and cultural difference emerged into mass culture and the media in ways that they had not since the last century—and with an intensity that far surpassed the struggles over immigration and ethnicity in the late nineteenth and early twentieth centuries. *National Geographic* did not report these issues. The struggles of the period are nonetheless part of the background to its 1950s coverage, and to the assiduous way in which the magazine averted its eyes from anything that suggested interracial or intercultural conflict.

Important changes in the leadership of the Society occurred in the 1950s, but this did not portend changes in style. Gilbert Hovey Grosvenor retired as editor-in-chief in 1954, but continued on as chair of the board. John Oliver LaGorce—who had worked beside Grosvenor since 1905—was appointed president of the Society and editor of the magazine. In 1957, after a preparatory period as associate editor, Gilbert's son Melville Bell Grosvenor took over LaGorce's roles as president/editor. A business-man at heart, Melville Grosvenor kept a close eye on membership figures and readership surveys. He introduced photographs to the cover of the magazine with great success, and initiated the Society's subsidiary product line with the first atlases and globes. He also greatly increased field budgets, which gave more shots to editors to select from, and gave them more leeway to construct a particular "Geographic" vision of the world.

Perhaps more important than changes at the top, which were carefully conducted to insure continuity, was the proliferation of staff at other levels during this period. Prior to World War II there had been only two staff writers/photographers. The *Geographic* still relied on diplomats, businessmen, and vacationing educators for many of its stories and photographs. By 1967, fifty full-time writers and fifteen full-time photographers had been employed, providing an opportunity for the staff to shape stories much more directly, and to play a more significant role in producing the magazine's images.

As the Vietnam War unfolded, the *Geographic* was caught in a quandary. Should it honor its tradition of upbeat, "fact-filled" war reporting? And how could it do so in an undeclared, as yet low-key war? Trusting in the past success of its war reportage, the Society began its coverage with a piece by Wilbur Garrett and Peter White in 1961, entitled "South Viet Nam Fights the Red Tide." In 1962 the Society sent photographer Dickey Chappelle to work on an article entitled "Helicopter War in South Viet Nam"—a piece that provided the first published photographs of American military personnel in action to the American public.[50]

Melville Bell Grosvenor stepped down from his positions in 1967; Melvin M. Payne took over the presidency of the Society; the editorship went to Frederick Vosburg for three years, and then to Melville's son Gilbert. Memberships had ballooned during Melville Grosvenor's tenure from 2.2 to 5.6 million. Perhaps his greatest contribution had been the hiring of a group of individuals known within the organization as "young turks"—highly acclaimed photojournalists from major midwestern newspapers who deviated strongly from the rather effete gentlemanly ethos of previous decades. This new cohort was interested in modernizing the appearance and content of the *Geographic*. They advocated more use of natural lighting in photographs, more white space in layout, and all-color issues. They also pushed for coverage of more controversial issues. Key among them was Wilbur Garrett, who was to serve as the magazine's editor between 1980 and 1990.

While the 1960s had seen modest changes—and resistance to change—in the magazine's style and content, conflicts became ever more central in the 1970s. Four articles published in 1977 served to draw public (and board of trustees) attention to the magazine's more issue-oriented and critical stance. The first of these was a story on Cuba by writer-photographer Fred Ward, which drew an angry response from the right-wing media-monitoring organization Accuracy in Media for its lack of criticism of Cuba's political system and its acceptance of a government official's prognostications of economic growth; it also angered board of trustees member Crawford Greenewalt, who was chairman of the board of E. I. du Pont de Nemours & Co., because one of Du Pont's chemical plants had been seized in Cuba.[51] The second was an article entitled "To

Live in Harlem." This story was less controversial for its focus than for its presentation to advertisers as an example of the "new" *National Geographic* magazine. A call to potential advertisers in the *New York Times* read: "The geography of Harlem: Poverty, dope, crime and people who wouldn't leave for a million dollars. . . . Isn't it time you took another look [at *National Geographic*]?" By suggesting that advertisers who took another look would find the *Geographic* more relevant and interesting, the announcement suggested that the magazine had been stodgy and less relevant in the past and that a major shift in editorial policy was occurring. The third article, entitled "One Canada or Two," covered the issue of Quebec's separatist movement. Finally, and perhaps most crucially, a spring article on South Africa—"South Africa's Lonely Ordeal"—drew outrage for its overt discussion of apartheid and the situation of black South Africans, and its disturbing photographs by James Blair of a black child's grave marked by the infant's white doll and a cardboard cross and of black maids holding a wealthy white couple's children. Despite the fact that it had been allowed to preview the story, and to recommend major changes, the South African government placed ads in major American newspapers accusing the Society of "anti-white racism" and serious misrepresentation of the facts.

In June of 1977, then chair of the Society's board of trustees, Melvin M. Payne, formed an ad hoc committee to determine whether the series of topical, controversial articles meant that the magazine's editorial policy was changing. Gilbert Grosvenor saw this as a direct threat to his prerogatives as editor. He argued that the magazine "had not deviated from its 89-year tradition of accuracy, timeliness and objectivity"; it was not the magazine that was changing, the world around it was.[52] Grosvenor's actions in publishing the articles were supported by both Melville Grosvenor and Frederick Vosburg, who warned Payne and the board that the magazine would be doomed if it did not reflect these changes in the world around it.

These changes were, in fact, not only in the world-at-large but also in the world of journalism, where conflicts within the press over coverage of the Vietnam War had "spilled the blood on the rug."[53] In a review of Vietnam War coverage, Susan Moeller has argued that the new style of Vietnam photographs broke with the aesthetic of the century's two World Wars. Instead of careful compositions of battles, Vietnam photographers focused on the plight of the individual soldier and civilian in the context of conflict. This new style—typified by such images as Paul Schutzer's photograph in *Life* of a Vietnamese woman carrying her blood-drenched child, Eddie Adams's *New York Times* photo of Brigadier General Nguyen Ngoc Loan executing a "terrorist" at point-blank range, or Huynh Cong Ut's picture in the *New York Times* of children fleeing a napalm attack—personalized the events of the war. In Moeller's words, at some point the American press realized that "American boys dying in Viet Nam *was* the story." [54]

According to Moeller, conflict within the ranks of the press over coverage of the war in part followed generational lines, with writers and photographers who had covered earlier conflicts less willing to break with past practices. Perhaps more significant, however, was the division (which only partly corresponded to generation) between photographers and reporters working out of Saigon, and those who remained in Washington. Washington-based reporters were far more subject to White House pressures on the quality of coverage; those in Saigon, to the realities of the war. The ascendancy of the Saigon contingent after 1968 played a role in changing the American public's view of the war; it also challenged, and changed, the existing set of journalistic conventions for covering world events.

In this context, Grosvenor and those who supported him believed that a continuing "Pollyanna" style of reporting would make the *Geographic* look increasingly shallow and out-of-touch. They believed that the public was becoming increasingly accustomed to grisly facts and critical coverage. If *National Geographic* continued to print only kindly and noncontroversial stories, they feared the loss of two elements crucial to their prior success. First, an increasingly sophisticated public would simply find their stories uninteresting—predictable and without punch. Carefully rendered versions of the idealized and exotic third world, which had formerly piqued interest, would present little competition to stories of the real-life drama and pathos of the Vietnam War. Second, the principle of "kindliness" was found increasingly to be in conflict with the principle of "absolute accuracy." Given media attention to conflicts in places like South Africa, "noncontroversial" stories about these locations would be opened to question. As *Newsweek* noted in its coverage of the controversy, "in any other magazine the articles on South Africa, Cuba under Castro, and life in Harlem would be considered tame—if not belated—attempts to report the issues of the day."[55] *National Geographic's* claim to present a factual representation would be weakened by its studious avoidance of the conflicts and violence that were covered by other sources.

In opposition to Grosvenor's view, the ad hoc committee established by Payne decried the "missionary instinct" of the magazine's recent coverage, arguing that "controversy is adequately covered in the daily press"; it suggested that the correct approach to coverage of controversy was to "state precisely what the current situation is, but don't take sides; you don't even quote people on either side."[56] Editors, perhaps correctly, perceived that even the recognition that multiple points of view existed made their claim to present an authoritative and objective account open to question. Coverage of social or political resistance movements not only suggested that the world was unstable, but that an omniscient, "unbiased" stance was not possible. Ultimately, the committee asked Grosvenor for a statement that the *Geographic* would simply not cover areas or issues that were "so emotionally charged that an objective piece cannot be written." Grosvenor complied by publishing a short editorial statement in 1978 that affirmed the *Geographic's* rejection of "advocacy journalism."[57]

That such coverage already appeared naive and "storybookish" to reading audiences of the 1970s is evidenced by the parody of the *Geographic* that appeared in Tim Menees's "Wordsmith" comic strip in 1976, referring to articles on "The Happy Ghetto: Training Ground for the NBA" and "Backpacking on the Ho Chi Minh Trail." It was further evidenced, somewhat ironically, by the *National Review's* defense of the magazine's Cuba story. "*National Geographic* is not ordinarily thought of as a fellow-traveling publication. . . . Indeed, there are few more refreshing magazines, few so beautifully designed to take the reader out of himself and give him an instant vacation from politics and other humdrum distractions." If the *Geographic* flattered Cuba in the article, it was only because "the magazine flatters everyone."[58] For an enterprise that still considered itself a "scientific-educational" establishment, this defense was almost as damaging as the criticism had been: it labeled the Society's work too definitively as entertainment, if not pabulum, and damaged its claims to present a factual account of the world.

Thus, despite the board's rebuff of Grosvenor and renunciations of "advocacy" in the editorial pages, the magazine continued to publish topical and somewhat controversial pieces. Environmental conservation has generally been seen as an important topic at *National Geographic*. Stories on environmental degradation began to be featured in 1970, and the magazine has subsequently published articles on the smuggling of endangered species, on hazardous waste, acid rain, and on the destruction of tropical rain forests. Environmental issues received significant coverage in the 1988 centennial issue. Articles on the Underground Railroad and the Vietnam War Memorial treated controversial (but now safely historical) themes.

Nevertheless, it was not long before Garrett had to go. His firing in 1990 has been interpreted as the product of long-standing ill will between Garrett and Grosvenor, who served as president of the Society during Garrett's tenure as editor.[59] But Garrett's removal also occurred during a period of market pressures: specifically, a time of declining readership and increasing production costs. Gilbert Grosvenor and the Society's board argued that, under these circumstances, the best strategy was to pay careful attention to market research and to launch a more determined endeavor to "give the public what they want": shorter stories, fewer articles on non-American topics, and less coverage of social problems. Garrett, on the other hand, apparently preferred to "give the public what it doesn't know it wants yet"—to play a greater role in shaping public tastes, rather than simply responding to them. Garrett's activist 1970s style did not win over a board of trustees that welcomed the right-shifting political sands of the 1980s and 1990s. "Beauty" had to take precedence over "truth." Politeness was more marketable than "politics." And after all, the American self-identity as rational, generous, and benevolent was at stake, as it had been since the magazine's inception.

Notes

1 See Howard S. Abramson, *National Geographic: Behind America's Lens on the World* (New York, 1987); C. D. B. Bryan, *The National Geographic Society: 100 Years of Adventure and Discovery* (Washington, D.C., 1987); Tom Buckley, "With the National Geographic on Its Endless, Cloudless Voyage," *New York Times Magazine*, 6 September 1970; Anne Chamberlin, "Two Cheers for the National Geographic," *Esquire*, December 1963; Geoffrey T. Hellman, "Geography Unshackled II," *New Yorker*, 2 October 1943; and Ishbel Ross, "Geography, Inc.," *Scribner's*, June 1938.

2   P. Pauly, " 'The World and All That Is in It': The National Geographic Society: 1888–1918," *American Quarterly* 31 (1979): 517–32.
3   John Higham, *Strangers in the Land: Patterns of American Nativism: 1860–1925* (New Brunswick, N.J., 1955), 108.
4   Pauly, " 'The World and All That Is in It,' " 521.
5   George W. Stocking, Jr., *Victorian Anthropology* (New York, 1987), 230.
6   See Stephen J. Gould, *The Mismeasure of Man* (New York, 1981).
7   Stocking, *Victorian Anthropology*, 233.
8   We describe the construction of cultural difference in the magazine via photographic conventions and reader response to them in a book manuscript, tentatively titled *Reading National Geographic*. See also Catherine Lutz and Jane Collins, "The Photograph as an Intersection of Gazes: The Example of *National Geographic*," *Visual Anthropology Review* 7 (1991): 134–49; and Catherine Lutz, "Intentionality, Race, and Evolutionism in Photographs of 'Non-Westerners,' " in Catherine Lutz and Jane Collins, *Reading National Geographic* (Chicago, 1993).
9   Pauly, " 'The World and All That Is in It,' " 518–19.
10   Abramson, *Behind America's Lens*, 33.
11   Pauly, " 'The World and All That Is in It,' " 521.
12   Abramson, *Behind America's Lens*, 48.
13   Pauly, " 'The World and All That Is in It,' " 527.
14   James Clifford, *The Predicament of Culture: Twentieth-Century Ethnography, Literature and Art* (Cambridge, Mass., 1988).
15   See, for example, Donna Haraway's description of how the African Hall of the Museum of Natural History encodes Western preoccupations with manhood, virile defense of democracy, and connection (or loss of connection) with nature (*Primate Visions: Gender, Race and Nature in the World of Modern Science* [New York, 1989], chap. 3).
16   Jean Baudrillard, *Le système des objets* (Paris, 1968).
17   Susan Stewart, *On Longing: Narratives of the Miniature, the Gigantic, the Souvenir, the Collection* (Baltimore, 1984), 163, 161, 165.
18   Abramson, *Behind America's Lens*, 141; and Bryan, *100 Years of Adventure*, 89.
19   Abramson, *Behind America's Lens*, 143.
20   Robert Rydell, *All the World's a Fair: Visions of Empire at American International Expositions, 1876–1916* (Chicago, 1984), 138.
21   Ibid., 66.
22   Ibid., 32.
23   Bryan, *100 Years of Adventure*, 90.
24   Abramson, *Behind America's Lens*, 61–62.
25   Roland Barthes, *Image, Music, Text*, trans. S. Heath (London, 1977), 21, 45.
26   See John Tagg, *The Burden of Representation: Essays on Photographies and Histories* (Amherst, 1988), 98.

27 Christopher Lyman, *The Vanishing Race and Other Illusions: Photographs of Indians by Edward S. Curtis* (New York, 1982), 29.

28 Bryan, *100 Years of Adventure*, 133.

29 Cited in Jean-Claude Lemagny and André Rouille, *A History of Photography: Social and Cultural Perspectives*, trans. Janet Lloyd (Cambridge, 1987), 108.

30 Tagg, *Burden of Representation*, 156.

31 Pierre Bourdieu, *Un art moyen: Essais sur les usages sociaux de la photographie* (Paris, 1978), 109.

32 James Guimond, "Exotic Friends, Evil Others and Vice Versa," *Georgia Review* (1988): 68.

33 Bryan, *100 Years of Adventure*, 128–33; and Abramson, *Behind America's Lens*, 118–19.

34 Paul Fussell, *The Great War and Modern Memory* (New York, 1975), 35.

35 Clifford, *Predicament of Culture*, 64.

36 Abramson, *Behind America's Lens*, 133–39.

37 Bryan, *100 Years of Adventure*, 205–13.

38 Ibid., 294–95.

39 Guimond, "Exotic Friends," 40–41.

40 See Neil Harris, "Museums, Merchandising and Popular Taste: The Struggle for Influence," in *Material Culture and the Study of American Life*, ed. Ian M. G. Quinby (New York, 1978).

41 John Berger, *Ways of Seeing* (New York, 1972), 141.

42 Abramson, *Behind America's Lens*, 179.

43 Bryan, *100 Years of Adventure*, 219.

44 Abramson, *Behind America's Lens*, 176–77.

45 Ibid., 7.

46 See George Lipsitz, *Class and Culture in Cold War America: A Rainbow at Midnight* (New York, 1981), 3, for a discussion of the distribution of benefits from wartime industrial expansion and the resulting concentration of capital in U.S. industry.

47 Guimond, "Exotic Friends," 61.

48 Ibid., 61–62.

49 Stewart, *On Longing*, 152.

50 Fred Ritchin notes that Dickey Chappelle (who was killed covering the war in 1965) also photographed an execution during this trip that was similar to the one with which Eddie Adams riveted the American public in 1968, but that the photograph was published only in "an obscure magazine" (not *National Geographic*): "The world was not ready to see the brutality of the war, nor searching for such a symbol of it" ("The Photography of Conflict," *Aperture* 97 [Winter 1984]: 24).

51 Bryan, *100 Years of Adventure*, 389.

52 Ibid., 390.

53 Susan D. Moeller, *Shooting War: Photography and the American Experience of Combat* (New York, 1989), 385.

54 Ibid., 397; emphasis ours. Many commentators have noted that the story politicians and the media told about the Gulf War of 1991 was that casualties were light. Here, too, the story was only whether or not Americans died, although the storyline that American military personnel were "not dying" also suggested, by implication, that this war was not Vietnam.

55 Tony Schwartz, "The *Geographic* Faces Life," *Newsweek*, 12 September 1977.

56 Abramson, *Behind America's Lens*, 240; and Bryan, *100 Years of Adventure*, 395.

57 Bryan, *100 Years of Adventure*, 395–96.

58 M. J. Sobran, Jr., "Tariff on Truth," *National Review*, 13 May 1977.

59 Charles Truehart, "The Great Divide at National Geographic," *Washington Post*, 7 May 1990.

Power, History, and Authenticity:

The Mowachaht Whalers' Washing Shrine

ALDONA JONAITIS AND RICHARD INGLIS

n 1904, George Hunt (a half-native, half-white resident of the Kwakiutl community of Fort Rupert, British Columbia), working for Franz Boas, then curator at the American Museum of Natural History, purchased a whalers' washing shrine from two Mowachaht chiefs for five hundred dollars and ten secret society songs.[1] Hunt wrote to Boas in July 1904: "It is the best thing that I have ever bought from the Indians." Indeed, this was Hunt's most impressive purchase: the shrine is the largest and most complex single monument ever acquired from the region. Moreover, with its eighty-eight carved figures, four carved whales, sixteen human skulls, and shed-like structure, the shrine is unique; it was the only artifact of its kind on the coast. In addition to the shrine, Hunt collected 152 other artifacts in the Mowachaht region, 12 of which were directly connected to whaling. He recorded sixty-five pages of text about the shrine and its ritualism, and took seven photographs of the structure.[2]

The published literature on the whalers' washing shrine is not extensive, and most references to the monument are based on a brief account published by Boas in 1930.[3] In 1922, a half-Mowachaht, half-Kyuquot woman who lived in Fort Rupert gave Hunt the following history of the origin of the monument. According to her, the shrine originally contained skulls, corpses, mummies, and kidnapped infants in cradles, all of which functioned to attract whales to the shore and beach themselves. After several generations, these human remains decayed. Because acquiring babies and corpses had become difficult, the owner of the shrine substituted them with wooden carvings. Although that story is the one familiar to Northwest Coast scholars, Hunt's unpublished manuscripts in the American Philosophical Society in Philadelphia provide interesting insights into the shrine and related whaling ritualism. In these texts, Hunt describes the carvings as spirits to whom the chiefs prayed for assistance in their rituals.[4] Chiefs and their wives went to the shrine to purify themselves by scrubbing their bodies with fresh water and hemlock boughs, and then slept inside the shrine on beds of skulls.

Boas was fascinated by the shrine when he saw his first photograph of it, and urged Hunt to do everything in his power to procure it for the American Museum of Natural History. This was not to be an ordinary acquisition for Boas; he had great plans for displaying the whalers' shrine when it got to New York. He asked Hunt to take as many photographs of it as possible, to facilitate the eventual reconstruction:

> If you can get it, it is our plan to build up a whole house just like the one in which the carvings are in, in one of our halls, and to put trees and vines and bushes made of wax around it, so as to make the whole thing look just as it looks now. For this purpose you must be very very accurate in all your photographs and in the numbers on the figures.

Boas's excitement about his reconstruction of this shrine in the museum is palpable. So is his insistence that Hunt do his job with special care, mindful of the need for "very very accurate" photographs. Boas was clearly anxious to create in the American Museum of Natural History a "natural" representation of this unique monument found three thousand miles away from New York.

═══

On 3 December 1989, we were driving to Gold River, British Columbia, anticipating our meeting with the Mowachaht band scheduled for the next day. The Mowachaht are Nuu-chah-nulth or Nootka Indians who live on the west coast of Vancouver Island, British Columbia. We had been writing a book on the whalers' washing shrine and wanted to propose forming a partnership with the band to design an exhibit of this unique artifact. A partnership seemed appropriate and long overdue. Though the shrine technically belongs to the American Museum of Natural History, culturally it belongs to the Mowachaht. We wanted their input.[5]

After we were introduced to the group, we described the proposed exhibition, offering a partnership to the Mowachaht. We stated that the American Museum of Natural History wished to have the community participate fully in the project, as equal partners. Should they determine that the washing house should not be displayed, we would agree—reluctantly, to be sure—to abandon the exhibition plan. Since the rights to the washing house belonged to the tribal chiefs, the three highest-ranking chiefs of the community went into closed session to discuss the request that the Mowachaht collaborate on this project. They agreed in principle to support it, and then asked for community approval, which was granted. At the end of these discussions, Jerry Jack, the second hereditary chief, speaking for the community, expressed appreciation and pleasure that this was the first time a museum had come to them to get their input on a project involving their own heritage.[6] Instead of initiating a repatriation of the shrine, they asked whether, as part of this endeavor, we could assist them in the creation of a new shrine, based on the one in New York, that would become the centerpiece of a cultural center they had been envisioning for years.

Although the result of our initial meeting with the Mowachaht was gratifying, and while we have both developed a warm relationship with them over the past several years, it would be dishonest to present too rosy a picture of the nature of working with native people. Today it is de rigeur for curators to involve them—as advisors, consultants, or co-curators—in museum representations of their culture. This is certainly an improvement over the situation in the past when a white, usually male, curator decided by himself the theme and content of an exhibition. It does not, however, solve the problems of the situation of native peoples in the contemporary world. Museums have far more relevance to the powerful—those capable of acquiring and housing art and artifacts—than they do to the disempowered. Moreover, there is no such entity as the native voice, one that speaks with authority for the entire community. There exist many voices, some of which speak for upholders of cultural traditions, others that address band and tribal politics, and still others that concern themselves with social issues. Only rarely are any of these speakers experienced in discussion of exhibition design and production. The encounter of different values, different priorities, often creates problems that can only sometimes be resolved.

=====

Boas wanted the whalers' shrine for several reasons, one of which was to represent in his museum the sole example of an extinct type of ritual artifact displayed in an "authentic" recreation of its original setting—vines, trees, and all. In his letter to Hunt dated 23 January 1904, Boas made explicit his requirements to ensure the accuracy of this representation:

> I do not need to tell you that we want to have the most detailed infor-
> mation. If there are explanations for the single figures, you must ask
> for them and get them. You must know what the whales are for, and
> what all the figures in the two middle lines are for, and what all the
> spectators are for, whose skulls are in the house, and what the skulls
> are used for, and what they are meant to be . . . You must spare no
> pains in making so valuable a find as yours known in all its features.

For Boas, the "authentic" shrine existed in Yuquot shortly before George Hunt acquired it. The goal of his museum representation was to present to the public the meaning it had for a "primitive" group in a neatly pack-aged "explanation" that would be true for all times. That is, the whalers' shrine was to be understood as a single cohesive monument, the sig-nificance of which was fixed at the moment of its "discovery" by the dominant society.

At the turn of the century, Boas believed that the most important object of anthropological investigation was the pure, pristine, and unaccultur-ated primitive culture that existed prior to white contact. Once native people succumbed to modernization and external influences, their cul-ture was judged corrupt, decayed, and, ultimately, no longer genuine.[7] Worried over the forces of change that influenced native societies, Boas and others sought to salvage what remained of precontact culture, and to reconstruct what they believed to have existed in the past. Despite his genuine goodwill, as well as the fact that he met many people, particu-larly the Kwakiutl, who on the surface may have appeared acculturated but nonetheless participated in a distinct and thriving culture of their own, Boas ended up reinforcing the notion of a stereotyped Indian who lived entirely in a world extremely foreign to our own, a world soon to be destroyed by the forces of progress. As a good many contempo-rary anthropologists and interpreters of anthropology have noted, Boas's conception of the primitive denies native people a place in history.[8]

The nature of anthropological investigations and representations has come under scrutiny in recent years. In the past, the authoritative (usually male and white), academically trained scholar conducted fieldwork from an "objective" point of view and then disseminated the "truth" about the people he had studied. Recently, anthropologists have begun to realize how that authoritative white perspective can create serious power asymmetries between the describers and the described, and have begun to question whether their discipline is in reality scientific, objective, and value-free. A good many contemporary theoreticians and practitioners, focusing on the asymmetric power relations inherent in ethnography, agree that the very process of studying and then representing native peoples implies that an authority has the power to select parcels of information about a group and present them as the whole truth. As Edward Said and others have stated, this process often unconsciously supports the continued subordinate position of people who do not themselves conduct influential ethnographic studies.[9] In recent years, self-scrutinizing monographs and collections of theoretical essays that analyze the nature of the anthropological endeavor have begun to pour out of university presses at a remarkable rate.[10]

This new anthropological self-consciousness, along with the recent skepticism about the benefits of modernization, the new openness to the vitality of contemporary cultures in the non-Western world, and the acknowledgment that native people do indeed have a history, has significantly shifted the anthropological paradigm away from a Boasian salvage mode to a celebration of cultural endurance in the postmodern world. Museums can no longer design displays that represent natives as timeless inhabitants of a mythic golden age of ethnic purity, but must, instead, portray them as participants in an ongoing history of creative and often ingenious responses to their encounters with dominant societies.[11] Including the voices of the natives explicitly recognizes them as contemporary inheritors of a historical tradition. That history, in turn, implicates the native/white relations that have had so many unfortunate consequences. Of course, this is why so many anthropologists are attempting new and creative ways to include the native voice in their cultural representations.

Can museums and native people enjoy genuinely equal relationships in the context of creating exhibitions? Probably not. The curators usually come from a privileged position within a university or a museum, while those whose culture is being represented are most often members of a culture subject to economic or social discrimination. True equality cannot result from dialogue, no matter how well intentioned; larger social change is necessary for native people to become equally empowered in the modern world. And such change is not on the horizon.

=====

Museums and their collections present interesting problems concerning the relationships between native peoples and members of the dominant societies. In the case of the North American and Canadian societies, regardless of the nature of native involvement in an exhibition, the artifacts themselves serve as a constant reminder of the imperial past. The majority of Northwest Coast artifacts in museums were acquired at the time when the Canadian government was systematically attempting to destroy the fabric of native culture. When Hunt collected the whalers' shrine, for example, the Nuu-chah-nulth could not legally engage in their most central ceremony, the potlatch.[12] Every ethnographic object in a museum, whatever the intention of the collectors (and Boas's intentions were extraordinarily progressive) is implicated in the historical reality of the nineteenth and twentieth centuries: the Western economic and social expansionism, ideologically premised in large part on a racism that often promoted brutal suppression of native culture. Ethnographic displays, even those that self-consciously attempt to counteract this historic reality by exposing it, cannot erase the events that led to the acquisition of museum collections.[13]

In addition to this generalized implication of their collections, museums themselves—or should we say more accurately, their architecture—significantly influence the message offered by their exhibits. This is certainly true of the message about the whalers' shrine made by the American Museum of Natural History, a large institution, marble everywhere. Probably because Franz Boas left the museum in 1905, just as Hunt's treasured purchases were arriving from British Columbia, the whalers' washing shrine has never appeared on exhibit. Instead, a model, no more than two feet square, is set up in the Nootka section of the Northwest Coast hall (Figure 1). An impressive monument, miniaturized to the point of looking almost like a dollhouse full of toy figures, appears within a context created by the institution itself, a context that imposes a forceful statement of the power of "manifest destiny."[14]

When visitors enter the American Museum of Natural History from the Central Park West entrance, they pass right by a remarkable statue of

Figure 1. Model of Mowachaht whalers' washing shrine in Northwest Coast hall, American Museum of Natural History. Photograph by J. Beckett and C. Chesek.

Theodore Roosevelt astride a large powerful horse, flanked quite subserviently on each side by an African-American and a native American. Then, in the immense Roosevelt rotunda, they can read the great man's celebration of power and manliness: "Only those are fit to live who do not fear to die and none are fit to die who have shrunk from the joy of life and the duty of life. . . . I want to see you game, boys. . . . Courage, hard work, self-mastery, and intelligent effort are essential to a successful life." [15]

Walking through the marble corridors and arriving at the Northwest Coast Indian hall, the visitor sees Indian culture neatly displayed in glass cases, replete with explanatory labels meant to render comprehensible to the casual visitor the complex customs of an alien and extinct people. The artifacts of the very native people who were demolished have been salvaged and now exist entirely within the context of a museum. The museum seems to be saying that it preserves the treasures of the world, treasures that have become part of its world, and ones it can represent on its own terms. The miniature of a shrine that once supported an active whaling cult, presented here in a glass case situated in an impressive exhibition hall, signifies the nonexistence of the cult.

Museums—particularly large, old ones like the American Museum of Natural History—continue to make architectural/spatial statements that may be considerably out of line with the intentions of those who work within them. By trying to bring the Mowachaht into the process of creating an exhibit on the whalers' shrine, we attempt to counteract the notion that the Indian inheritors of these traditions have vanished. We cannot, however, alter the message made by the museum itself. It is no simple matter to integrate successfully the native voices from a small community on western Vancouver Island into this institutional symbol of the achievements of American wealth and progress.[16]

———

The present museum environment of the whalers' shrine miniature is but one element in the history of the monument that began in the late eighteenth or early nineteenth century, when we believe it to have been originally made. A series of photographs taken of the shrine in situ by George Hunt in 1903 and 1904 constitute other important elements in that history.[17] We take it as a given that photographs, to quote Fredric Jameson's discussion of architectural pictures, are "illicit substitutions of one order of things for another, the transformation of the building into the image of itself, and a spurious image at that. . . . We consume so many photographic images of . . . buildings, coming at length to believe these are somehow the things in themselves."[18] This is certainly the case with the whalers' shrine photographs, which many assume, without questioning, to be pictures of the "real thing." Because the entire shrine has never been on display, these photographs have assumed an even greater significance than they might have otherwise had.

We have determined that Hunt took the photograph illustrated in Figure 2 in 1903, when he first saw the shrine; he took the other six pictures the next year, after he had purchased the shrine. In the first image of his newly discovered treasure, an otherworldly quality expresses Hunt's powerful response to this extraordinary monument he has just discovered in a pristine and unspoiled glen. Here, emerging from overgrown brush, is the abandoned shrine of an extinct whale cult. In the foreground are out-of-focus salal bushes that seem to protect the shrine. They ward

Figure 2. Mowachaht whalers' washing shrine in 1903. George Hunt photograph. American Museum of Natural History neg. no. 104479.

off invaders, even the camera's eye. A bright glow issues forth from a sloping plank that underlines a skull seemingly suspended in the air. Soft late autumn light coming from the south, or front of the shrine, bathes the figures, and seems to make them radiate from within. Peeking from behind the central post, a silently staring, half-hidden figure leads a line of carvings. To its left a brightly illuminated, erect, tall figure opens its mouth, ready to speak. To its right stand five figures, each one more obscure than the former. At the back of the shrine are yet more carvings, individuals, each with a different emotion. Some have open mouths, as if singing; others smile; one seems to be frowning. The sunlight that illuminates the forehead of the third figure from the right brings attention to its expression of worry, or perhaps of surprise. On the ground are a large carved whale facing the haunting figures and five human skulls lined up in a row, some glowing in the sunlight. Since only the right side of the shrine appears in the photograph, what is on the left side remains a question. Mystery pervades this image, with skulls emerging from decaying humus, and individualized figures, some dynamic and engaged, others remote and obscure, emerging from a tangle of vegetation.

A year later, Hunt took another picture (Figure 3), the shrine's most

Figure 3. Mowachaht whalers' washing shrine in 1904. George Hunt photograph. American Museum of Natural History neg. no. 104478.

published illustration, one that differs dramatically from the 1903 photo. This photograph of the entire shrine is bilaterally symmetrical, with the central frontal pole bifurcating the picture plane. One large figure peers out from the left of this pole, another from the right. The figures here look static, and project a feeling of quiet, perhaps even a sense of abandonment. Hunt stood at some distance from the entire assemblage of central figures with their expressionless stares, remote rear figures, and rather obscure side figures. The two central figures serve almost as sentries protected by a tangle of salal bushes. The rows of smaller figures at the rear look like soldiers lined up; all their heads, brows, noses, and mouths are at the same level, making them appear uniform, depriving them of the individuality so clear in the earlier shot.

In addition to this full view of the shrine, Hunt took five additional photographs, two of the central part (Figures 4 and 5), one of each side (Figures 6 and 7), and one of a chief singing in front (Figure 8). By reading these photographs, we can reconstruct Hunt's movement into the monument: he approaches its front outside (Figure 3), enters to the right of the

Figure 4. Mowachaht whalers' washing shrine in 1904; central line of figures. George Hunt photograph. American Museum of Natural History neg. no. 104475.

central line of figures (Figure 4), and finally stands before the back row (Figure 5). The play of bright light and deep shadow on the surfaces of the figures creates a sense of drama that only partially offsets the coolness, aloofness, and inaccessibility of the carvings. One must consciously scrutinize these images to discover their considerable differences; it is almost as if the photographic process has quashed their individuality and expressiveness. The left and right sides (Figures 6 and 7) are somewhat more dynamic, with figures positioned at sloping angles, some with faces in profile or three-quarter view. These photographs, more so than the others, reveal major age differences among the carvings. Some are more decomposed than others: in Figure 6 the moss-covered carving at the far left is almost entirely rotted away, the lower jaw of its neighbor equally decayed; in Figure 7 the figure in the right foreground, almost inseparable from the surrounding leaves and bushes, seems about to return to its organic origins.

Figure 5. Mowachaht whalers' washing shrine in 1904; close-up of figures at rear. George Hunt photograph. American Museum of Natural History neg. no. 104474.

What strikes one about the assemblage of 1904 photographs, which should be read both as individual images as well as an integrated group, is the focus on the center and back of the shrine. Hunt devotes four pictures—the overview, the line of central figures, the rear, and the chief—to this area and provides us with only one shot of either side. This may be a response to Boas's directive to obtain as much information about the figures as possible, for, according to Hunt, the group of carvings at the rear are characters in a story about whaling ritualism. In his documentation, dated 22 February 1905, which accompanied the glass plate negatives as well as the photographs, Hunt explained his notations that identify these characters: he stated that he marked "the whales and chief with x and speaker with v and singer with xi and some of the human skulls where the whaler goes to sleep xii after washing on the right hand side of the back end of the house." Although we have not been able to locate the original print with Hunt's marks, we believe it to be Figure 5. The figure Hunt refers to as the "chief" is in all likelihood the figure connected to the whale by means of a rope tied around his neck, the open-mouthed

Figure 6. Mowachaht whalers' washing shrine in 1904; left side. George Hunt photograph. American Museum of Natural History neg. no. 104480.

image next to him the "singer," and the lower figure next to the whale the "speaker." Perhaps because these were the only carvings about which he could obtain information, Hunt took more photographs of them than any others.

These photographs record a major transformation the shrine underwent from what it was in 1903 to what it became in 1904. We believe that the conditions under which Hunt took the photographs each year differed considerably, even though on both occasions he carried with him cumbersome equipment to produce the five- by seven-inch glass plate negatives. It had not been easy for him to gain access to the shrine on his initial visit. The Mowachaht considered shrines dangerous places that could harm those without the right to enter them; even the chiefs who used the shrine needed to ritually purify themselves before entering. When he expressed interest in seeing the shrine, one of the chiefs who owned it asked if Hunt was a shaman. Knowing that only those with proper

Figure 7. Mowachaht whalers' washing shrine in 1904; right side. George Hunt photograph. American Museum of Natural History neg. no. 104482.

spiritual credentials were allowed to see the structure, Hunt responded affirmatively. To test him, the chief presented Hunt with a sick person. As Hunt wrote to Boas, "I was Lucky to get the man Wel, and as soon as he was Made Wel, I was aloud to go" (Hunt to Boas, 9 June 1904). Hunt then took a quick, rushed shot of only part of the front of the shrine; although Hunt's demonstration of shamanic powers had given him access to the shrine, the chief may have been reluctant to permit a photograph of so sacred a monument. A year later, the circumstances were quite different, for once Hunt consummated the purchase of the shrine, he could take as many pictures of his new possession as he wished. He did so carefully, deliberately, and even took a photograph of one of the chiefs wet from ritual bathing (Figure 8), an indication of the openness with which the shrine was now treated. In 1903, the chief, his traditions, and the magical potency of the shrine dominated. In 1904, the power relations had changed, and Hunt was quite in control of everything.

Hunt's exhilaration at discovering this treasure is palpable in the early photograph. As is clear from the intensity of the letter he wrote when

Figure 8. Chief Sesaxalas singing by the whalers' washing shrine in 1904. George Hunt photograph. American Museum of Natural History neg. no. 104476.

he saw it, Boas responded with similar exhilaration to the temptation presented by Hunt. Despite his initial passion about the shrine, Boas the scientist reappeared in his instruction to Hunt to take "very very accurate" pictures to use in the reconstruction of the newly purchased prize. The 1903 shot is magical, with its softer texture (almost out of focus), and light that appears to emerge from the inner soul of the figures, the planks, and the poles of the shrine. The 1904 full frontal picture has a far more sterile quality, a sharp-edged clarity that denies the monument's magicality. The second shot is for the record: an accurate accounting of all the features of the monument. The soft glow of a late autumn light is replaced with harsher summer light that creates hard edges and deep shadows. It is ironic that in order to represent the shrine that initially captivated him, Boas commissioned a series of shots which, by their very scientific nature, are comparatively dry and lifeless.

The first photograph seduced Boas to pursue the purchase of the shrine, while the second suggests his intention of dismantling the structure and its contents, removing it from its overgrown setting, and ultimately reassembling it in an institution thousands of miles away. With none of the persuasive celebration of the shrine's magic that pervades the 1903 shot, the 1904 picture signifies that the shrine will not remain in this pristine environment. Indeed, it communicates the future absence of the shrine from that site. In so doing, it partakes in the process of appropriation that will soon provide the monument from Vancouver Island with another meaning. By heralding this removal, the 1904 photograph further signifies the transformation of the whalers' washing house from cultural treasure to ethnographic artifact.

The cultural treasure captured before the forest engulfs it forever fits nicely into the salvage paradigm. Here *was* a monument whose magic, so evident in 1903, is as lost to the Mowachaht as is their whaling culture and its related ceremonialism. The wistful melancholic response to this disappearing culture that now has a place only in museums pervades another photograph Hunt took in 1904 (Figure 8). The image of one of the two chiefs from whom he purchased the shrine, Sesaxalas, hauntingly suggests the end of whaling ritualism among the Mowachaht. The carving to his right, as well as several of the more shadowy figures in the rear, have open mouths, as if joining the chief in a concert of their last whaling song. This photograph seems to communicate with sad finality the loss of a tradition that provided the shrine with its meaning and thus, with its compelling power. No museum exhibit could restore the human dimension of the chiefs who sang their whaling songs in the presence of those spirits that would soon be gone from this remote spot on Vancouver Island. This connection to tradition was lost when the whalers' washing shrine left Yuquot. But it was not lost forever.

The components of the whalers' shrine, after they arrived at the American Museum of Natural History, were only once reassembled in a non-public area, presumably in order to see what the acquisition looked like. After that, the carvings, the skulls and the elements of the shed remained safely in storage, only occasionally being removed for scholarly study. The anonymity inherent in its new dismantled condition and its location among the thousands of other ethnographic artifacts in the museum's storerooms signify its disassociation from the west coast of Vancouver Island, from whaling ritualism, and from the Mowachaht. Ironically, it was the image of the shrine in situ that maintained its mythic memory. As a sacred treasure located on a remote site, the shrine was to reappear twice in the twentieth century, not in a museum, but once in a silent movie released in 1914, once in a 1989 television show.

In 1914, the photographer Edward S. Curtis released the feature-length In the Land of the Head Hunters. The film's "boy gets girl—boy loses girl—boy gets girl" plot would be quite conventional were its actors and actresses not Kwakiutl Indians wearing pre-contact-style cedar bark clothing, its setting not a reconstructed mid-nineteenth-century Kwakiutl village built for the movie near Fort Rupert, about sixty miles away from Yuquot on the east coast of Vancouver Island, and its principal advisor not George Hunt.[19] In addition to scenes of feasting, dancing, and hunting, this film includes one unforgettable scene of three canoes speeding through the water, at their helms proud dancers impersonating a bear, a bee, and a thunderbird. It also, incongruously, includes an episode in the Mowachaht whalers' shrine.

At one point, the hero embarks on a spirit quest on "the island of the dead" to acquire supernatural power. He walks through a forest, discovers a skull lying at the base of a tree, and then enters a setting unmistakably based upon Hunt's photograph of the right side of the Yuquot shrine. Simple carvings of anthropomorphic figures line the sides and rear of a structure, with only the lack of a roof and the inclusion of skulls hanging from ropes differentiating this cinematographic version of the shrine from the original. The hero proceeds to hang a skull around his neck, lies down and falls asleep in a reference to the Mowachaht ritual practice of spending a night on the bed of skulls to obtain power.

In the Land of the Head Hunters was not the success Curtis had hoped it would be, and the film fell to disuse. Only in 1973, after Northwest Coast Indian art historian Bill Holm and his colleague George Quimby rediscovered the footage, added a soundtrack, and rereleased it under the title In the Land of the War Canoes could the public once again view this remarkable production. And only then could they see the episode of the hero entering a re-creation of the whalers' washing shrine, which the movie fails to identify as Mowachaht rather than Kwakiutl. It still remains obscure as to why Hunt and Curtis included a replica of a Mowachaht shrine in a movie about the Kwakiutl; we must assume that Hunt either described the shrine to Curtis or showed him his photographs, or did both. Perhaps Curtis responded viscerally to the dramatic potential of this extraordinary assemblage of anthropomorphic figures, carved whales, and human remains, and using an artistic license to which Hunt presumably agreed, appropriated them from one group and assigned them to another.

In 1989, the same shrine, neither identified nor misidentified, appeared in an episode of the Canadian television series Danger Bay entitled "Ancient Spirits." Two teenagers on a camping trip stumble upon a site with carvings and skulls (but no shed) clearly based on the Yuquot shrine. When they bring their photographs of the place to a museum archeologist, he identifies it as an ancient Indian whaling shrine, "not touched since the time of Captain Cook." Although the girl thinks the shrine should stay hidden in the woods, her father reassuringly says that it's better for it to be in the museum, where "everyone can see it." It turns out, however, that the archeologist, craving the excitement of retrieving something so special and unique, "an artifact that represents a way of life that has vanished," removes the artifacts from their site, fabricates a story about thieves stealing them, and demands a ransom of $100,000 for their return. Naturally, he is found out and arrested. This television show has everything: a nostalgic allusion to the vanished primitive, an archeologist cum thief, a verification of the public value of museums. Of course, what is left out is the contemporary native voice, which would lend a dissonant note to the neatly packaged story, which reassuringly concludes with the shrine's safe storage, for perpetuity, in a museum.

Hunt's photographs are not only records of what the shrine looked like in 1903 and 1904. Neither are they just signifiers of the appropriation process, important as that may be for understanding its history. The pictures are not only representations, but also genuine parts of the whalers' shrine as we know it in 1993; they are part of the authentic artifact. Authenticity is an issue of central concern to those who both create and write about museum exhibitions of native people.[20] Obviously, the museum's two-foot-square model is not the authentic whalers' shrine. Would it be any more authentic if we took the carvings out of storage and positioned them within a reconstruction of their original context, informed by the 1904 photograph, as Boas dreamed? We don't think so. The shrine would be special, of course, and would impress museum visitors. However, they would probably still perceive the shrine as a cultural artifact of a people frozen in time, a people without history. It would be an artifact impoverished by the lack of connection to a living people.

Of particular value in our analysis of an authenticity that includes the history of an artifact is the concept of "wrapping" described by Jameson in relationship to architecture.[21] Simplified considerably, wrapping as an analytic device assumes that (in the case of the topic at hand) the artifact is the core of an entity that changes as a result of the layers of meaning applied to it. We can attempt to decipher how the original whalers' shrine has been "wrapped" by new levels of meaning produced by representations that refer to it; those representations do not just form layers that sit on the original authentic artifact, but actually incorporate that original piece to create a new entity, a two-or-more-part whole with a "resonance" among its component parts. Hunt's photographs of the shrine are just one layer of wrapping; other layers include the published illustration of those photographs, what scholars and others have written about it, what native people have said about it over the years, and what the movie and television industry has made of it. All these wrappings, which interact with each other, create a composite entity considerably different from the original shrine that once stood in a forest; always at the core of this wrapped artifact stands the shrine itself: magical, unique, and compelling.

The authentic object is not an artifact frozen in time, made by a people fossilized in a golden age of ethnic purity. Instead, the authentic object consists not only of the artifact itself, but also of its meaning to the variety of different peoples for whom it has come to have significance, as well as the added meanings that have come about as a result of its varied representations. This is a somewhat less romanticized notion of what "authentic" might mean, less static in its conception, founded, appropriately, upon the historical events that have affected the original artifact, and less pure in that it acknowledges the roles played by the powerful in those historical events. The authentic artifact—in this case the whaling shrine— always undergoes an evolving process that takes into account new interpretations, new analyses, new perceptions over time. In *Gone Primitive*, Marianna Torgovnick warns that the romantic notion of the primitive still exists.[22] Yet it is somewhat doubtful as to whether the general public will be as receptive to the presentation of this kind of impure authenticity as it is to the painfully nostalgic representation of the Sioux in *Dances with Wolves*.

One of the most fascinating aspects of the evolution of the whalers' washing house photographs concerns their meaning to the Mowachaht people of today. Up until very recently, no member of this community had ever seen the entire shrine, which is still in storage at the American Museum of Natural History. For years, the photographs provided them with the only concrete images they had of this treasure. As we mentioned earlier, our initial encounter with the Mowachaht community was to invite them to be partners with us on the whalers' shrine exhibition. To initiate this partnership, we invited the political leaders of the community, Norman George, Larry Andrews, James Dick, and Arnold James, as well as the Nuu-chah-nulth Tribal Council chairman, George Watts, to visit the museum. From 11 to 14 March 1990, they saw the washing house figures as well as the skeletal material acquired along with it, the gallery in which it would be erected, the conservation laboratory, and the exhibition department. In addition to meeting the administration, they met many members of the staff who would be working on the exhibit. Later that week, Art Thompson and Tim Paul, Nuu-chah-nulth artists, visited the museum to share with us their perceptions on the shrine carvings as artworks, and to discuss their views on how a museum artifact, new traditions defined in the 1990s, and past legacies might interact in the creation of a new shrine that could become a significant component of this entire project.

Figure 9. President of the American Museum of Natural History, George D. Langdon, presenting Larry Andrews, speaker for Chief Maquinna of the Mowachaht, with a photograph of the whalers' washing shrine, March 1990. In the foreground are George Watts, Nuuchah-nulth Tribal Council chairman, and William Moynihan, director of the American Museum of Natural History. Photograph by D. Finnan.

During the visit of the Mowachaht to New York, the president of the museum, George Langdon, gave to the delegation from Gold River an elegantly framed print of the full-view whale shrine photograph with the statement, "To the Mowachaht, with best wishes from the American Museum of Natural History" (Figure 9). This photograph, which records the transition the whalers' washing house underwent from sacred treasure to museum artifact, now appears in a new and different context. An official of the museum offered to a representative of the Mowachaht community the 1904 image that tells of another transition, enhanced considerably by the wrappings it has undergone over the many decades since Hunt first directed his camera lens to it: the photograph, which now hangs in the band office in Gold River, signifies that the shrine is once again a cultural treasure, but one quite different from that appropriated in 1904.

That initial visit to New York was just the start of the dialogue. After that visit the two of us returned to Gold River in March, May, August, and January to continue discussions with members of the community. In February 1991, Chief Ambrose Maquinna, his son Mike Maquinna, Sam Johnson, and Max Savey came to New York. We returned to Gold River in April to plan future meetings both in New York and Gold River. The nature of these discussions, and their ultimate result (which at this point is not fully predictable), will unquestionably add new wrappings to the Mowachaht whalers' washing shrine.

═══

Our dialogues with the Mowachaht community have occurred within the context of a topic of considerable interest to native people throughout Canada and the United States, to the public and, especially to the media: repatriation of native treasures to their originating communities. Ever since historian Douglas Cole described the circumstances under which Hunt purchased the whalers' shrine in his 1985 *Captured Heritage: The Scramble for Northwest Coast Artifacts*, discourse on the monument has included speculations on its possible return to the Mowachaht. Hunt had encountered serious difficulties in 1904, first because two Mowachaht chiefs, each of whom claimed ownership of the monument, disputed each other's right to sell it, and second because both were concerned that their community would protest its removal from Yuquot. These chiefs ultimately accepted his payment of five hundred dollars (and ten secret society songs) with the stipulation that Hunt would take the shrine away in secret. This narrative of disputed ownership and clandestine removal has led some to believe that the shrine was acquired in an inappropriate fashion, making it a prime candidate for repatriation. Indeed, although we have anticipated a Mowachaht request for the shrine back, it has not been forthcoming.

The media have found the whalers' washing shrine story fascinating. In the spring of 1991, after the second visit of the Mowachaht chiefs to New York City, three separate articles on the whalers' shrine appeared in British Columbian newspapers, each illustrated with Hunt's photographs. The best of them, Sid Tafler's "Secrets of the Chiefs," the cover story of the March 7–13 *Monday Magazine*, recounts both Boas's 1930 description of the shrine and also the story of Hunt's acquisition. In the April 18 edition of the *Times-Colonist*, Katherine Dedyna's headline reads

"Return of Whaler's Shrine to B.C. Depends on Decision by Natives," which refers to our efforts to work with the Mowachaht on a possible exhibition of the shrine in New York and the Royal British Columbia Museum. And, on May 25, *The Vancouver Sun* carried Mark Hume's story, "Reviving Dark Forces," which asked "Should [the shrine] be returned to British Columbia, from where [it] was covertly taken almost a century ago?" Then, early in 1992, on *The Journal*, a Canadian Broadcasting Company television news magazine, Eric Rankin moderated a fifteen-minute segment on native people and repatriation, a section of which dealt with the Mowachaht shrine. In addition to providing some information about its history, and showing Hunt's 1904 photograph, Rankin states that "the American Museum of Natural History bought it under shady circumstances," and later suggests that "being more sensitive [to native people] may mean giving it back." The shrine, no longer only an artifact of considerable power to those chiefs who used it for whaling magic before 1904, nor simply an image appropriated by filmmakers or television producers, now plays a role in an international dialogue between natives and museums in both New York and Victoria, a dialogue that has entered the even larger world of the media and the public opinion they both reflect and shape.

Leaving aside the legal matters of ownership, the practical concerns of preserving fragile artworks, and the more universal issue of who has the right to maintain and display cultural property, the theme of repatriation contributes new facets to this analysis of the whalers' washing shrine. Does returning artifacts correct the past excesses and occasional insensitivities of museums and their collectors? Are those who request repatriation embracing a nostalgic concept of the pristine primitive existing in a premodern community that nonnative scholars have endeavored to discredit? Can a native community retrieving one of their past treasures from a large prestigious institution enjoy a genuinely satisfying experience of empowerment that has relevance to their position in contemporary society? The photographs that have appeared and reappeared in such diverse contexts raise a last question: how would these scholarly and popular representations that have brought to the fore this issue of repatriation differ had George Hunt's acquisition included only the artifacts themselves and not his seven memorable black-and-white images of the whalers' washing shrine? The perceived reality of the shrine is so deeply embedded in those pictures that it would be difficult to imagine the nature of this discourse in their absence.

=====

Even as they have added new wrappings to the whalers' washing shrine, the dialogues with the Mowachaht and their visits to New York City have unwrapped some veils of photographic representations that have prevailed over the decades since 1904. Regardless of whether the eventual outcome is an exhibition or repatriation (or both), the reopening of museum storage facilities for the Mowachaht to actually see these elements of their cultural heritage turns the focus of the shrine's history away from its photographs and once again to its material component parts. This in turn raises questions about how the involvement of the Mowachaht with these sculptures, skulls, and architectural elements intersects with the quest for authenticity.

Walter Benjamin worried, among other things, about the problem of authenticity in "The Work of Art in the Age of Mechanical Reproduction." Benjamin associated authenticity with the aura emanating from the solidarity of a community directly experiencing a unique work of art that is "embedded in the fabric of tradition."[23] Once art could be mechanically produced, and the community no longer joined together to experience it directly, it lost the aura that Benjamin thought irretrievable.

When the whalers' washing shrine left Yuquot and was no longer embedded in Mowachaht ritual traditions, it lost its original aura. That aura cannot be recaptured. No amount of realistic contextualization—no wax trees, vines, and bushes—can restore the significance of the human dimension to the shrine in its New York location. Neither the appropriation process nor the history of the Mowachaht can be reversed; whaling ritualism will probably not be revived; the nineteenth-century magic of the chief and his wife cannot be recaptured.[24] But since the shrine, with all its wrappings, is now something different, we can envision a different, more contemporary aura resulting from the involvement of the Mowachaht today.

What is the role of curators in this process? We can facilitate the involvement of the Mowachaht with the shrine by obtaining funding for planning the exhibit and by working with them in this planning process. In addition to these concrete contributions, we can also try to sensitize others to the cultural biases that make such exhibits possible, that put the artifacts into our hands. The history of much twentieth-century anthropological thought reveals a considerable conscious effort to combat racism and promote social equality. Both Boas and Claude Lévi-Strauss certainly tried to do this. A leitmotiv that runs through much contemporary anthropological writing—as well as literary criticism—is self-consciousness about inherent hierarchies in the descriptive process, about the white male orientation of so many texts and their (most often unconscious) endorsement and support of the values that underlie Western industrial society. One goal of self-scrutiny is to contribute to the liberation of those people who have so infelicitously been named the "Other." Nevertheless, curators ought not deceive themselves with the idea that they can achieve an equal relationship with groups such as the Mowachaht simply by bringing them into our institutions. As long as places like the American Museum of Natural History hold treasures like the Mowachaht whalers' washing shrine, those of us who work at such museums have an obligation to discredit stereotypes by presenting a history of the artifacts— before, during, and after their appropriation—while making it very clear that the voices speaking that history belong to the dominant culture.

Earlier we expressed some caution about being too optimistic about the prospects of working successfully with native people on projects like a museum exhibition. Although anthropologists and art historians are increasingly self-conscious about how they write and speak of native people, it is still easy to fall into mythologizing romanticism about re-empowering Indians. In this case, to believe that bringing Indians into museums and offering them a voice will allow them to become successful spokespersons for their culture is to ignore the reality of British Columbian Indian history (as well as Canadian and American Indian history in general), in which for decades those in power have run reserves and governed native communities. That history cannot be denied. Indeed it is always an implicit, if not an explicit element in our current discussions— it is part of the "wrapping," part of what has become, for better or worse, the "authenticity" of the Mowachaht whalers' shrine.

Notes

1   Versions of this paper were presented by Aldona Jonaitis at the University of British Columbia and the Whitney Museum Symposium on Art and Technology in March 1991. See Douglas Cole, *Captured Heritage: The Scramble for North-*

west Coast Artifacts (Seattle, 1985), 161–62; and Aldona Jonaitis, From the Land of the Totem Poles: The Northwest Coast Indian Art Collection at the American Museum of Natural History (New York, 1988), 182–85, for descriptions of the purchase of the shrine. George Hunt was an initiated member of the Kwakiutl hamatsa society; the two Mowachaht chiefs wanted ten of the songs associated with that secret society.

2   See Ira Jacknis, "George Hunt, Collector of Indian Specimens," in Chiefly Feasts: The Enduring Kwakiutl Potlatch, ed. Aldona Jonaitis (Seattle, 1991), 176–224.

3   Franz Boas, "Religion of the Kwakiutl Indians," Columbia University Contributions to Anthropology (New York, 1930), 10: 261–69.

4   We will be publishing these texts in our full-length study of the whalers' shrine.

5   In 1978, Parks Canada wanted to install the washing house shrine in an Interpretation Center they planned to build in Yuquot (or Nootka)—the original home of the Mowachaht, who now live in the community of Gold River, and the location from which the shrine was removed. Peter Bennett, the Parks Canada general director, was asked to make an inquiry about repatriation of the artifact. The American Museum of Natural History was at that point willing to send the shrine to British Columbia on a long-term loan basis. But the project to create the center in Yuquot never got underway, and the whalers' shrine remained at the museum. In 1980, the Nuu-chah-nulth Tribal Council Museum Committee planned a museum/cultural center of their own, to be built somewhere on the West Coast; they are still hoping to accomplish this goal. Although they would like the shrine to become the centerpiece of their project, the Council has yet to request the return of the shrine.

6   Involving native people in museum exhibitions of their own culture is not a new phenomenon. See Alan Hoover and Richard Inglis, "Acquiring and Exhibiting a Nuu-Chah-Nulth Ceremonial Curtain," Curator 4 (1990) 272–88; and Robin Wright's introduction to her A Time of Gathering (Seattle, 1991). The American Museum of Natural History has only recently begun to involve natives in museum exhibitions.

7   James Clifford, "Of Other Peoples: Beyond the 'Salvage' Paradigm," in Dia Art Foundations Discussions in Contemporary Culture, ed. H. Foster (Seattle, 1987), 1: 122. See also Virginia Dominguez, "Of Other Peoples: Beyond the 'Salvage' Paradigm," in the same collection.

8   See Johannes Fabian, Time and the Other: How Anthropology Makes Its Object (New York, 1983); and Eric Wolf, Europe and the People without History (Berkeley, 1982).

9   See Marcia Tucker, "Mechanisms of Exclusion and Relation: Identity," in Discourses: Conversations in Postmodern Art and Culture, ed. Russel Ferguson et al. (New York, 1990), 91–92; and, in the same collection, Phil Mariani and Jonathan Crary, "In the Shadow of the West: An Interview with Edward Said," 93–103.

10 See Roger Sanjek, "On Ethnographic Validity," in *Fieldnotes: The Makings of Anthropology*, ed. Roger Sanjek (Ithaca, 1990), 385–418; *The Interpretation of Dialogue*, ed. Tullio Maranhao (Chicago, 1990); *Modernist Anthropology: From Fieldwork to Text*, ed. Marc Manganaro (Princeton, 1990); and *Writing Culture: The Poetics and Politics of Ethnography*, ed. James Clifford and G. E. Marcus (Berkeley, 1986).

11 For more analysis of the power relations inherent in displays of native artifacts in nonnative museums, see George Stocking, "Essays on Museums and Material Culture," in *Objects and Others: Essays on Museums and Material Culture*, ed. George Stocking (Madison, 1985); Tony Bennett, "Museums and 'The People,' " in *The Museum Time-Machine: Putting Cultures on Display*, ed. Robert Lumley (London, 1988); Aldona Jonaitis, "The Creation of an Exhibition," in Jonaitis, ed., *Chiefly Feasts*, 21–69; *Exhibiting Cultures: The Poetics and Politics of Museum Display*, eds. Ivan Karp and Steven Lavine (Washington, D.C., 1991); *Museums and Communities: The Politics of Public Culture*, eds. Ivan Karp, Christine Mullen Kraemer, and Steven Lavine (Washington, D.C., 1992). The best and most recent publication on this topic is Michael M. Ames, *Cannibal Tours and Glass Boxes: The Anthropology of Museums* (Vancouver, 1992).

12 The Canadian government passed an anti-potlatch bill in 1884. The bulk of the Northwest Coast collections in museums were acquired between 1880 and 1910. See Cole, *Captured Heritage*.

13 Attempts to expose historical contexts can sometimes be misunderstood. The Royal Ontario Museum last year put on an exhibition called "Into the Heart of Africa," which was intended to provide information about racism. The black community in Toronto, however, felt that the exhibit celebrated racism. See Enid Schildkrout, "Ambiguous Messages and Ironic Twists: *Into the Heart of Africa* and *The Other Museum*," *Museum Anthropology* 15 (1991): 16–23.

14 For an analysis of how other Northwest Coast artworks presented in the American Museum of Natural History reflect the power of the institution, see Aldona Jonaitis, "Franz Boas, John Swanton, and the Creation of New Haida Art at the American Museum of Natural History," in *The Early Years of Native American Art History*, ed. Janet Berlo (Seattle, 1992).

15 See Donna Harraway, "Teddy Bear Patriarchy: Taxidermy in the Garden of Eden, New York City, 1908–36," in *Primate Visions* (New York, 1989), 26–58. See also Mieke Bal, "Telling, Showing, Showing Off," *Critical Inquiry* 18 (1992): 556–594, for another reading of American Museum of Natural History halls.

16 See Fredric Jameson, *Postmodernism, or, the Cultural Logic of Late Capitalism* (Durham, 1991), 128.

17 Our research on the actual carvings has revealed that they were made at different times. The oldest shrine figures date back to about the late eighteenth century, while the newest were carved in the 1880s.

18 Jameson, *Postmodernism*, 124–25. Gerald Vizenor asserts that photographs "of

tribal people . . . are not connections to the traditional past; these images are discontinuous artifacts in a colonial road show" (see his "Socioacupuncture: Mythic Reversals and the Striptease in Four Scenes," in *Out There: Marginalization and Contemporary Cultures*, ed. Russel Ferguson et al. (Cambridge, Mass., 1990), 411–19.

19 Bill Holm and George Quimby, *Edward S. Curtis in the Land of the War Canoes* (Seattle, 1980).

20 Dean MacCannell has questioned the notion of authenticity in *The Tourist: A New Theory of the Leisure Class* (New York, 1989). In "Beyond the 'Salvage' Paradigm," James Clifford argues that

[new] definitions of authenticity (cultural, personal, artistic) are making themselves felt, definitions no longer centered on a salvaged past. Rather, authenticity is reconceived as hybrid, a creative activity in a local present-becoming future. Non-western cultural and artistic works are implicated by an interconnected world cultural system without necessarily being swamped by it. Local structures produce *histories* rather than simply yielding to History. (126)

For other insightful discussions of authenticity, see Ames, *Cannibal Tours and Glass Boxes*, especially chapters 7, 8, 13, 14; and Brian Spooner, "Weavers and Dealers: The Authenticity of an Oriental Carpet," in *The Social Life of Things: Commodities in Cultural Perspective*, ed. Arjun Appadurai (Cambridge, 1986): 195–236.

21 Jameson, *Postmodernism*, 101–03.

22 Marianna Torgovnick, *Gone Primitive: Savage Intellects, Modern Lives* (Chicago, 1990), 246.

23 Walter Benjamin, *Illuminations* (New York, 1969), 223.

24 It is of interest that the Makah of northwestern Washington state, cultural and linguistic relatives of the Mowachaht, have recently been discussing resuming whaling. In keeping with earlier ritual practices, the Makah have decided to prohibit women from handling whaling implements held in storage in their tribal museum. This situation raises fascinating questions about differing perceptions on authenticity and traditionalism.

The Ecology of Images

ANDREW ROSS

T   he *Target-Rich Environment*. At least two urgent needs emerged from the war in the Persian Gulf. First of all, the United States Congress ought to sit down and draft a constitutional amendment that would ensure the separation of press and state. That will take a long time, and a much better Congress than any money can buy, but it would do well to protect against the kind of collapse, all too clear from the first hour of Gulf combat, of the distance conventionally observed between the corporate media and the corporate state, respectively engaged in the ratings war over images or the strategic war over oil resources.

The technically sweet aesthetics of the TV war that many people compared to a Nintendo game was the culmination of what other critics have increasingly come to call the military-industrial-media complex, concentrated in the hands of fewer and fewer conglomerate owners. Consequently, the logic of the TV ratings war became an integral part of many viewers' experience of the minute-by-minute progress of military operations in the Gulf. Everyone seemed to become a media critic. Many even became Baudrillardians without knowing it, repelled by everyone else's (and never their own) fascination with the simulacra of war cooked up by the Pentagon and the networks (a simulated aerial view of Baghdad from an F-111 pilot's perspective—who would not want to see that?). Members of the Institute for Defense Information, a group of disaffected Pentagon ex-employees, confirmed what many suspected: that, in view of a job well done by the networks, the Pentagon had decided not to release their own independent footage and propaganda in the United States. To top it all, antiwar protesters (including myself) marched, not to the Pentagon, but to the TV network buildings. Denied access to the corporate workings of military industrialism, intellectuals and activists feel they have at least one foot in the door of media making, but the opportunities for "linkage" suggested by the phrase "military-industrial-media complex" often went begging in the rush to paint media professionals as craven or warmongering. While the TV anchors drew the heat, the industrialists and the generals were laughing all the way to the bank.

That is not to say that critiques of the media's role in the war were not justified, especially when they extended to exposés of the TV war's exploitation of popular pleasures embellished by racism and xenophobia. However, in a war openly fought for control over dwindling oil resources (the model, now, for the twenty-first-century eco-wars for which dystopian science fiction has so long prepared us), we cannot forget that the nightly firework display in the Gulf skies and the spectacle of laser-guided smart bombs homing in on their targets were also an explicitly seductive advertisement for another thirty years of the permanent war economy, sustained by the uninterrupted flow of cheap fossil fuels. Such images, when put alongside the images of burning Kuwaiti oil fields, were part of a story being told about the ecological significance of war politics.

Perhaps the most telling Pentagon images in this respect were those shot by a camera mounted on a GBU-15 glider bomb en route to destroying the al-Ahmadi Sea Island terminal's pumping mechanism, which, we were told, controlled the flow of four hundred million gallons of Kuwaiti oil spilling recklessly into the Gulf. Here, then, in this official Pentagon footage, we were offered the visual perspective of the United States Air Force as Captain Planet, waging war against eco-terrorism in what must surely also rank as the first photo-opportunity for politically correct militarism. The prelude to this bizarre footage was best summed up in the previous day's three-inch high headlines in the scab edition of the New York Daily News: SADDAM ATTACKS EARTH!—a headline worth an appearance in any bad SF movie. Media treatment of the ecological consequences of the spill itself was no less adventurist and no less fantasmatic, varying dramatically in assessing the size of the slick or the flush-out cycle of the Persian Gulf (anything from two years to two hundred years). In the absence of any footage of Iraqi soldiers themselves, the slowly spreading oil slick in the Gulf quickly came to embody, for Western audiences, many of the diabolic features attached to the pseudo-biological "Arab threat." The

meaning of the slick no longer lay simply within the traditional iconog-
raphy of corporate oil spill images, incomplete without stock footage of
an oil-drenched seabird. Narratives of war, and the new image-arsenal of
"eco-terrorism," gave this oil slick layers of additional meaning. When it
was not a "military obstacle" or "logistics problem," in Pentagon parlance,
the slick was yet another mess for the West to fix with its wondrous technology. Most pernicious of all, however, the slick came to personify (oily)
Arab treachery, whether it signified the dark, inscrutable evil of Saddam
Hussein or the sinister, inexorable spread of Islam/Arab nationalism.

   If the oil slick became the leading ecological actor during the war itself,
the spectacle of the burning Kuwaiti oil wells played the starring role in
the media war's denouement. This sooty spectacle very quickly satisfied
a number of needs: first, a Western and, I suppose, specifically Christian
desire for images of hellfire appropriate to wartime, images that were
widespread in the wake of bombing raids on Baghdad and Basra, but denied us by military censorship; second, the sense of an ending to the war's
narrative, recalling for Western audiences the real oil-related purpose of
the war and its economic significance for Bush's New World Order; and
third, in the midst of extensive ecological commentary about climatic
effects, acid rain, equatorial holes in the ozone layer, and monsoon failure in the Indian subcontinent, a need to believe that there is no life in
a desert, and thus there is no desert ecology to devastate. The oil slick
and the burning wells were the images of ecological spoliation we did
get to see. Forget the "moonscape" created by B-52 carpet bombing, the
targeted bombing of over forty biochemical and nuclear facilities, or the
systematic destruction from the air of the water and sewage infrastructure
of Iraq. Forget the catastrophic erosion likely to be caused by the breaking
of the desert's top surface, held in place by a crust of living microorgan-
isms. Forget the environmental devastation begun with the installation of
the two armies—the garbage, sewage, and toxic waste created by two vast
alien populations totaling over one million in a desert whose ecosystem
is in many ways more delicate than that of the Gulf. Those are stories that
could not be told, either because of Pentagon censorship or because they
require more than a sound-bite analysis and a set of atrocity images. This
is not to dispute the disastrous scale and consequences of the oil spill
and the burning wells, about which the Pentagon had ample forewarning
from their own environmental impact studies, commissioned from the

Sandia National Laboratory in Albuquerque (among others). But nothing else could compete, in media terms, with these twin spectacles, which were left to fill out the environmental story by themselves. It is a story in which the United States military, the biggest polluter in its own country, generating a ton of toxic waste every minute in peacetime, was featured in the Captain Planet role of combating environmental damage. This was one of the more obscene aspects of the war—the bestowing of ecological sanctity upon a military institution that makes a mockery of public review of the toxic effects of its weapons testing (especially nuclear) and production of war matériel in the United States, while national environmental laws are nonbinding for overseas activities. (The Bush Administration's wartime decision to exempt military observance of the 1970 National Environmental Policy Act was implemented in only one instance, and circumvented in many others, for fear that a general exemption would raise too many questions.)

=====

Credible Forms of Lust. If we are to make proper sense of such events and such images, it is high time that we had more of a green cultural criticism, if only to help us see why all wars, and not just this one, are now ecological wars in every sense of the term. When I started thinking about this paper, I looked around for published work in the field of film and media studies to build upon, and found media-oriented theoretical discussion of ecological issues to be very thin on the ground. One of the few related discussions I found was in Susan Sontag's book On Photography (1977), at the end of which she called, somewhat metaphorically, for an "ecology of images":

> Images are more real than anyone could have supposed. And just be-
> cause they are an unlimited resource, one that cannot be exhausted
> by consumerist waste, there is all the more reason to apply the con-
> servationist remedy. If there can be a better way for the real world to
> include the one of images, it will require an ecology not only of real
> things but of images as well.[1]

A decade earlier, in her book Against Interpretation (1966), Sontag had made a similar kind of call for an "erotics of art." This call was answered loudly and clearly in literary and cultural criticism of the subsequent two decades: the kind of criticism that has focused on the libidinal, or psycho-sexual relationship between language and desire, and images and plea-sure. By contrast, there has been precious little in the way of a response to Sontag's call for an "ecology of images." It is unfortunate but perhaps instructive that we may have needed images from war to provide the im-petus for belatedly responding to Sontag's call, and for seriously debating the consequences, for cultural criticism, of an "ecology of images." At the start of a decade that will play host to a green cultural criticism, re-directing attention to the suppressed (at least, in the last twenty years of cultural theory) "nature" side of the nature/culture equation, nothing seems more important than to debate the ecological role and charac-ter of images; not only the use of images to tell ecological stories, but also the ecology of the image industry itself, considered in all aspects of production, distribution, and consumption.

My remarks here on this neglected debate will be speculative and ex-ploratory. Whatever immediate shape this debate will take, I will venture that it may well divide itself along lines similar to those once used to dif-ferentiate feminist film criticism into two schools of thought: "images of women" film criticism on the one hand, and what came to be known as feminist film theory on the other. "Images of ecology" could well be distinguished from discussion of the "ecology of images" in a way that may resemble the distinction between those critical schools that once focused, respectively, on images of women, positive and negative, and on the production of gendered divisions within the filmic narrative, the filmic "apparatus," and the filmic spectator. I do not intend this to be a hard and fast analogy, but there exists, I think, a minimum of common elements and conditions to make the link between these respective kinds of analysis—analysis of the meanings of images, and analysis of narrative and technical logic.

To begin with what looks like the easier category, what are "images of ecology"? Aside from the long history of "images of nature" in the genres of nature and wildlife photography, films, and documentaries, there has appeared, over the twenty-year existence of the ecology movement, a genre of image in which the "environment" figures quite distinctively as a narrative element, usually endangered and in some advanced state of degradation, but also often in a state of repair, reconstruction, or even in pristine good health. In recent years, we have become accustomed to

seeing images of a dying planet, variously exhibited in grisly poses of ecological depletion, and circulated by all sectors of the image industry, often
in spots reserved for the exploitation fare of genocidal atrocities. The cli-
chés of the standard environmental image are well-known to us all: on
the one hand, belching smokestacks, seabirds mired in petrochemical
sludge, fish floating belly up, traffic jams in Los Angeles and Mexico City,
and clearcut forests; on the other hand, the redemptive repertoire of pastoral imagery, crowned by the ultimate global spectacle, the fragile, vulnerable ball of spaceship earth. These images, which call attention to the
actually existing state of the environment, are intended to have different
meanings from the traditional genres of images of nature (notwithstand-
ing the obvious caveat that "Nature" itself has played host, historically, to
a whole spectrum of shifting meanings). It is in this respect, then—the
conditions of representation under which the ecology of a depicted environment becomes a narrative agent—that we can speak of "images of
ecology" in recent years, as well as the critical language used to describe
these images and narratives as either "positive" or "negative" images and
narratives.

I will have more to say later about images of ecology, because I do not
want to assume that we have a self-apparent understanding of the power
of these images. In other words, I don't mean to suggest that it is, in a
sense, the more *vulgar* of the discussions I will be pursuing here, and that,
having briefly pinned it down, we can move on to higher things. For the
time being, however, I am obliged to devote some time and space to the
question of whether images have an ecology in their own right, if only
because it is a less widely recognized idea in the first place. To do so, we
must consider the social and industrial organization of images—the processes by which images are produced, distributed, and used in modern
electronic culture—and ask if there are ecological arguments to be made
about those processes.

Sontag's discussion of photographic images is a starting point. In On
Photography, a book about the "ethics of seeing" the world through the
voracious filter of image consumption, she argues that the world is consumed and used up by our appetite for images. In Sontag's view, the world
has been reduced to a set of potential photographs; its events are valued
for their photographic interest, and large sectors of its population have
become "tourists of reality" as a result. While she sees the act of the pho-

tographer as "essentially an act of non-intervention," the knowledge that an audience gains through images is always gained cheaply; it is always knowledge at "bargain prices." Sontag is careful to avoid reproducing the jeremiac tones of those who, historically, have lamented the popularity of the image over the reality, but there is no mistaking the repulsion that wells up below her fascination with modern image-addiction. "Industrial societies," she writes, "turn their citizens into image-junkies: it is the most irresistible form of mental pollution."[2] Surely Sontag has in mind here some Judeo-Christian meaning of "pollution," as applied to the moral equilibrium of the mind-body, and marked by the perversion of that balance. She is clearly invoking the older, moral stigma of spiritual pollution to describe our complicity with the overconsumption of images and the consequent depreciation of the world's reality-resources. But there remains a persistent distaste in her comments. Later in the book, the same charge returns, this time more overtly embellished, in a mode that would come to preoccupy Sontag in her subsequent writing, with the metaphors of sickness:

> The possession of a camera can inspire something akin to lust. And like all credible forms of lust, it cannot be satisfied; first, because the possibilities of photography are infinite, and, second, because the project is finally self-devouring. The attempts by photographers to bolster up a depleted sense of reality contribute to the depletion. Our oppressive sense of the transience of everything is more acute since cameras gave us the means to "fix" the fleeting moment. We consume images at an ever faster rate, and, as Balzac suspected cameras used up layers of the body, images consume reality. Cameras are the antidote and the disease, a means of appropriating reality and a means of making it obsolete.[3]

When Sontag speaks of photography as a "credible form of lust" (just exactly what an "incredible" form of lust might be is left for the reader to toy with), an addictive pleasure for which we ultimately will have to pay the consequences, she seems to want to convey a strongly moral or religious sense of retribution. I find this appeal disturbing, and quite objectionable. If we consider its implications in the context of Sontag's later commentary on the history of "illness as metaphor," we might complain about her own perpetuation of that particular discursive history, exemplified here by the description of visual technologies as both "the antidote and the disease."[4]

For me, Sontag's remarks about image addiction can best be placed in the context of ecological arguments about the historical role of science and technology in the domination of the natural world. In this light, camera technology can be seen as an embodiment of what ecologists have called the rationalist project of mastering, colonizing, and dominating nature; a project whose historical development now threatens the global ecology with an immediacy that is all the more ironically apparent to us through those very "images of ecology" that have become standard media atrocity fare in recent years. My reading of Sontag's arguments is that they take this ecological thesis one step further, into the realm of the epistemology of images. I would summarize her discussion of the capacity of images to "deplete" reality in the following way: just as ecologists have spoken of the "carrying capacity" of a bioregional economy, so too are we invited to think of the production and consumption of images as a central element in our social habitat; just as the technological overproduction and overconsumption of raw materials can wastefully exhaust the carrying capacity of a natural economy to sustain itself, so too a similar tendency in image production and image consumption diminishes our capacity to sustain a healthy balance of life in the social world of our culture. There comes a point, if you like, when one image too many destroys the global "commons." This is perhaps a rather crude way of drawing out a working analogy from Sontag's comments, but I don't think it is an unfair one; and I have put it in these terms because they highlight more clearly the question that troubles me about this analogy.

Can we talk about technologies of cultural production and cultural consumption in terms that so clearly parallel the way in which ecologists have talked about the effect of similar technological processes upon a natural economy? To be sure, there are already many common elements, on both sides of the analogy, not least of which is the profitable organization of technologies within the film and image industry, and I will have more to say about that topic presently. But the differences are also worth considering. Just as it is important for social ecologists to think about technologies as fully *cultural* processes, not restricted by definition to hardware development and economic growth, so too it is important for us, as cultural critics, to think of the cultural processes we study and

talk about as meaningful in ways that are not always technologically determined. The advantage, then, of the analogy that I have sketched above
is that it invites us, as cultural critics, to think more about the technological underpinnings of the culture that we study. The danger of the
analogy is that it also invites us to forget what we think we know about
the specificity of images themselves—how they are received and used for
all sorts of purposes, not least of which, in this particular case, the ways
that images of ecology can actually be used to activate public and popular
support for the repair of our local and global ecologies. And it is here that
I find Sontag's analysis finally disappointing, because it leaves virtually no
room for the kind of green cultural criticism that I think might help to
make a difference.

In addition, Sontag's remarks are in every respect consistent with the
school of silly thought that rails against image overload in our modern
information society. Information glut has become a favored object of
attack from both the right and the left. Even on the level of the quantitative argument, I have never been happy with this response, since I
have always assumed that most people in this world would rather have
a surfeit of information (whatever that means) than a scarcity. But information is not the same thing as intelligence or knowledge; its quantity
tells us no more about its reception than a quantitative estimate of the
number of proliferating TV channels, or the number of viewing hours
clocked up by the average couch potato, can tell us about the uses made
of those television images selected by any particular viewer. That, after
all, is supposed to be the job of cultural studies, which assumes that
competent viewers of images have their own, highly organized ways of
making sense of the "glut" of images available to them. Even less useful
is the response of postmodernist theorists who see the helpless victims
of information overload as schizoid or paranoid casualties of forces beyond their control. To my mind, the most useful critiques of information
culture are still those that focus on the economic organization of information and its technologies, ever advancing new and profitable ways of
restricting access to information and making it an ever more scarce commodity. Contrary to the image-glut school of thought, which leads the
moral crusade against the overavailability of information, it is quite clear
that getting access to information today is just as uneven and as expensive
as ever; this is as true in the tradable global market, where information is

a primary commodity, as it is in the home, where it is increasingly difficult, for example, to receive a decent TV signal without paying through
the nose for cable. Besides, most of the public commentary that warns
us about the dominance of images in our politics and our everyday lives
issues from within the "media" themselves—media owners, media professionals, media critics—that is, groups with a vested interest in seeing
the image business as all-powerful.

=====

The Anti-Reality Principle. For an ecological analysis of the process of creating
image scarcity, one need look no further than the economic organization
of the film industry in the age of the megahit. In Hollywood, the medium-
priced picture is disappearing fast as the film industry increasingly organizes itself around two markets: the blockbuster market ($15 to $100 million for production, up to $10 million for wide release, and up to $50
million for global advertising and distribution), and the much cheaper
direct-to-video/cable market. In the blockbuster market especially, the
familiar industrial process of recycling and recombining images, narratives, and themes has been streamlined with all of the rigor and efficiency
available to modern management and marketing techniques. In this context, the principle of recycling is both conservationist and conservative;
the industry wants to maximize its gain on tried and true resources—
formulae proven to be profitable—but the result runs directly counter to
the ecological spirit of preserving and encouraging diversity. The result
more and more resembles an image monoculture. That ever greater and,
some would say, wasteful sums of capital are devoted to recycling the old
in pursuit of the transnational megahit has the net effect of drastically
reducing the chance of cultural diversity in mainstream film production.

The increasingly crucial role of special effects in the megahit business
is geared to the industrial principle of obsolescence. The "look" of films
made only a few years before is outdated by the technologically advanced
effects of today's computerized cameras and postproduction image pro-
cessing. It is only in the realm of countercultural or subcultural taste
where camp nostalgia for the shlocky, low-tech, low-budget look (early
stop-motion model effects) of past futures runs high that this industrial
principle is displaced if not directly challenged. Yet, with the increasing
monopolization of first-run houses, and the concomitant extinction of

revival houses and venues for screening avant-garde films, the channeling of this redemptive taste culture into the video rental business has itself become a lucrative subsidiary market that does not cut into the mass-release theater circuit, and, in many ways, supports its mainstream economy. One of my favorite comments on the ecology of image production comes from the princely parodist of the bad taste circuit, John Waters, ever ready to turn a popular cliché to good use: "At least I've never done anything really decadent, like waste millions of dollars of other people's money, and come up with a movie as dumb as *The Deep* or 1941. The budgets of my movies could hardly feed the starving children of India."[5]

A more exhaustive account of these tendencies is obviously required if we are to have anything like an ecological analysis of image production. It's my hunch, however, that we are likely to find that many of the economic and technological processes in the image industry call out for similar kinds of critiques that ecologists have brought to bear upon other industrial processes. We are just as likely to find differences, however, for which the application of ecological principles to the field of culture do not have quite the same meaning as they do in the field of technology. The wasteful exploitation of finite resources to manage and control the production of scarcity among general consumer products is an industrial principle that cannot be entirely carried over into an analysis of image production and consumption. Image consumption may not be subject to the same quantifiable processes as those that govern the consumption of other industrial products. If it makes any sense at all to talk about the image "waste stream," then our own position, as consumers within the watershed of the stream, is quite different from our position in the material, consumer-product waste stream. Images can be used, and reused, in ways that most consumer goods cannot. Proponents of cultural studies, for example, who speak about "consuming" signs and images often forget that "consuming" a Pepsi ad is quite different from consuming a can of Pepsi. So, too, complaints about the "visual pollution" of billboards invite the same kind of second-level critique. That billboard space can be used as a medium for pro-ecological messages further confounds the metaphor.

Cinephiles, archivists, and media critics have long been horrified by the scandalous lack of conservationism within the film and TV industry: the studios' throwaway attitude toward film prints (the meltdown of

Erich von Stroheim's Greed for thirty cents of silver nitrate is the mythical horror story par excellence), the instant obsolescence of TV film, and the cavalier decisions about use of capital and resources that are made in pursuit of the final cut. There is no question that ecological critiques of the history of the photochemical and photographic industry would expose an even more sordid narrative about the chemical underpinnings of the film economy. You do not need to have lived in Rochester, New York, as I have, to know something about the life-threatening history of the image industry's major supplier, Eastman Kodak, consistently among the worst polluters of major United States corporations. The history of the common use of materials like nitrocellulose in film stock and in explosives production has long been an element in film historians' accounts of the image industry whose film technologies invariably were and are a direct spin-off from military research and development.

In War and Cinema (1984), an especially prescient book for the Gulf War, Paul Virilio offered a historical analysis of the importance of film technology to military-industrial interests. In his account of the transformation of the modern battlefield from a Cartesian arena of warring objects to a simulated arena of pictures and sounds, Virilio examines the crucial role of camera technology in what he calls the "logistics of military perception."[6] This history runs from the emergence of military photography in the American Civil War, through the military use of propaganda film units and Nuremberg-like staged spectacles, to the advent of planetary war vision with spy satellites and advanced simulation technologies. It is a history in which film technologies are fully and materially embedded in the logic of destruction; in which the video-equipped warheads and electro-optically lit battlefields that we saw in the Gulf are continuous with earlier strategic uses of aerial photography in World War I, a war of which D. W. Griffith, the only civilian filmmaker authorized to make propaganda films at the front, said that he was "very disappointed with the reality of the battlefield" (soldiers seldom, if ever, actually saw the enemy).[7]

The camera's contribution to what Virilio calls the "dematerialization of reality" on the battlefield seems to me a more telling story about the destructive potential of image-making technology than that offered by Sontag. Here, the logic of photography—the dematerialization of reality— goes hand in hand with the apparatus of war, devoted to the destruction of reality. This is a materialist epistemology, as distinct from Sontag's idealist epistemology, in which images figure as the means of *depleting* reality. In Virilio's history, the camera is a material participant in the apparatus of destruction. Sontag insists that the world today exists only to be mined and ransacked for images, but there is no principle of immediacy at stake in this knowledge because there is no finite limit to the quarrying.

Although I believe that there is an important difference between these kinds of analyses—Virilio's and Sontag's—I am not comfortable with the opposition, nor do I think that we can simply appeal to the superiority of the materialist over the idealist critique, in the last instance, as it were. Ideas and images are constitutive of the world in ways that can counter their role as technological recruits in the war against environmental reality. And that is why a discussion of the ecology of images—the ecology of image production and image consumption—of the sort that I have briefly pursued here must make room for some understanding of the role played by images of ecology. For neither Sontag's nor Virilio's critique takes account of these instances when images (of destruction and/ or ecology) are actually used to debate, or even to contest, the consequences that both critics lament—the material disappearance of the real. In short, images of ecology are also produced, consumed, and used in ways that can help to counteract the destruction of the natural world.

=====

Images of Ecology. In turning back, then, to the question of "images of ecology," we must recognize that any proper account of them covers a broad spectrum. At the most visible, activist end of the spectrum are agitprop images that are directly employed within and by the ecology movement to mobilize sympathy, support, and action for environmental causes; what we could call images of ecology *for* ecology. At the other, more sublimated end of the spectrum are images that have some kind of ecological content and that are incorporated into the everyday fictions of public and popular culture; images of ecology that are not necessarily *about* ecology. This spectrum is not, of course, a flat political spectrum— it does not simply run from left to right—and I will try to show how and why this is so.

While the ecology movement has made very good use of images of environmental degradation and repair alike, there is no naive faith in their power as political images in their own right. If such images speak about the exhaustion of the ideologies of progress that have sustained technological growth and development in the West, the socialist bloc, and, increasingly, the third world, the images themselves cannot, of course, say very much about such ideologies. Rather, the story is told by the narrative context in which they occur, a problem that is aptly demonstrated by the coverage of the oil spill and burning wells in the Gulf, or by the widespread use of "images of ecology" in advertising by the most environmentally destructive of the major industrial corporations. For those and other reasons, ecologists tend to be suspicious of the use of images in themselves as a medium of information. In this respect, we can say that discussion of the images of ecology has already moved beyond the assumption that images in themselves have a fixed political meaning for audiences as either "positive" or "negative," and thus as "good" or "bad." It is not yet clear, however, whether discussion of this issue has fully addressed the means by which forms of representation—narrative logic and point of view—can bring political meanings to bear upon the nature of the information provided about ecological matters. In the examples that follow I will try to show how a focus on narrative logic and point of view can provide a way of linking critiques of the ecology of images and images of ecology.

My first example is from the more activist end of the image spectrum. The ecology movement may be exceptional among new social and political movements in making an overriding appeal to scientific information for proof of the justice of its claims. One of the favored visual forms of organizing eco-statistical information is the cartographic—maps and graphs are science's privileged genres of imagery—and one of the most commercially successful genres of ecology publications is state-of-the-world atlases. These atlases exploit the fact that the global image is the most stable form of information about a highly unstable environment. Joni Seager's *Atlas Survey of the State of the Earth* is a typical example, a breakdown, from page to page, of the degradation of the world's resources: the state of the rain forests, population increase, energy budgets, acid rain, drinking water, food supplies, sewage, air quality, firewood, petrochemical pollution, coastal erosion, the wildlife trade, genetic diversity, toxic waste, the timber trade, and so on.[8] For the most part, atlases like Seager's, or the *World Wildlife Fund Atlas of the Environment*, or Michael Kidron and Ronald Segal's more political *New State of the World Atlas*, accept the current organization of global territory according to the sovereignty of nation-states, and their eco-statistics are broken down into the share accorded to national economies (Kidron and Segal's book, at least, seems to be assembled as a cumulative statement against the absurdity of the nation-state system).[9] These maps are not, then, utopian kinds of images; they seldom organize the field of representation by bioregion.[10] Nor are they dystopian in the ways that reflect the new global economy or global culture; they do not adequately represent the influence and power of transnational corporations. Nor does the form of per capita statistics help to differentiate the average citizen's share from the disproportionately destructive contribution of the military, government bureaucracy, or industry within any given nation-state, each citizen in that state sharing differently according to region, color, and class.

While these images are produced for activist purposes, their form is not an activist one inasmuch as it does not imagine a world organized differently. They accept the current political and economic organization of the world as ostensibly controlled by existing nation-states. Their representational form is also one that accepts the cartographic legacy of imperialism, the very historical perspective that has exploited the privilege of seeing "the big picture." The eco-atlas may finally be an elite form of representation; its point of view is ultimately that of a new elite of planetary eco-managers. Here, then, is an instance of how the representational form of the image is a major component of the political meaning of the information conveyed by the image.[11]

A similar kind of argument could be made about eco-statistics themselves, a staple of ecological arguments made in the public sphere. Just as the eco-atlas inherits and accepts the imperialist perspective of military logistics, so too the persuasive citation of eco-statistics borrows its shock appeal from the rhetorical stock-in-trade of military statistics. The arsenal of statistics about eco-atrocities in the global environment is often used to create a climate of fear in the same way as the merchants of war have profited from the statistics of nuclear kilotonnage, projected megadeaths, and strategic firepower. The result of this dystopian climate of shock and terror is not necessarily empowering; it feeds into survivalism, the lowest form of ecological consciousness, especially when these statistics are simply projected into the darkest of doomsday futures.

Another privileged genre of images of ecology is the narrative documentary, with its roots in the nature and wildlife film. The noncable context for this genre in the United States is almost exclusively public television, with its demographic appeal to the concerns of a predominantly white, neoliberal, middle-class audience. (On cable, the Discovery channel presents a host of nature and ecological features.) In the wake of Earthday 1990, the fall schedule of PBS programming was almost entirely devoted to environmental documentaries, culminating in the lavish, ten-hour miniseries *Race to Save the Planet*, an attempt to narrate an ecological history of the development of human cultures in a form akin to that middlebrow classic of public television programming, Kenneth Clark's BBC series *Civilization*. Contextualized by liberal, "quality," Hollywood performers (it is introduced by Meryl Streep and narrated by Roy Scheider) and characterized by its laboriously pious narratives and monotonously conscientious tone, *Race to Save the Planet* was advertised, in slots for PBS's annual fall fund-raising campaign, as exemplary of "television that lets you take action." The rhetoric of this appeal to a PBS audience was brilliantly appropriate: not activist TV, nor TV about activism, but TV that reaffirms its audience's identity as liberal-minded people who are accustomed to taking for granted their social identity and position—middle-class and predominantly professional—as always already "active" (rather than "activist") in the world.

In considering the use of images about ecology drawn from the more articulate, or even activist end of my spectrum, I have pointed, all too briefly, to the political importance of representational forms and narratives, heavily contextualized by their appeal to particular histories—imperialist, corporate, and professional-managerial—and particular communities—planetary managers of the eco-elite, and consumers with high- to middlebrow taste. Similar considerations are no less evident if we turn to more popular genres.

With the recent revival of ecological concerns in the public mind—thanks to Bhopal, Chernobyl, Exxon Valdez, the Gulf War, the greenhouse effect, and the rain forests—narratives about environmental repair have begun to surface in popular genres. The TV networks have been flooded with scripts and proposals for ecologically minded shows and series. TBS launched Ted Turner's personal brainchild, the cartoon show *Captain Planet and the Planeteers*, and a host of other children's features—*Widget, Dark Water, The Toxic Crusaders*—are either airing or in trial runs for syndication. The 1990 fall TV season also saw the shaky debut of two eco-cop shows, E.A.R.T.H. Police and Super Force, while Voice of the Planet, TBS's ten-hour Gaia-inspired New Age adventure series made a brief initial appearance in February 1991. On a less salutary note, the first cyberpunk film of the 1990–91 season, Richard Stanley's low-budget Hardware, featured a grisly futuristic narrative about overpopulation: "Welcome to the 21st century. Guess what's become the planet's most endangered species?" The answer? Fertile women, who are hunted down by military cyborgs to reduce overpopulation.

Hardware's twisted ecological story line is worked through a familiar blend of generic SF formulae. In the last twenty years of popular entertainment, especially in science fiction, the ecological "look" of the future has been governed by a dark dystopian imagination, feeding off the imagery of global degradation. The cultural power of this imagination has long transcended the vestigial influence of images and narratives of progressive futurism that were the standard diet of early science fiction films like Things to Come. The historical role of SF film, with its power to "colonize" the temporality and spatiality of the future, is paramount in any discussion of the ecology of film images. From the slew of 1970s SF dystopias—Colossus: The Forbin Project, The Andromeda Strain, THX 1138, Silent Running, Westworld, 2001, Soylent Green, Dark Star, A Boy and His Dog, Logan's Run, The Late Great Planet Earth—which fully absorbed the urgency of ecological concerns about overpopulation and pollution in the wake of the energy crisis, to the more recent cyberpunk genre—Escape from New York, the Mad Max trilogy, Blade Runner, The Running Man, The Terminator, Robocop, Cherry 2000, Max Headroom, Millenium, Brazil—the degraded bio-future has become a dominant landscape in Western cultural imaginary. (The exception, of course, is the temporary revival of the conservative version of progressive futurism in the nostalgic Hollywood theme parks of Lucas-Spielberg.)

One might balk at the irony of the film industry persistently devoting vast sums of money to producing images of futureless futures. In most of the cyberpunk films, this dark future is merely a generic backdrop, a convention whose profitability is tried and tested. Different contradictions arise, however, when the genre aims at producing a utopian future. In its action-adventure version of the "race to save the planet" and liberate its population, Paul Verhoeven's 1990 summer SF film, Total Recall, offered the best recent example of a blockbuster film that attempts to include a utopian eco-narrative. It is not an eco-friendly film, however. The planet in question is Mars, and the population is a federal worker colony, physically mutated by radiation as a result of inadequate working facilities, and organized into underground rebel cadres fighting against enslavement by a primitive capitalist exploiter. Air is a commodity whose price is controlled by the capitalist mogul, while the colony's mineral mining production, ruthlessly protected by the imposition of martial law, is used to fund an eco-war on Earth between northern and southern blocs.

While the film is structurally governed by the promotional requirements of its being a Schwarzenegger vehicle, the ecological components of the narrative are everywhere foregrounded. On Earth, pristine environmental spaces—assumed now to be extinct—are simulated for the purposes of tourism and domestic therapy, while advanced mind technologies, freely used for entertainment and politics alike, are used to manufacture human memories in pursuit of the perfect artificial ecology of the mind. In every respect, *Total Recall* tells a plausibly and explicitly Marxist tale about the destructive, alienating conditions of primitive capitalist exploitation and production. Again, one might stop to speculate about the irony of such a film, since its very existence tells an otherwise astonishing story about the domestic absorption of Marxist critiques of capitalism within mainstream Hollywood film. But this is not my intention here. What concerns me is how the Marxist critique is employed to resolve the film's narrative in a way that works against the proto-ecological critique.

With the aid of the resistance forces on Mars, the Schwarzenegger figure succeeds in utilizing ancient Alien technologies to create an Earth-friendly atmosphere for the colony. The capitalist's power is broken, and the shlocky appearance of sunny, blue skies at the end of the film heralds a brave new world for the liberated workers. Here, the Alien technologies are also explicitly Marxist; they are "alien" to the monopoly-regulated system of capitalist production because they are employed in the service of all—everyone gets air, and it is free. As technologies, however, they are finally "alien" to the planet's ecology. The process of terraforming the planet is achieved through macroengineering and macroproduction; the vast Alien reactor is employed to melt down the planet's ice core and generate an oxygen-rich atmosphere. In the final sequence of the film, then, the planet's core resources are almost entirely exhausted in three minutes flat in order to create friendly conditions for its liberated human population. Nothing could be more explicitly Marxist than this narrative about using macrotechnology to free humankind from servitude to Nature. Nothing could be more explicitly anti-ecological.[12]

At a time when these once-progressive narratives about emancipation through maximized technological production have been challenged to the point of exhaustion, here is a Hollywood film that is at last comfortable with such narratives, and that poses them as solutions to an ecological predicament. I present it here as an example of the ways in which ecological concerns are being articulated as images of ecology in popular entertainment—not in any ideal form, but in the impure context of other popular or generic narratives (even Marxist ones) that have meanings, often counter-ecological meanings, of their own. In the final analysis, we have to consider, of course, that the dramatic narrative of *Total Recall*, favoring the spectacle of ecological reparation, is itself a product of the eco-logic of industrial cost-efficiency, balancing massive and wasteful expenditures against the promise of box-office profit.

=====

The Owls Are Not What They Seem: A Postscript. To my mind, this essay would be incomplete if I did not close with some comments about a TV show that monopolized much of the conversation of film-literate audiences in the United States during its brief run from spring 1990 to spring 1991. Almost from the first time I saw the opening credits of *Twin Peaks*, I have been inclined to watch this show about a northwestern logging town as a commentary about environmental and ecological questions. If *Twin Peaks* is one of our first examples of ecological camp (*Green Acres* was a weak, but likely, earlier candidate), as I think it is, then it surely will not be the last.[13] One of the enduring effects of *Twin Peaks* is its influential reshaping and reimagining of the Pacific Northwest at a time when urgent ecological questions are being asked about the timber economy of that region. Recent political debate about these issues has centered on the protection of the northern spotted owl (even though it is only one of the many animal and fish species threatened by the clearcutting of old-growth forests). It is this owl that increasingly got a bad press in *Twin Peaks*, since Bob, the mystery killer entity, seems to be associated with the owls in some way, and since, according to Laura Palmer's diary (the commercially available version), Laura's own psychosexual history was haunted by attacks by owls, imaginary or otherwise. In light of the current ecological challenge to the timber industry, it is hardly surprising that *Twin Peaks* takes place in a lumber town where the surrounding environment is depicted as harboring threatening, evil forces, likely aliens, for whom the owls may indeed be serving as telepathic communicants, perhaps even the Log Lady's log as well. The owls, we are repeatedly told, "are not what they seem," and may in fact turn out to be benign agents in the narrative. Nonetheless, the environment is one in which Nature, in Lynch's work generally, is seen as hostile, and complicit with the threat to human life in a small town. This is evocatively suggested by the opening credit sequence—the metonymic links there are between the birds, the brute facticity of industry and its pollution, the inexorable sharpening of the teeth in the sawmill, the shot of a small town beseiged by the shrouded, secretive environment, the sublime violence of the waterfall, and the ominous undertows concealed in the eddies, all reinforced by Badalamenti's theme music, where the strings on top are a familiar referent from film melodrama, and the bass melody below is a sinister undertone.

In view of this demonizing of the environment, no sequence was more crucial in the show than the scene in the April 1990 pilot in which the sawmill is shut down for the day by its female owner, Josie, against protests by its female manager, Catherine. Here we saw the spectacle of a conflict over labor, a conflict between two women who, it is significant, are the two people who seem to be in charge of primary economic production in this town. In this scene both women commit transgressive acts. Josie shuts down the mill, and Catherine gratuitously fires a worker—the first and only mill worker, as far as I am aware, to appear in the entire series (you wonder where all these workers are—it's a big mill in a small town after all). Neither Josie nor Catherine will be forgiven for such transgressions. Alongside the firing of the worker—the first intimation that all of these workers, eventually, will lose their jobs, after the mill is arsonized—the halt in production at the mill is the first public sign that there will be a crisis in the community. This crisis is generated by the death of a woman, Laura Palmer, and publicized in the pilot by the transgressive acts of these two women. You did not need to be a feminist film theorist to know that these were very bad signs indeed, and did not augur well for the future of women in the series.

In the light of the ecology movement's "threat" to the male work force of the northwestern logging industry, it is perhaps no surprise to come across this story about a small town whose lumber economy is thrown into crisis by actions involving women, both alive and dead, and by mysterious environmental forces that involve owls and aliens. Toward the end of the series run, the environmental subtext became an overt focus of Twin Peaks life, when Benjamin Horne launched a campaign to save the pine weasel as part of his scheming ambition to thwart Catherine's property development ambitions. Perhaps it is also fitting that it is Josie, an Asian woman, who has power over the economy, and who halts the mill, since the northwestern timber industry has been dependent on the Asian market as its prime export market over the last decade. It is Josie's face, staring into a mirror as she applies her lipstick, that composes the first shot in the pilot—a completely gratuitous shot, but one that suggests an origin for many of the resulting crises in the show: femininity, foreignness, and dreamy narcissism (dreamy narcissism being the mould for many of the other female characters in the show, especially Donna, the willful romantic, and Audrey, the village vixen). With a figure like Josie in charge of so many of the determinants of the show, it is no wonder that the masculine revenge of the show would be slow but sure, and perhaps only fully apparent after the fact, rather like Hegel's Owl of Minerva, which spreads its wings only at dusk.

Notes

1 Susan Sontag, On Photography (New York, 1977), 179.
2 Ibid., 11, 24.
3 Ibid., 179.
4 On the other hand, Sontag's remarks about "credible forms of lust" may remind many of us of the debate, within film theory, about psychoanalytical descriptions of the role of sexuality in visual pleasure. As it happens, I don't think this is a productive path to pursue—for the following reason. For Sontag, the visual—the field of vision—is not an element in the construction of reality, as it is for most film theorists. Images, for her, are fundamentally a substitute for reality. In her model, image addiction ultimately determines our diet—our need to "consume" more and more images reduces our tolerance for more nutritious encounters with reality. The result à la Balzac (a man of considerable girth, it should be remembered) is a thinner body of attention

to the real world. The operative model of health in this analogy is strictly biological; there is no room for psychosexual or even biocultural determinants.
In this respect, there seems to me to be little common ground between feminist film theory's assumption that "perversions" are a normative aspect of
our relation to images, and Sontag's view that our addiction to images is a
fundamentally unhealthy, even immoral, perversion.

5   John Waters, Shock Value (New York, 1981), 272.

6   Paul Virilio, War and Cinema: The Logistics of Perception (London, 1989).

7   Griffith's comment reminds us of so many discussions about the lack of any
visible enemy sightings in the Gulf War, not only for TV audiences, but for
combatants themselves. Saudi gravedigging teams were delegated to each
Allied unit in order to dig the mass graves for the Iraqi dead. While this action
officially was taken for religious reasons, the result was that Western soldiers
were prohibited from seeing the people they had killed. (Griffith, quoted in
Virilio, War and Cinema, 15.)

8   Joni Seager, Atlas Survey of the State of the Earth (New York, 1990).

9   Geoffrey Lean, Don Hinrichsen, and Adam Markham, World Wildlife Fund Atlas
of the Environment (New York, 1990); and Michael Kidron and Ronald Segal, The
New State of the World Atlas (New York, 1987).

10   For the best bioregional map of the world, see Miklos D. F. Udwardy, S. Brand,
and T. Oberlander, World Biogeographical Provinces Map (Berkeley, 1975).

11   Gaia: An Atlas of Planet Management, produced by the Gaia Project (gen. ed. Norman Myers, London, 1984) explicitly attempts to avoid the "gloom and doom"
ethos that pervades the genre. Presented under the aegis of the Gaia hypothe-
sis—that the planet is a living biosphere with its own global life-support
systems and feedback mechanisms—it is a more adventurous and inspiring
survey of the state of the earth's ecosystems and resources. The maps use
projections based on either Gall's cylindrical projection—to counter the traditionally Eurocentric cartographic perspective—or the more recent Peters
projection, which more accurately represents the true land mass of the con-
tinents. But the maps are only one of a host of visual images (tree diagrams,
larder diagrams, three-dimensional globes, and creative low-tech depictions
of ecosystems) designed to illustrate statistical information. The polemical
overview of the survey, however, is that of planetary management—responsible stewardship of global resources—and therefore meets the gaze of the
World Bank and other global organizations created to police the natural economy of the planet according to laissez-faire market principles.

12   Those who know the film will remember that the plot itself doesn't seem
to "work," since the Alien reactor can be activated only by a three-fingered
Martian fingerprint, and not by the human hand of Quaid that Verhoeven

utilizes to do the job. Dan O'Bannon, the original scriptwriter, has argued that this inaccuracy is symptomatic of the film's overall failure. In O'Bannon's script, Quaid, who discovers that he is the resurrection of a Martian race in a synthetic human body, uses the Alien technology to totally recall his own identity. The ending chosen by Verhoeven, in spite of its diegetic flaws, seems to me to be more faithful to the film's social ambition (Carl Brandon, "*Total Recall*: Dan O'Bannon on Why It Doesn't Work," *Cinefantastique* 21 [April 1991]: 36–37).

13 By the time of the fall 1990 season, a 900 number, called the Twin Peaks Sheriffs' Office Hotline, was being operated by Lynch-Frost Productions. The phone line recapped the previous night's episode and included new clues and information—a portion of the revenue was to be set aside for "environmental causes." The environmental questions raised by the show cannot, of course, be divorced from the historical psychopathologies of David Lynch himself; his history, for example, as an Eagle Scout from Montana, who fondly recalls camping trips in the northwestern forests with his father, a research scientist with the United States Forestry Service who wrote his dissertation on the ponderosa pine.

Academic Writing and the Uses

of Bad Publicity

GERALD GRAFF

Whatever the long-range import of the stream of attacks on "political correctness" in the university in the 1990s, one thing that seems clear is that while nobody was looking a great change has been taking place in the relationship between the concerns of the academic humanities and the nonacademic public. Academics and journalists may be at war, but the war would not be possible if the antagonists were operating in wholly separate arenas. I want here to try to outline some features of the situation, and to suggest how its pressures may force academics to become better at communicating with their students and the public.

Everyone knows the accusations against academic writing: it is overrun with indecipherable jargon; it deals with rarefied subjects that only a specialist could love; it is ingrown and autistic, turning its back on lay audiences; it is probably like this on purpose, for only by creating an excluded class of so-called "lay" people can an academic field legitimate itself as a "profession." The humanities are more vulnerable to these charges than the sciences, since they lack the practical payoff that publicly justifies the scientific forms of specialization and jargon.

All these charges are old, at least as old as the emergence of professionalized American universities a century ago. But now to these old charges a new one has been added—the charge that the academic humanities are not only opaque and narcissistic, but obsessed with power, ideology, and (the most unanswerable charge of all) "political correctness." On top of the professional humanities' time-honored reputation for being incomprehensible, they are acquiring a new reputation for being politically obnoxious.

Of course these political pretensions are considered something of a joke: how laughable that those who claim to put their scholarship and teaching to the service of social change pursue their project in vocabularies that are impenetrable to the people who supposedly are to benefit from their agitations. Here is how the novelist and critic David Lodge puts it:

> English and literary studies have reached a point in their theoretical development when they've become incapable of communicating to the layman at the very historical moment when they've most needed to justify their existence. The brightest and most innovative young people in literary criticism are as impenetrable as nuclear physicists. The Left-wing intelligentsia is trapped in a kind of ghetto that only they understand, and so can't bring leverage to bear on the body politic.[1]

So goes the standard charge. And yet there is something about it that doesn't quite add up: If "the Left-wing intelligentsia" were really as inept at communicating its ideas as Lodge and others make it out to be, would everyone be getting so worked up? If academic writing were as obscure as people say, why would they be making so much fuss about its political threat? Something must be getting through to someone or there would not be pounding of tables and shaking of fists.

It seems the left intelligentsia can't win: it is damned if it is obscure, but damned even more when it is clear, since its message is one that many people do not want to hear. But I suspect that lurking behind all the jokes about the obscurity of new theories is a fear that these theories may become all *too clear*, that they may start exerting all too much "leverage" on the body politic, especially if they go on being taught to undergraduates.

Of course, when Lodge says that literary studies have reached a point "when they've become incapable of communicating to the layman," one would like to ask him if that past ever really existed in which those studies were significantly better at communicating to lay audiences. Here is another way in which a double standard is at work when the new forms of criticism are singled out for their obscurity, as if so-called traditional literary studies had at some earlier time been wonderfully accessible to the masses, who could not wait to read the latest *Journal of English and German Philology* article by Leo Spitzer, A. O. Lovejoy, or René Wellek. To most people outside academia, the phrase "traditional literary studies" has always evoked approximately the same degree of recognition as a word like "problematize" evokes today—which is to say, none.

What we don't know, however, is whether things will stay this way. The notion that academic literary studies have always been opaque to most people and probably always will be is too easy and reassuring, telling us that nothing can or need change. The fact that "problematize" would be opaque to most Americans today does not mean it will necessarily continue to be tomorrow. If the word "deconstruct" has begun to appear occasionally in the newspapers (though usually misused to mean "attack"), then "problematize" may soon have its day. "Phallocentric" has already appeared in a New Yorker cartoon, and as the Anita Hill–Clarence Thomas hearings and other recent trials have shown, the controversies over race, class, and gender that have erupted inside the academy only mirror those that are taking place outside. This rapid process of assimilation suggests why the joke that the new academic radicals are really ineffectual poseurs may mask the fear that they will not remain ineffectual enough.

The common assumption that the academic humanities are narrowly specialized and deal only in esoteric matters has been becoming less and less true for some time. If the academic humanities are over-anything, they are overgeneralized, not overspecialized. For a generation now, the academy has actually penalized narrow specialization in the humanities and reserved its highest rewards for work that propounds sweeping cultural theories and broad interdisciplinary generalizations, and that promises to revise the paradigm for thinking about its subject.

To see the signs of this change one need only look at the terms in which academic books are promoted. Does Oxford University Press boast that its current list in criticism is more highly specialized than that of Harvard University Press? On the contrary, the claim is inevitably that one's books are "path-breaking," and just because such claims may be four-fifths hype does not change the fact that a shift in priorities has taken place, even a path-breaking one, if you'll pardon the mixed metaphor.

The turn away from specialization can also be seen in the terms in which scholars now couch grant proposals and letters of recommendation. No professor would like to hear that a referee for a National Endowment for the Humanities (NEH) grant had written, "What I like about this project is that it's so narrowly specialized." Indeed, grant application forms themselves now often ask for an explicit statement of how the proposed project figures to change the world. This is true of the grant application forms of the NEH, whose chair during the Bush administration published a report complaining that humanities research is hopelessly specialized.

What critics like the Bush-era chair of the NEH mistake for specialization are in fact new languages of *generalization* that they either don't understand or don't like, or both. The most prominent of these new languages of generalization is "theory," the language in which all that problematizing I spoke of a moment ago is being done. To problematize the dominant assumptions of the culture is not a more specialized activity than to defend those assumptions, at least not in the sense in which a dissertation on, say, "The Passive Voice in Old Icelandic" used to be called specialized. But talk of problematizing assumptions does look specialized to those who do not understand what "problematize" means or who are unsympathetic with the thing itself.

In response to which you may say: well, if academic humanists *look* specialized to outsiders then that's as good as *being* specialized, isn't it? In a sense, yes. But I want to suggest that the relations between academic and lay discourses have been changing in a way that demands thinking again about the question of who is accessible to whom and who speaks for the generality. When women's and ethnic studies programs are attacked as "specialized," the word is obviously being used as an ideological slur, as in attacks on "special interest groups" in the campaign rhetoric of the Republican party. But once the word "specialized" is used to mean "having a political agenda," it no longer means "obscure" or "narrow," quite the opposite. What is offensive about feminism and ethnic studies is their aggressively *general* claims about culture, not their pedantic narrowness.

I am suggesting that the recent war over literary studies has already made the debates within those studies a little less mysterious to outsiders than they were before. I know this claim will seem farfetched and perhaps even fatuous in the wake of the gross misrepresentations of the new academic trends, amounting to a virtual smear campaign, which have appeared in the press since 1990. The popular picture of what academic trends are all about has been drawn almost entirely by their harshest detractors, and it is an absurdly inaccurate picture. Anyone who got his or her information strictly from the editorial pages would conclude that literature departments have virtually stopped teaching anything but rap songs and rock videos—except for the rare occasions when they assign a canonical text in order to trash it for its racism and sexism.

And yet this very antagonism between the academic and journalistic worlds is actually a sign of increased closeness. Formerly the concerns of academic humanists would not have even merited a journalistic put-down. That editorialists have been attacking literature professors testifies to the extent to which the internal battles of the academy have become the same battles being fought outside. The furor over "political correctness" illustrates this linkage, as when the attacks on "PC" hardly pause to distinguish between the issue of ethnic slurs in student dormitories and the issue of revising the literary curriculum. Debates over the validity of a feminist or postcolonialist interpretation of The Tempest overlap with debates over affirmative action, which in turn overlap with debates over the rights and status of minorities in American society. The very antagonism and anger of the culture war suggests that the academy and the public are no longer distant from one another, but are fighting over the same issues.

Furthermore, even gross misrepresentations can enable truths that were not generally visible before to leak out. There is a certain risk in broadcasting accusations of crimes against the humanities: you may create an opportunity sooner or later for the accused to tell their side of the story to an audience that otherwise would not hear it. You may create a public scene that did not exist previously in which the orthodox representations of reality can be contested. As inaccurately as the academic scene has been represented in the press, the publicity generated by recent conflicts means that freshmen coming into a college (or perhaps even high-school) literature course will probably be aware of issues that students a decade ago would not have heard of.

These freshmen are likely to be aware, for example, that their teachers radically disagree over what literature is, how to read and teach it, and what the social function of language, literature, and composition studies should be. They will also increasingly be aware that their teachers' disagreements have something to do with conflicts over multiculturalism, feminism, and sexuality that are rampant outside the university in the culture at large.

I sometimes think that if the critics of the new trends in the humanities reckoned their own interests more coolly, they would keep quiet instead of giving so much prominence to ideas and practices that would otherwise have remained obscure. This thought first dawned on me in 1984, when William J. Bennett, then chair of the National Endowment for the Humanities and soon to become secretary of education under Ronald Reagan, published his famous "To Reclaim a Legacy" report, in which deconstruction, Marxism, feminism, and other theories appeared prominently in the list of insurrectionary influences that Bennett blamed for undermining humanities education and humanistic values.

Though dismayed at the cartoon version of the new theories presented by Bennett, I could not but be impressed that one of the most powerful politicians in America considered these theories important enough to be worth abusing over the space of many columns in his report. Up to then I, along with many others, had thought of literary theory as a largely ineffectual enterprise, despite its global pretensions; but the alarms sounded by Bennett and others in his wake forced me to reconsider. Perhaps Bennett and his friends knew something I didn't.

Then, too, when Bennett and others spoke of "theory" as if it were a unified front with a rigid party line, his gesture tended to create a solidarity among his targets that had not existed before. I still suspect that all that keeps today's disparate feminisms, deconstructionisms, postcolonialisms, and Marxisms from splintering into a welter of hostile factions is the unity that results from being unfairly lumped into a single "politically correct" movement.

On the other hand, these factions do speak with something like a common voice if you view them from the standpoint of people like Bennett, who don't regard the distinction between a deconstructionist critique of the Arnoldian tradition and a Marxist or feminist critique as terribly important. The new oppositional criticisms may be at odds with one another over many things, but they do have a significant common cause in their premise that cultural standards that have been taken for granted as natural and normal are cultural and ideological constructions; in their view that culture is a text whose meanings are sites of conflict rather than preestablished givens; in their dissatisfaction both with traditional humanistic values and the claims of value-free disinterestedness. Here is why opponents of these trends cannot afford just to shut up and let them run their course. There is too much risk that new ways of reading and thinking will continue to make an impact on undergraduates.

So there may be something, after all, to the show business maxim that bad publicity is better than no publicity at all. At least it can be better if it *offers an opportunity to reshape and transform the terms of the publicity.*

Admittedly, that is a big if, for it remains to be seen whether such an opportunity actually presents itself. But it also remains to be seen whether academics can take advantage of the opportunity, or can help create it. To put it another way, what is certain is that the opportunity to recast the terms in which the academy is being publicly represented will not present itself if academics who reject the current misrepresentations do not fight to create that opportunity.

So far, academics have been slow to respond. It is almost as if things have happened too fast. Until recently, there was little reason to think anyone was listening to academic radical discourse except other academic radicals, and thus the emergence of a situation in which there is suddenly great curiosity about that discourse, most of it hostile, has seemed to take those radicals by surprise. Then, too, having trained themselves for two decades to speak in voices that would be resistant to co-optation by the dominant discourses, academic radicals find themselves almost without an idiom in which to contest the misrepresentations being made of them. Yet the hostile temper of the new public curiosity makes it all the more necessary that it be engaged on its own terms, and in a voice that the curious can understand.

Though academic radical critics often refer to people like Secretary Bennett and Allan Bloom, their writing is not addressed to the Bennetts and Blooms or to the people who read and agree with them. Too much academic radical writing still assumes an addressee who already takes for granted the basic assumptions of academic radicalism, or at least does not need to have them spelled out. Thus the right has been able to co-opt the rhetoric of democracy and populism, and turn labels like "elitist" and "authoritarian" against the academic left.

This tendency to preach to the converted seems to me a deeper problem than the more talked about ones of jargon and obscurity. What turns away lay audiences more than jargon and obscurity, I think, is the failure to take their lay assumptions into account, except as instances of a mystified consciousness that must be unmasked. Not that conservatives (and liberals) do not preach to the converted as often as radicals do. But then, radicals have less luxury to engage in this practice, at least if you accept their own premise that their converts are in the minority. Preaching to the converted makes sense only if you assume you are winning.

It is no longer enough for radical critics to demonstrate again and again in their work that what passes in our culture for apolitical common sense is often hegemonic ideology, even if this is perfectly true. The people who most need to hear this message not only don't agree with it, they don't understand it. The notion that "everything is political," which is such a commonplace inside the academic left, remains a strange and counterintuitive notion to most who are outside it. If their minds are to be changed, they need to have such formulations explained to them not just in language free of jargon, but in ways that respect their resistance and take their counterarguments seriously. The fact that their resistance may itself be ideologically conditioned is all the more reason why it needs to be respected if one hopes to overcome it.

The same comment applies to the current call for an oppositional curriculum, a transformative educational practice, a pedagogy of the oppressed. A pedagogy of the oppressed makes sense if there is prior agreement among teachers, students, and others on who is oppressing whom and what should be done about it. But as long as there is no such agreement in American schools and universities, as there is not and never has been, oppression cannot be taken for granted as a given. One has to ask what role will be played in a radical curriculum by teachers and students who don't at the moment particularly desire to be radical.

Radical educational theorists like Paulo Freire, Henry Giroux, and Stanley Aronowitz seem in their writing to assume a teacher who is already committed to social transformation and simply lacks the lesson plan for translating the commitment into classroom practice. The premise, in other words, is that radical pedagogy is for those who have already decided to be radicals, and that the others will pretty much stay out of it, as presumably they will want to anyway. Hence the tunnel-vision style of the writing of these theorists, which speaks of but never to those who oppose its premises.

In *The Pedagogy of the Oppressed*, Freire attacks the Leninist model of education in which movement leaders impose their teleological revolutionary blueprint on students. "It is absolutely essential," Freire writes, "that the oppressed participate in the revolutionary process with an increasingly critical awareness of their role as Subjects of the transformation." But though Freire ostensibly gives the oppressed the autonomy to decide for themselves what their transformation will look like, it is clear that for Freire the oppressed are free to decide only within certain limits. If a student were to end up deciding that he or she is not oppressed, or is not oppressed in the way or for the reasons Freire thinks, one suspects that Freire could not count such a decision as an autonomous one.

Again, Freire says that libertarian education "starts with the conviction that it cannot present its own program but must search for this program dialogically with the people."[2] But Freire never considers seriously the possibility that the program preferred by the people might conflict with that of the pedagogy of the oppressed. The sentimental assumption is that really deep down, inside our authentic selves, we are all Christian Marxists.

The same tunnel vision appears in current discussions of the institutional prospects of cultural studies, which has all but become a code term for left studies. I have argued on behalf of cultural studies elsewhere and I don't intend to reverse myself. But if the concept of cultural studies makes no place for conservative ideas of "culture" as well as radical ones, it is likely to become yet another recipe for the self-marginalization of the left.

I raise the curriculum issue in a discussion of academic writing because I suspect that whether academic radicalism can stop preaching to the converted in the Freire-Giroux-Aronowitz style and can start speaking to those outside its ranks will depend to a large extent on changes in the curriculum and in other institutional structures. Preaching to the converted is a function not just of the personal traits of academics but of institutional organization.

I have in mind the fact that professors teach for the most part in closed classrooms, where they are rarely exposed to the objections that would be made by their colleagues down the hall or on other parts of the campus. A literature student today can easily go from one course in which the validity of traditional beliefs about culture is taken for granted (and thus not explicitly stated) to another course in which it is taken for granted (and thus not explicitly stated) that these traditional beliefs have been problematized, demystified, and exploded.

This is not only bad for the students, who are prevented from getting a clear view of what is at issue in this and other major cultural conflicts and thus are prevented from becoming active participants in such conflicts instead of passive spectators. It is just as bad for the teachers, who are screened from the sorts of challenges to their assumptions that they need in order to make themselves clear to people outside their immediate circle, including their colleagues. Academics would speak and write more accessibly if they taught in situations that forced them to engage those who disagree.

I am suggesting there is a connection between the academy's notorious unintelligibility to nonacademics and the fact that most academics teach in isolation from colleagues. At first sight, my point may seem counterintuitive. If one professor teaching alone is obscure, would not a connected chain of professors teaching in relation to one another and their courses simply reproduce and multiply that obscurity? There is indeed always that danger, but I believe there are strong reasons why professorial intelligibility has to be seen as a collective project.

The most important of these is the fact that human identities acquire definition only in relation to a community. When academics teach their courses in isolation from their colleagues, they are bound to seem mysterious to students who do not already possess the academic community's identifying codes. Take the case of a student who goes from one literature teacher who makes frequent admiring reference to "the Western humanistic tradition" to another teacher who refers to the "hegemonic ideology of the dominant order." Since our student never sees these two teachers in dialogue with each other, he or she may fail to recognize that they are referring to the same thing, that is, that they are in disagreement. Our student is likely to be confused about the nature of both positions, which make sense only in relation to one another. These two teachers need each other in order to clarify their identities to that student.

After all, the teacher who defends humanistic tradition becomes intelligible only if you know that this tradition is under attack, just as the teacher who makes the attack becomes intelligible only if you know what is being said in defense. Your ability to construct either position, much less to identify with either or to move to some third position, depends on having a sense of the conversation. But that conversation is precisely what is effaced by a curriculum composed of disconnected courses. The curriculum, in effect, asks students to enter into a conversation that they never see, that it in fact withholds from them.

Certain progressive teachers claim they overcome such confusions among their students by candidly identifying their positions "up front" at the start of every course. On the first day of class, these teachers announce, "I'm a Marxist," or "I'm a feminist," or "I'll be teaching this course from a Marxist-feminist point of view." Though such candor is no doubt preferable to concealment, it does not eliminate the problem. For one thing, no matter how earnestly the teacher may assure the students that they won't be expected to defer to the teacher's avowed Marxist-feminism or whatever position it may be, many students have a hard time believing they won't be. For another thing, students need to know that their teachers' self-identifications are themselves not beyond challenging. But how are students to know this when the teacher's colleagues—the only ones likely to have the confidence and sophistication to challenge the teacher's self-identification—are not present?

Often at academic conferences I have attended, when a speaker has prefaced a talk by saying, "I'm a Marxist-feminist," someone else has responded, "You call yourself a Marxist-feminist, but you sound like just a bourgeois liberal to me." This contesting of identifications takes place frequently at academic conferences but rarely in classrooms. For few students are able to challenge their teacher's self-identification, and they do not experience the sort of open community conversation of the type that takes place at conferences that could provide them with models for how to do it.

Some would say this is all to the good—who wants to see the kind of professional one-upping that goes on at conferences take over our classrooms? The trouble is, the structures that screen out professional one-upping also screen out the process of intellectual growing up. Since the conflict of self-identifications occurs only in a constricted form in the classroom, students naturally find it hard to understand the self-identifications of their teachers, much less to form their own intellectual identifications.

And in fact, most undergraduates probably do not form intellectual identifications at all, for they are not really expected to, as we betray when we assume that the teachers will bear labels like "deconstructionist" and "New Critic," but the students will not. Such an assumption in effect concedes that undergraduates are not really part of our academic intellectual community and probably don't want to be, that they naturally pass through our courses regarding the clash of "isms" to which they are exposed as a game reserved for the faculty whose terms should properly remain alien and mysterious.

A curriculum made up of noncommunicating courses effaces the background of collective contexts and relations that academics need in order to clarify themselves to nonacademics. Even the Emersonian loner, the Walden Pond isolato, has symbolic meaning only in relation to a community that is not Walden. When the academic community is reduced to a set of Walden Ponds without links to the rest of the intellectual country, the conditions of its intelligibility are impaired, and then teachers must spend a good deal of their time laboriously repairing the links that should never have been severed to begin with, laboriously reconstructing the contexts represented by their colleagues in the next room or right down the hall.

The culture war, with its all-out assault on the academy from the right and the center, compels rethinking the conditions of academic-lay communication. It has clearly pushed the academy into a phase of its existence in which it can no longer afford to bumble on in colorful and charming incoherence about its concerns. And for the dissenting wing of the academy, now so routinely and irresponsibly libeled by people who have no idea what it is saying, the stakes are even higher.

If those of us who identify with the dissenting wing of the academy do not get better at engaging with those who disagree with us, we will only lose ground to those who defame us as politically correct authoritarians. In short, then, those of us in the academy who are sympathetic to the changes that have been taking place in the humanities have suddenly been presented with an unprecedented opportunity to gain a measure of control over the way we appear to the larger world. And I think we will have ourselves largely to blame if we fail. As long as we are unable or unwilling to speak for ourselves in public, it figures to be our detractors who will speak for us.

Notes

1   David Lodge, quoted by James Atlas, The Book Wars: What It Takes to be Educated in America (New York, 1990), 57.

2   Paulo Freire, The Pedagogy of the Oppressed (New York, 1970), 118–21.

Ideology, Energy, and Cultural Criticism

MARK EDMUNDSON

When Lenin was living in Munich, more than fifteen years before the journey that took him to the Finland Station to spur on the Russian Revolution, he worked all day every day of the week, with one exception. On Sunday afternoons Vladimir Ilyich, his wife Krupskaya, and whatever visitors were on hand repaired to a local restaurant where the generally abstemious revolutionary ordered a good cut of meat and washed it down with a stein of local beer. His meal completed, he and his companions went off for a walk through the town. When Lenin was in an especially good mood, he'd break into song. His favorite number was one that touched on the subject of ideology: "Your doctrine is false," the chorus ran, "freedom can be fettered, but freedom can't be killed." Then back home to work, often well into the night, on his correspondence and to compose editorials for Iskra about the fall of capitalism.

Lenin was a devoted revolutionary and practical politician whose characteristic works have titles like *What Is To Be Done?* He hadn't much time for theorizing about the states of bourgeois consciousness. Marx, of course, did. A well-known passage from the *Contribution to the Critique of Political Economy* is, overall, representative of his views on the question of ideology. "The mode of production," Marx observes there, "conditions the social, political and intellectual life process in general. It is not the consciousness of men that determines their being but, on the contrary, their social being that determines their consciousness."[1] And if someone's social identity entails ownership of the means of production, then his consciousness will, almost inevitably, be skewed, his doctrine false.

Roland Barthes has said that modern myth—but he might just as well have said ideology—is the transformation of history into nature: a fine pocket definition, provided you know what history and nature are.[2] Marx thought he did. History is materially motivated class struggle: a condition of flux; nature is unregenerate, cyclical, eternal. Bourgeois hubris consisted in believing that capitalism was the "natural" (therefore eternally just) fulfillment of material strivings endemic to human beings at all times. The free market was human nature translated perfectly into social form. Given Marx's confident view of the world, the concept of ideology follows with ease. Those whose place in the human food chain—in which the great capitalists, as Marx memorably said, devour the lesser—inhibits them from seeing the truth are creatures of ideology: they live and breathe false consciousness.

Two events have intervened to make the view of ideology sustained explicitly by Marx and by and large implicitly by Lenin more difficult to hold onto. The first, and surely the most important, is the fall of communism throughout the world. The internal collapse of the Soviet Union and the breakup of its foreign empire cast virtually everything associated with Marx and his thought into discredit, at least for many. The fate of Russia has been broadly taken as witness to the fact that Karl Marx was comprehensively wrong.

The second event, an earlier and far lesser one, is the onset and dissemination of what goes under the name of post-structuralist thinking. Can one take, say, Lacan seriously when he associates the drive to possess the truth with the quest for that supremely determining nonentity, the phallus, and still talk about ideology? For to use ideology as an analytical category, mustn't one have a verifiable and verified doctrine to oppose to bourgeois error? "Like it or not," Foucault has said, ideology "always stands in virtual opposition to something else which is supposed to count as truth."[3] How much of Marx would remain intact after a Derridean reading had brought his latent religious affiliations—the teleology, the apocalyptic vision, the prophetic identification, and the rest—to the fore?

For a while the effect of a lot of left-wing theorizing was to preserve the notion of ideology in a form that Marx could at least dimly recognize, while at the same time being responsive to those influential theorists who undermined claims to fixed truth. Post-structuralist theory seemed to scare high-thought Marxists away from any but the most recondite notions of ideology. In the work of Althusser, Macherey, and the Terry Eagleton of *Ideology and Literature*, one finds attempts, often rather strained, to keep talking about ideology but to do so in ways that won't entirely traduce post-structuralist skepticism.[4] The result in these writers is often that the notion of ideology is refined to the point where it loses significant force.

But lately the notion of ideology, in its strong form, has been making a comeback. With the recent turn to cultural criticism, it has, to some, seemed necessary to have a term that crystallizes the assumed differences between the critic's vocabulary and the cultural languages under analysis. The holding action against intellectual challenges to ideology seems to have won out. For now, with the advent of cultural studies, the term and its correlatives are passing again into general intellectual exchange.

But does cultural criticism really need the notion of ideology? What would happen if those of us interested in the study of art and culture gave it up? What would happen if we replaced the Marxist version of critique with one that comes out of the American pragmatic tradition, one that does not rely on the truth/ideology distinction in however displaced or refined a form? What would be lost, what gained, by such an intellectual shift?

To begin to answer these questions, I want to look quite critically at what is probably the most recent important move in the holding action against post-structuralist and pragmatic thinking that I have been describing: Terry Eagleton's *Ideology: An Introduction*. A skimming reader of Eagleton's book might think he was aiming to intervene on the ideology debate so as, at last, to pull the term from circulation. For he finds every theorist of ideology whose work he considers (and that includes Marx, Engels, Althusser, Lukács, Adorno, Bourdieu, Habermas, then Rorty and Fish, among others) to be in some crucial ways inadequate. Eagleton's most common move when he's discussing Marxists from the classical tradition is to locate what he takes to be maiming paradoxes in their work. If, as Marx insists, all thought is socially determined, then isn't his thought on the subject of ideology itself so determined, itself ideological? Lukács, in *History and Class Consciousness*, argues that the only true perspective on society is the proletariat's. But from what vantage might that perspective be validated? Not from the proletariat's point of view, surely; that would be sheer tautology.

Eagleton's criticisms of his Marxist predecessors are vaguely post-structuralist: he thinks he's locating significant epistemological fault lines in
their writings. Often these are points where expression and intention—
or the figurative and the literal—seem to part company. When it comes to
his postmodern contemporaries, Eagleton is inclined to excoriate them
for leading readers toward relativism. In other words, he uses something
like a post-structuralist stance to discredit the canonical Marxist writers
and—implicitly—a classical epistemology to undermine the postmodern
types. Though Eagleton does find things to applaud about the majority
of the figures he considers, the most energetic impulse in the book is,
if not dismissive, at least severely critical. It sometimes looks as though
Eagleton is opening the door to the elephant's graveyard and ushering
the behemoths in one by one. In his conclusion, one half expects, he
might be ready to close the gate and lock it.

But that is not what happens. The conclusion begins by promising to
summarize Eagleton's own views on how ideology ought to be understood. To this task he devotes three dramatically vacuous pages. The nadir
comes when Eagleton admits that "it is doubtful that one can ascribe to
ideology any *invariable* characteristics at all."[5] Not much later England's
premier Marxist literary critic signs off. What's going on here? Didn't
Eagleton owe his readers a comprehensive final chapter where, in clear
and persuasive terms, he justified the perpetuation of ideology as a category, describing how he thought the term ought to be used and to what
effect?

But such a question, I think, mistakes the real task of this book. *Ideology: An Introduction* isn't so much an intellectual enquiry as it is an act of
defiance. At a historical moment when Marxism, as an intellectual movement and as a script for practical politics, is being discredited nearly
everywhere in the world, a leading Marxist theorist publishes a book that
insists on taking seriously one of Marxism's hoariest and, I believe, least
essential concepts, as though nothing has changed. Aside from an obfus-
cating reference to the "post-capitalist states of the Eastern bloc," Eagleton
hasn't a word to say about his contemporary historical context. Publishing a book now in which ideology survives as a concept based on the
writer's willingness to trash its every manifestation, but without giving it
up, is—one cannot avoid the conclusion—a profession of religious faith
in the midst of worldly adversity.

Actually the current situation would seem an ideal opportunity for tough self-scrutiny on the left, some questions about what, if anything, in orthodox Marxism remains tenable. Or why not use this as a chance to end the left's investment in the cult of Marx's personality? Why not widen the tradition of leftist thought by looking back at other thinkers and organizers who have been devoted, by their lights, to achieving human equality? Or why not begin a reappraisal of the vast field of Utopian writing, from Plato through More and beyond, in order to form a fresh tradition of resistance to human exploitation, given that the Marxist tradition, admirable as it may be in parts, has proved a failure thus far?

Why has it failed? Perhaps in part because Marx's vision was more literary than analytical (if indeed there are any analytical or cognitive vocabularies that enable us to predict the future's approximate shape): the narrative of capitalism's fall through overweening hubris grants the reader many of the satisfactions to be found in tragic form. (Literary form—the setting up and fulfillment of expectations in the reader—may be understood in part as a protest against the formlessness of much political history.) Thinking of the bourgeoisie as a modern version of Oedipus, enmeshed in dramatic ironies, blithely sowing the seeds of its own downfall, has a poetic appeal that may cloud other sorts of judgment.

For the crises that Marx predicted, in many ways quite correctly, have been, if not dispatched, at least attenuated: by Keynesian deficit spending, by the opening up of new markets (Lenin called imperialism capitalism's ultimate stage) and the creation of "false needs," as well as by the evolution of a working class partially insulated by unemployment compensation and the beneficiary, or victim, of Henry Ford's idea that laborers ought to be able to afford the cars they sweat over on the assembly line.

Nor can one neglect the fact that no Marxist revolution took place in any nation where capitalism had brought the means of production to a formidable level: historically it has always been a matter of socializing poverty. On have come the thugs then to simulate the capitalist stage with five-year plans, temporary suspensions of democratic process, the murder of kulaks, dissenters, Jews, and other people in the wrong place at the wrong time, threatening to spike history's plan.

And yet there remains something compelling at the heart of Marxist thought. As Eagleton briskly puts it, "A socialist is just someone who is unable to get over his or her astonishment that most people who have lived and died have spent lives of wretched, fruitless, unremitting toil. Arrest history at any point whatsoever, and this is what we will find."[6] Those who agree with this version of history past and present (and I do) cannot want the ethical imperative that drove Marx (along with a lot of rancor and a pride one can only call aristocratic) to pass out of mind. What has to happen so that, after the revolutions of 1989, some people will still share Eagleton's astonishment?

Perhaps to start with, cultural critics should consider detaching themselves from the notion of ideology. In the strong form in which Marx used the term it is embarrassingly susceptible to the criticisms of Derrida and William James: to be brief, it lets you play at being God—bad news for the mere mortals in proximity. In the refined usage of mandarins like Althusser and Macherey, the word is so exquisitely elaborated that it passes into sheer conceptual vapor, of little or no experiential use to anyone. Perhaps Marxism, if it is to survive as a tenable intellectual form, must give up on Hegel and his displaced theological ruminations about the movements of the World Spirit (the Spirit that Marx relocated in the material dialectic and that Lukács in *History and Class Consciousness* tricked out in worker's garb and renamed the proletariat) and become genuinely practical, something of this world. What would a pragmatic Marxism, a Marxism in the spirit of Dewey and James, look like?

The first step in concocting such a pragmatism would be shifting the burden of responsibility. One would need to understand the concept of ideology not as a name for the public's irrational resistance to the truth, but rather as an excuse, the excuse leftist intellectuals have arrived at for their inability to persuade other people to talk and think as they do. The burden of being a pragmatic public intellectual lies in convincing people to switch vocabularies, to jettison those they've grown used to in the interest of other ways of talking. To the pragmatist, one ought to adopt a vocabulary not because it gives perfect access to something real out there in the world, but because it helps you live better. It helps you, as William James would say, to get what you want.

Pragmatism denies the existence of ultimate truth by asking of a new vocabulary not whether it unlocks the secrets of nature or brings one into contact with the noumenal world, but by asking what happens experientially when you take the vocabulary up. Pragmatism is experimental; it tests truth by trying it out, or imagining its trial in life. A pragmatist is likely to be hospitable to Jacques Derrida's effort to cast out all the conceptual fetishises that Western culture has latched onto in an effort to reachieve the stability that comprehensive religious faith seems once to have offered. Yet in Derrida's urge to displace every commitment by employing what one might call an unqualified irony, a pragmatist is likely to see another form of absolutism, an absolute romance of the negative.

Pragmatism itself has an ironic view of truth. It understands investments in persons, ideas, and institutions as provisional, as being open to change, yet it sees some measure of commitment as necessary for a fruitful life. Like Marxism, pragmatism is committed to historicism, and thus understands that what's good in the way of belief must respond to changing cultural circumstances. The power to make effective judgments will be severely limited by one's historical context. But unlike the Marxist, the pragmatist isn't devoted to thinking her way out of a given historical context in order to arrive at a secure version of where history is going to go. She doesn't want to work her way imaginatively to the end of history and then look at things from there, as both Marx and Hegel did. Pragmatism steers its way between Derrida's obsessive skepticism and the obsessive quest for stability that informs conventional religion and its many cultural descendants, orthodox Marxism included.

I find pragmatism's epistemological views to be good ones. That is, I find that William James and Richard Rorty are fair enough guides to how one ought to conceive of one's responsibilities and opportunities as a citizen in contemporary America. But it is worth adding that, especially in the criticism of art, pragmatic thinking can be debilitating. Because pragmatism, like it or not, is a philosophy. Like any philosophy, it propounds and elaborates a special terminology, a sequence of buzzwords like work, cash-value, contingency, open-endedness, and the rest. People committed to a philosophical position are often prone to go to art to see their favorite concepts endorsed.

So when Richard Rorty tells us that what matters most in poetry is the fact that it dramatizes contingency, reminding us that the world we have could be much different than it is now, and will be different in time, he's pointing to what is surely an important facet of many poems.[7] At the same time, he's disposing us to forget how much of art concerns itself with continuities as well as with the more general task of enlarging our experience by telling stories and using verbal figures that aren't satisfyingly encompassed by any existing set of concepts. Used as a grid for analysis, rather than as spurs to action and reflection, pragmatic terms can be just as confining as any other kind, perhaps more so in that pragmatism's buzzwords tend to be visceral, kinetic terms that make you feel that you're in there mixing it up with whatever issue happens to be at hand. Which is only to say that the pragmatic jargon tends, like any other, to solidify over time and, as Emerson puts it, "to hem in the life." But by inspired substitution of terms, inspired troping, one can, I think, help ensure that pragmatism doesn't solidify as a collection of keywords, or what Burke calls master-tropes. Pragmatism has got to earn and re-earn the vitality it often rather cavalierly advertises as its birthright.

With this much said, I can go on and describe what I mean by a pragmatic Marxism. Someone wishing to continue, one hopes in highly revised form, Marx's legacy would stop talking about how the Marxist hermeneutic provides the ultimate horizon within which all other methods of interpretation find ultimate containment. She would instead become, if not an investment capitalist out and out, at the very least a capitalist of ideas. Rather than using a lot of theoretical footwork to preserve Marx's epistemological pretensions in the midst of a critical moment rightly skeptical of transcendent claims, she might appeal to fellow citizens in a more or less accessible language. She would not argue that the Marxist analysis is the ultimate this or that, but that given the other competing terminologies in circulation, the Marxist vocabulary could help you get what you want, or what you ought to want—a less cruel, more humane world.

In this case one would take, for instance, the labor theory of value, with its assertion that workers deploying their socially necessary labor time, not capitalists putting their investments at risk, are the true creators of value, and advance it as an ethical, rather than a scientific view. Someone who holds pragmatically to the labor theory of value believes that in all probability each human being has only one turn on earth such that the time—the finite, ever-diminishing time—of an individual life, is the highest value and *should be* the standard for measuring all other worth. *Should be* the standard: which is something much different from saying that the labor theory of value, by the grace of Marx's authority and equations, *is the law.* A pragmatic Marxist would look at an argument to the effect that the great venture capitalist is the sole creator of wealth and thus due every comfort, while the workers are no more than bolts on the wheel of progress, as wrong, yes, but on the same epistemological level as the labor theory of value. The capitalist-as-hero line is just another idea in circulation that one must argue against or displace, persuading free people that it's a bad way to think and providing something better.

To stop talking about the conflict between History and Ideology would, from the pragmatic point of view, provide this advantage: Marxists would have to see themselves as citizens like anybody else, with no special claims to superiority. They would have to change their tone of voice from the missa solemnis theoretical drone to something suited to an exchange between equals. In fact, one way to characterize pragmatism overall is as an idea about truth (truth as what's good in the way of belief) that gets people talking in a tone of voice that's more ironic, provisional, tolerant, and urbane, and that puts metaphor-making—not the sending of well-drilled, strategically deployed concepts into argumentative battle—at a premium.

A change in tone of voice isn't much, perhaps, if what you'd actually like to do is eclipse the metaphysics of presence, or put man under erasure, or discredit ideology with a blast of high-voltage theory. One of the foibles of the intellectual left in America, I think, has been its devotion to an all-or-nothing policy: total revolution, or complete withdrawal from all forms of practical politics. "These professors," Edmund Burke observes of another time (and another sort of professors), "finding their extreme principles not applicable to cases which call only for a qualified, or, as I may say, civil and legal resistance, in such cases employ no resistance at all. It is with them a war or a revolution, or it is nothing."[8]

A pragmatic Marxism might, to point to one specific possibility, have the effect of producing fewer well-armored theorists and more Christopher Hitchens-type intellectual journalists. Hitchens, whose work appears regularly in Harper's and The Nation, and sporadically in most any national publication that tolerates liberal or left-wing views, is probably by now more than a bit player in the nightmares of reactionary politicians throughout America. He has read history, and in particular American history; has versed himself in nonglamorous sorts of matters, like the committee protocols of our legislature and our national political parties; writes extremely well, with a large range of literary reference; and has a gift for getting mad not about Capitalism and Exploitation and Repression, but about S&L crooks, Bush's "tilt" toward Iraq which may have prompted the Kuwait invasion, or the rise of disturbing kinds of nationalism among our good friends the Germans. A shrewd reading of the limits of our current economic and political order informs Hitchens's work, but he makes that reading persuasive implicitly, by recourse to specific events, current issues. You can find yourself agreeing with part of what Hitchens says, find yourself informed and provoked but not finally in full accord: his isn't the take-it-all-or-leave-it mode that one meets in high theory.

There are at present any number of left-leaning academic theorists in America who possess at least a share of Hitchens's energy and intelligence. If fifty such people went pragmatic, started sounding less like Hegel and more like John Dewey (of whom it was observed by Henry Steele Commager that no public debate was clarified until he'd had his say), I think they would do palpable good. They'd also, one must add, be running a risk. The institutions in which most of them work refuse to value pragmatic, accessible writing very much. What gets promotions and stature are forays into generality, into theory. Any assistant professor who spent years writing muckraking articles for the local newspapers about poverty in the surrounding county would probably be in trouble at promotion time. But shouldn't radicals earn their status as radicals by taking a risk now and then? And shouldn't they have the sense to doubt the professional standards of excellence that institutions, and especially elite institutions, enforce upon them? Consider, for instance, what might happen if all of the liberal and left-wing professors in America spent their research energies over the next five years on local, not "universal," issues: on local poverty, local corruption, local elementary education.

But from the point of view of the critic who wants to hang on to the notion of ideology, the arguments I have been making so far are shot through with idealizations. Reference to things like a free marketplace of ideas, a dialogue among citizens, and recourse to a common language gives my game away. For from the Marxist point of view, a key weakness of pragmatism lies in its overestimation of human reason and the contextual freedom of the human subject. The pragmatist's use of everyday parlance is thought to signify a capitulation to received (that is, ideological) ways of thinking which have thoroughly permeated common speech. Using theory's alien and alienating language is, accordingly, a first step in protesting against such linguistic accommodations. It was comparable criticism that made one of William James's most devoted and admirable readers, W. E. B. Dubois, wish that as a Harvard student he had paid more attention to the likes of Freud and Nietzsche and a bit less to the local pragmatists.[9]

And what about unconscious inhibitions that prevent people from accurately perceiving what is good in the way of belief? What about the human tendency toward regression, the conservatism of the drives, and all the limitations imposed on the ego by the id and the superego? For one resource of theories of ideology is how well they coincide with the Freudian theory of repression. Suppose that the mechanisms that produce repression of the Oedipal scene and its corollaries also inhibit conscious access to the truths of class conflict. Such a view—and it is anything but a weak one—has been effectively argued by Herbert Marcuse and others associated with the Frankfurt School.

It is true that James is not terribly concerned with unconscious forces within the self that are antithetical to the actively enquiring mind. As Howard Feinstein's engaging book, *Becoming William James*, persuasively shows, James struggled hard to make himself the attractively healthy spirit he eventually became.[10] And yet, one may think that there is something too well-balanced, too Apollonian in James's voice. Orwell said of H. G. Wells that he was too sane to understand the modern world, and D. W. Winnicott, the closest we have to a distinguished psychologist who is also, as Adam Phillips indicates in his fine book on him, a pragmatist in something of a Jamesian mode, remarked that we are poor indeed if all we are is sane.[11] Both of these observations are much too harsh to apply to James, but they do begin to touch on his limits.

But the limits of William James are not the limits of pragmatism. To integrate the Freudian/Nietzschean critique, pragmatism might start by undermining the impoverished mapping of the mind that Freud and most theorists of ideology share. For this is an area in which the available stock of language falls far short of experiential nuance. Could one persuade Wordsworth, who works to capture the sharp particularity of every subtle fold and permutation of the inner life, that there are only three governing states of the mind—unconscious, preconscious, and conscious? When one recognizes that "the unconscious" and "repression" are absolutes, terms no less transcendent than "heaven" and "God" (Kenneth

Burke called the unconscious Freud's God-term), one begins to see them as what they are: precipitates of theory's will to power. And if there are no *absolute* repressions, then the possibility of mental freedom—the freedom to change one's mind—always exists. On such freedom, the pragmatist will, at the least, be willing to wager.

But what about the question of language. Isn't accessible language inevitably a hostage to ideology? Can one speak a common language to free citizens? Or is the harsh discourse of theory necessary to shock our contemporaries from their presumptions? This question is best answered by posing another. Can those who have spoken the hyper-sophisticated languages of ideological theory say that they are satisfied with the effects they've had on American political and cultural life over the past couple of decades, the theory years? Have they effected any of the transformations they've dreamed of? If the answer to these questions is no—and I do not see how it could be anything but—then why not try something else?

Another advantage that the pragmatic tradition presents to the left— beyond its focus on the local and particular, its insistence on competing truths over and against one large Truth, and its fondness for the idiomatic—is that it allows for, in fact it demands, self-reflection in a way that classical Hegelian Marxism does not. Emerson, who is the founder of the pragmatic way, has any number of moments in his work where concepts akin to ideology come into action. He speaks of poverty, of nature, of fate, destiny, experience, and limitation. These states are inseparable from humanly inadequate social forms, dead institutions, norms that suffocate. But Emerson never underestimates his own attraction to deadening forms. When he turns brutally against limitation, he turns against those elements in himself that take satisfaction in maintaining needless limits.

The theorist of ideology in the Marxist mode is not an autobiographer, or even that engagingly indirect kind of autobiographer, the accomplished prose stylist. "Style," said J. Robert Oppenheimer "is the deference that action pays to uncertainty." By that he means, I would guess, that human actions, whether physical or symbolic, are, because undertaken by circumscribed individuals, inevitably constrained in what they can encompass and achieve. Style records an awareness of such constraint as well as the daring involved in challenging it by speaking or acting at all. The transpersonal theoretical style—if it is a style at all—will trifle with no such human difficulties.

Nor do I recall a time when our major contemporary theorists of ideology have had a word to say about their own implication in it. Does the leftist professor who works in a distinguished institution, giving grades and helping to select the best and the brightest for entrance through the portals of law, medicine, and business, not have a stake in the system as it stands? And might such dual allegiances be conducive to a few misprisions? Can the professor work the productive mechanism with one hand and try to jam it with the other?

A more important question along these lines comes out of a passage in Hannah Arendt's book *Between Past and Future*. "The educators," she writes there, "stand in relation to the young as representatives of a world for which they must assume responsibility although they themselves did not make it, and even though they may, secretly or openly, wish it were other than it is."[12] The notion of ideology works to absolve the advanced intellectuals of the responsibility that Arendt feels they must accept in order to introduce others to the world. One of the most productive kinds of tension that can arise in a classroom, I think, derives from the willingness of teachers to identify themselves, even if ambivalently, with existing social forms and submit those forms, and implicitly themselves, to the critical attention of students who are—in the temporary and artificial environment of the school—free of many entanglements. For a teacher to join students in their legitimate freedom to doubt everything is the quick route to acclaim, but it fails to convey to students just how tough established social forms can be. Professors who partake of bourgeois comforts and deride the system in an unqualified way aren't owning up about the compromises they had to negotiate in order to get where they are. They're making life look too easy.

This in turn brings up some questions associated with the issue of professionalism. How do left-wing intellectuals distinguish between a creditable desire to write a more socially aware literary criticism than has been the norm in the academy and their professional, and very material, need to say something—anything, one sometimes thinks—that the foregoing generations haven't said, simply to make a place for themselves in the field, to support their families and pay back their school loans? (Harold Bloom's theory of influence anxiety, with its description of the creative strife between poets of different generations, has many uses in literary studies, but for understanding the institution of academic literary criticism now, with its generational warfare, it seems to me unequaled.[13] And what about the other end of the scale, academic stardom? Is it worth asking what happens to your Marxist critique when you ascend to a high-paying chair in literary studies?

I'm not saying that simply because the Marxist theorist takes home a good check his doctrine is necessarily false (bad in the way of belief), nor that every young Marxist Literary Group member is an upwardly mobile sheep decked in lupine black leather. The market is a kinky, quirky game, often more radical in its effects than the radicals. It's only that indictments of America coming from the cultural left would be more persuasive if they contained just a little self-scrutiny, perhaps even self-indictment. In *Ideology: An Introduction* Eagleton is interested in excoriating the others, the capitalist roaders, and leaving himself, those readers who agree with him, and, too, all of those countries with pretensions to Marxism out of the picture. Could we hear a word, maybe, about ideology in China, or in preelection Nicaragua? Not in this book. Ideology is a capitalist vice, the only indigenous vice, it seems, we don't manage to export.

In fact, I'd go so far as to suggest that the best available critique of "ideology" coming out of England now may be one associated not with Terry Eagleton or any other professional thinker, but with Eagleton's contemporary, Mick Jagger. The Rolling Stones, in songs like "Sympathy for the Devil" and "Highwire," throw themselves in with the party of greed and destruction and give you—in their hard-driving, aggressive sound and I'll-piss-anywhere attitude—a dose of the high that power brings. The part of you that goes uninhibitedly over to these songs (if it does) is the part that, alone and untranslated, is anything but appalled by smart bombs and the like. The Stones are ironic about such investments (most of the time), and a lot of the strength of their popular art is in its ability to let you have the power rush and to make you ask a few questions about it, too. They can do this because they're honest enough to admit their attractions to all the tasty vile things that celebrity lays on their table. Put down your *Ideology* and put on your *Flashpoint*, as Carlyle no doubt would have phrased it.

When you do that, you'll be able to gaze for a while at *Ideology*'s cover, a rendering of "Industrialized Peasants" by Georg Scholz. The peasants are a couple, presumably man and wife. The man, gripping a Bible, has the look of a sanctified sadist: wearing preacher's garb, sitting bolt upright, with vicious drawn mouth, vicious empty eyes, he looks like he's poised to recite one psalm more, then go upstairs and whip the children for their share in Adam's crime. His wife is a heap of offal shoveled into a black dress. In one hand she's cradling a baby pig. There is a cretinous expression on her face and a screw through the top of her head. Now presuming that a critic of Eagleton's stature has some say-so over his covers, what are we to make of this kind of gesture? An attempt, maybe, to hold up the mirror to resistant readers? I'm reminded of an old National Lampoon cover: a photo of Spot with a revolver at his head and the words, "Buy this magazine or we kill the dog."

But it would be shallow to write off the entire appeal of positions like Eagleton's to snobbishness, opportunism, or displaced religious fervor— though none of these possibilities ought to be dismissed out of hand. There is another dimension to this matter, which puts the pragmatic response under more pressure than anything I have discussed so far.

"Your doctrine is false," sang Vladimir Ilych, then went off to change the world—for good or bad it is difficult to say, but change it he surely did. The Russian Revolution would have had a different shape without him. And central to Lenin's achievements, I think, was a more or less Manichaean worldview: true and false, history and ideology, and proletariat and bourgeois. Within the context of such fixed contentions, men and women will do extraordinary things, for they are fighting for principles. They are on the side of the gods and anything is possible. "Your doctrine is false"—intellectually all but void, maybe, but a way of thinking that can get work done: remember Lenin slaving at his desk until well into the night. Can the sense that one's truth is good in the way of belief generate comparable energies? How many of the fifteen thousand who stood in front of the Russian parliament defending Boris Yeltsin and democracy and who—it is probably no exaggeration to say it—changed the world forever were pragmatists? How many thought they were fighting for a definitive truth against equally palpable lies?

In fact, even James, one of the most impressively urbane thinkers America has yet produced, resorts at a memorable point in his writing to a sort of Manichaeanism: "If this life be not a real fight," he says in "Is Life Worth Living," "it is no better than a game of private theatricals from which one may withdraw at will. But it *feels* like a real fight." [14] It does feel, in other words, as though the world is divided between opposing forces, and that the good fully needs our efforts.

When in the remarkable interview that followed the publication of "The White Negro," Richard Stern pushed Norman Mailer, the most conspicuously Emersonian writer at work in America now (as James was in his time), to expound on the hipster's ethics, Mailer said that he felt God was in danger of dying. "He is not all-powerful; He exists as a warring element in a divided universe, and we are part of—perhaps the most important part—of His great expression, His enormous destiny; perhaps he is trying to impose upon the universe His conception of being against other conceptions of being very much opposed to His."[15] God and the devil are in contention, the outcome in doubt. This God needs us as much, if not more, than we him. It feels like a real fight.

As Diana Trilling remarked, a lot of sophisticated people who admire Mailer (ambivalently, of course) speak about this as one of Mailer's key metaphors. But for Mailer it's not really that at all: he believes the story of the embattled god out and out. And Mailer, whatever else one may say about him, commands energy; he does more work in a year than most ambivalent sophisticates can in a decade. "It feels like a real fight"; "Man's fate . . . is tied up with God's fate": neither is quite the same as that very pragmatic, and quite moving, line in Wallace Stevens: "So, say that final belief / Must be in a fiction. It is time to choose."[16]

If you are resolutely secular, believing that when you die you probably rot, will you risk your life for contingent truth? Are there people who can see their possibilities for heroism against a less exalted background than the heights of absolute value? It is such people that a whole line of pragmatic poets, philosophers, and critics has worked to bring into being. The wager of this Jamesian line is that strong commitments to contingent ideas—final beliefs invested in fictions—are possible. One does not, to this way of thinking, need a Wagner overture or Lenin's marching song resounding from the wings in order to act decisively. How this experiment will work out, no one can say. But it is not a mean thing to be alive amidst the possibilities that it offers.

Notes

1   Karl Marx, *Contribution to the Critique of Political Economy* (Chicago, 1911), 11–12.
2   Roland Barthes, *Mythologies*, trans. Annette Lavers (New York, 1972), 109–59.
3   Michel Foucault, *The Foucault Reader*, ed. Paul Rabinow (New York, 1984), 60.
4   Terry Eagleton, *Ideology: An Introduction* (New York, 1991).

5 Ibid., 222.

6 Ibid., 82.

7 See Richard Rorty, *Contingency, Irony, and Solidarity* (New York, 1989), 23–43.

8 Edmund Burke, *Reflections on the Revolution in France* (New York, 1968), 155.

9 See Cornel West's remarks on Du Bois in *The American Evasion of Philosophy* (Madison, Wisc., 1989), 138–50.

10 Howard Feinstein, *Becoming William James* (Ithaca, N.Y., 1984).

11 Adam Phillips, *Winnicott* (Cambridge, Mass., 1988).

12 Hannah Arendt, *Between Past and Future: Six Exercises in Political Thought* (Cleveland, Ill., 1963), 189.

13 See Harold Bloom, *The Anxiety of Influence* (New York, 1973).

14 William James, *The Will to Believe and Other Essays in Popular Philosophy* (Cambridge, Mass., 1979), 55.

15 Norman Mailer, *Advertisements for Myself* (New York, 1959), 380.

16 Wallace Stevens, *The Palm at the End of the Mind: Selected Poems and a Play*, ed. Holly Stevens (New York, 1972), 18.

Invoking Culture: The Messy Side of "Cultural Politics"

VIRGINIA R. DOMINGUEZ

I am an anthropologist. I am supposed to be a student of culture. Until joining the faculty at the University of California–Santa Cruz in the fall of 1991, I taught in Duke University's Department of Cultural Anthropology.[1] I subscribe to *Cultural Anthropology*, the newest major journal in the field of anthropology. I have even regularly taught my Duke department's introductory course entitled "Introduction to Cultural Anthropology." But I am quite uncomfortable talking about "culture," and I am less and less alone among my colleagues.[2]

That fact might be curious, but not noteworthy, were it not for the history of the discipline. For most of the twentieth century, anthropologists have followed the lead of German-born Franz Boas in employing a concept of culture deliberately antithetical to the old elite German notion of Kultur.[3] Fighting the racist underpinnings of evolutionism and the assumption of privilege that went hand in hand with European imperialism, anthropologists asserted that culture was a property of all human communities, and that it wasn't a reference to an aspect of a society or an arena within social life but, rather, to the whole of society as constituted by particular perceptions of the world and largely reinforced by particular forms of social, economic, and political organization. Antielitism meant a reconceptualization of culture so that it would describe, explain, and apply to all people, and not just to a few privileged populations or classes. "Culture" was strategically invoked to wrest it from the elite and make it a property of the masses. Social class was rarely their analytic unit in the early days, but the mission was still to democratize culture by universalizing its applicability.

As holistic representations have come under scrutiny, especially in the past two decades, anthropologists have noticed the greatly exaggerated picture of pristineness, purity, consensus, and order painted by many of the early antielitist ethnographic texts.[4] A school of cognitive anthropologists has responded by trying to restrict culture to patterned cognitive processes—schemas, classifications, and metaphors.[5] Self-labeled interpretive anthropologists, among them Clifford Geertz, have sought to locate "it" in "public webs" of meaning.[6] British social anthropology has tended to relegate culture to something conceptualized and studied by American anthropologists.[7] Yet despite the critiques, the worries, and the reconceptualizations, at least part of the Boasian legacy remains. I have never met an anthropologist not firmly committed to a populist (rather than elitist) sense of culture.

As these changes have occurred, it has been easier to see the social and political dimensions of scholarly talk about culture, and with them the broader politics of invoking culture. Some of us anthropologists react by increasingly avoiding invoking culture for the purposes of analysis,[8] and have both sympathy and criticism for the contemporary "cultural studies" movement within the humanities. From an anthropological perspective, the commitment to liberate culture from elite forms, claims, and conceptions is commendable but late in coming, and not exactly new. The commitment to employ culture at a time when anthropologists are suspicious of its referentiality or validity seems, on the other hand, curious—making us wonder why. Why, when the concept of culture has such an elitist history, would sympathetic antielitists contribute to its discursive objectification by trying to argue for the value of other things in terms of it?

So culture stays with us, but not, I shall argue, because it is simply a part of life. Rather, because we think and act in terms of it, and we make strategic social and political interventions by invoking it. I am calling that propensity to employ culture (to think, act, and fight with it) "culturalism."

=====

The issue is broader and deeper than the canon debate and far more global in reach than the current American obsession with "multiculturalism." While we are arguing over the content of canons of knowledge, disputing the value or need for canons, and pointing out the patterns of exclusion evident in curriculums, publishing practices, funding agencies, and museums, we are ironically reinforcing the perception that there is such a "thing" as culture and that it is something of value. But why is culture something of value? Perhaps more important, why does so much of cultural politics around the world stop short of asking that question?

Two processes converge and overlap to create this late-twentieth-century culturalist moment. The first is global in scope and begrudgingly Eurocentric; the second, societal in scope and importantly "self"-oriented.[9] In both, criticism is central though not always obvious. Some of it is "about art," "about literature," and "about music." Much of it, however, is about other things explicated in terms of culture.

To understand what is involved we need to shift the question we're asking. We need to move away from asking *about* culture—what belongs, what doesn't belong, what its characteristics are, whose characteristics are being imposed and whose are being excluded—and toward asking *what is being accomplished* socially, politically, discursively when the concept of culture is invoked to describe, analyze, argue, justify, and theorize.[11]

A different view of culture and cultural politics emerges when we look socially at the discursive practices of invoking culture, and when we allow ourselves and our own discursive practices to be part of what we study. Specifically, I believe we can get a great deal of mileage from asking (1) when it is that certain things get called "the culture" and others do not; (2) when it is that one sector of society invokes a cultural argument to explain a social, political, or economic reality; (3) when it is that governments make a point of developing and articulating an explicit "cultural policy," while others do not; and (4) when it is that reformist or revolutionary governments call for social, economic, and/or political change by earmarking culture as a preeminent arena for their struggle.

This "thing" that anthropologists have for decades taken to be what we study, describe, decipher, and theorize about can be, and often has been, an ideological mechanism for subordination and social control. A parallel kind of awareness has emerged in literary studies. We have all noted how over the past decade culture has been increasingly earmarked by intellectuals from the so-called third world or an American minority as a necessary, and conceivably effective, site for resistance. Witness the work of Gayatri Spivak, Trin Min-Ha, Edward Said, Ariel Dorfman, and

Henry Louis Gates, Jr. But they have, almost uniformly, in my opinion, not taken their critiques far enough. I repeat: Why do they all go along with the discursive objectification of culture when it is precisely that—a historically situated discursive object with a particular European origin and Eurocentric history?[11]

An obvious answer is that something is being socially and politically accomplished in each and every case, though it is often not what the invokers of culture themselves proclaim or believe. It is common for government institutions, social activists, and intellectuals to claim to represent large groups of people—"the nation," "the ethnic group," "the peripheralized minority," "the educated classes."[12] It is also common for that representation to be more imagined than documented. What invoking culture then accomplishes may have more to do with the social and political aspirations of the invokers than with the stated goals of an activist movement, a gatekeeping movement, or a government policy. I am not so much questioning the honesty of those who invoke culture when they do so, as I am questioning the seeming transparency of the reference to culture.

=====

While anthropologists and humanists in the United States debate the best way to conceptualize culture, many, if not most countries in the world today valorize culture enough to issue official "cultural policies," create staff ministries or institutes of culture, and provoke opposition movements articulating alternative "cultural policies."[13] National visions, nationalist ideologies, and national identities are all implicated, and with them issues of unity, distinctiveness, self-esteem, and civility.[14]

What is involved in calling policies *cultural?* Outsiders looking in might have so naturalized a concept of culture that they might not think twice, unless, of course, what they see in a foreign setting fails to match their sense of the kinds of things culture refers to. Herein lies the rub. It is simultaneously true that the nature of culture is far from obvious, and that its continued discursive deployment suggests sameness and shared understanding.

That paradoxical fact highlights the importance of conceptualizing culture as something invoked rather than something that is. It strikes me that there may be more merit in asking why so many people have an investment in circumscribing "the cultural" (when there are so many arguments about it) than in continuing to debate its ontology. It seems to me that the time may have come to ask questions about our debates and our discussions rather than about whether we are right within those debates and discussions.

It is in this light that "cultural policies" may be illuminating. The fact that so many countries have cultural policies needs to be explained, not taken for granted. The fact that they function as symbolic capital, to use Pierre Bourdieu's term, is not a corollary of, but rather a reason for, their existence.[15] To so function, cultural policies presuppose (1) the objectification of "the cultural"; (2) clarity in the reference to culture; and (3) the belief that government has a say in the shape of a country's culture and that nations are valued and identified by their cultural characteristics. Each of these presuppositions points to ways of raising questions about our debates and discussions.

(1) *Objectification of "the cultural."* Calling something a cultural policy implies that there is an arena of life to which it refers that is separable from other arenas for which there might be other types of policies. The discursive carving out of such a thing produces a belief in its referentiality, its "real" existence outside discourse.

Ramifications of this phenomenon are sometimes straightforward, but often unanticipated and paradoxical. It is easy to see that fights over particular cultural policies could be heated and prolonged just like fights over particular economic policies, foreign policies, or energy policies. It is the foreseeable effect of a proposed activity, budget cut, or platform that is the focus of the heated and prolonged debate.

It is less easy to see other consequences of calling something a cultural policy. Consider the nature of this discursive object as it appears in governmental uses and political discussions. To have a cultural policy—and have it mean something other than everything associated with human beings or everything associated with a particular society—it has to be differentiated from other types of policies. That process of differentiation circumscribes the cultural in ways that make it incompatible with the old anthropological holism. An anthropologically holistic concept of culture would include economic organization, political processes, intergroup relationships, and technology as integral components of a population's culture, not separate from it.

The logical result is discursive differentiation. The historically situated result is discursive differentiation of a particular inherited sort. While the very notion of a cultural policy does not allow the rebellious, populist, holistic Boasian sense of culture to be employed, two other forms of "the cultural" seem to be "natural" adoptions: either the old German and French notions of Kultur/Culture (and derivative United States notions of high culture) or enclave notions of culture that distinguish between minority populations and dominant populations. In Kultur, two types of differentiation coexist: a distinction is made between certain things deemed to be the content of Kultur and other things, and a distinction is made between the people associated with Kultur and those not associated. In enclave notions of culture, there is the appearance of holism but a fundamental differentiation is nonetheless always produced: only small, minority, peripheral, or controlled populations are described holistically, while the dominant population employs substantive differentiations to refer to itself, its activities, and its characteristics. Both of these notions of the cultural are European in origin and have gone hand in hand with class differentiation in Europe and European attitudes toward the rest of the world, especially in the past two centuries.[16]

Unanticipated and contradictory ramifications of articulating cultural policies follow from this fact. Foremost among them is the problem of articulating a cultural policy as a way to fight postcolonial domination. Many non-European countries, especially those long subjected to direct colonial domination by European powers, indeed make concerted efforts to establish cultural policies that highlight and celebrate forms of creative expression thought to have been developed before the establishment of European hegemony. This is typically perceived to be a form of resistance. Yet it is arguably more a continuation of a form of European ideological hegemony than an example of resistance. Resistance, it is true, is evident in the inclusion of items, genres, and forms not associated with European elites in the category officially identified as cultural; resistance, however, is not evident in the common adoption of a notion of the cultural defined conceptually (as an area of life) in the footsteps of the hierarchical, elite European sense of distinction, value, and aesthetics. Few, if any, of those postcolonial countries' official cultural policies encompass the whole country's economic practices, governmental structures, or technologies; many concern performances, museums, archeological sites, publications, and the areas of greatest distinction in education.

(2) *Clarity in the reference to culture.* The discursive objectification of the cultural, combined with the widespread distribution of talk about it, policies about it, and political struggles focusing on it, fosters the presumption of sameness and shared understanding even when people debate the merits and demerits of including specific things under its rubric. This presumption, in turn, raises the stakes in social and political struggles that invoke culture. For the conviction that there is something to be articulated, cherished, shaped, and claimed invites people to want to articulate it, cherish it, shape it, and claim it. It becomes a thing of value and, as a thing of value, it behooves people to invoke it.

The presumption is interesting because it flies in the face of a great deal of evidence that is not hard to come by. Consider the problem of reference for students of cultural politics. Let us say we choose to work on the relationship between cultural policies and national identities. What do we include in our conceptualization, and what do we exclude? We could, of course, proceed by examining formally articulated statements issued by branches of a country's government, officially dubbed as that country's cultural policy. Such distillations of what culture is or should be, and of the kind of intervention state institutions make or should make in that "sector" of the country's life, are useful data, but of a particular sort. They tell us the kinds of activities that are promoted and those that are discouraged by people with determinate positions in a country's power hierarchy. Most students of cultural politics concentrate on the policy side of the concept of cultural policy—who is pushing what activity and why. Lost in the explicit struggles is the less obvious but nonetheless crucial way in which certain things are being pushed by invoking culture in the first place.

Official articulated cultural policies are examples of situated, motivated practices of invoking culture. If, as students of national identities and cultural policies, we chose to ignore the official cultural policies and concentrate on other phenomena we read as signs of governmental cultural policies or as extragovernmental, autonomous, semiautonomous, or resistant practices that either we or some of our informants interpreted to be matters of culture, both the data and their scope could end up being quite different. Consider, for example, four different conceptualizations of the possible object of study: (a) clearly articulated official policies issued by government institutions and deemed by these institutions to be about the nation's or the region's culture; (b) practices and patterns not explicitly targeted by any official cultural policy but that researchers identify as sociocultural consequences of government policies (however labeled); (c) public discourse about culture, the range of agreement and disagreement about it and its significance, and the social and political circumstances in which that public discourse exists; and (d) discursive and nondiscursive practices outside government circles that researchers identify as forms of cultural accommodation, innovation, or resistance because their very existence at a particular time and place indexes (or comments on) established institutions and hierarchies of power in the country at large.

These are significantly different things that could all well serve as references for discussions on cultural politics, and, in fact, do. A telling example is the experience of a group of researchers who gathered in June 1990 at the East-West Center in Honolulu for a week-long workshop on "cultural policies and national identities."[17] Eight scholars (four anthropologists, one folklorist, two sociologists, and a political scientist) had been asked by the Institute for Culture and Communication to write position papers on cultural policies and national identity in the primary country of their own research. Five of these were also native-born citizens of the country on which they were asked to write. The sixth was binational; the seventh, Beijing-born though Taiwanese by ancestry and citizenship; the eighth, an American with years of experience and professional contacts in his research country. Included were position papers on Singapore, Thailand, New Guinea, Japan, the People's Republic of China, and the United States.

Several of us were brought in to comment on the papers, offer comparative suggestions, and help develop a research agenda for the group. These participants added representation from Taiwan, the Solomon Islands, and New Zealand, and substantive knowledge of several Pacific Island countries, Nicaragua, and Israel. I should add that all but one of the participants had obtained graduate degrees (or at least postdoctoral fellowships) from North American universities and were quite proficient in English.

The papers, without exception, were thorough, lengthy, substantive, and insightful, but one thing I cannot say about them is that they shared an obvious subject matter. Three papers dealt with the People's Republic of China. One took as its subject matter "Chinese minority policy and the meaning of minority culture."[18] A second examined the lively public debate and discussion in the 1980s, especially among intellectuals, on wenhuare, translated as "culture fever" or "culture mania."[19] The third conceptualized its topic as the historical and contemporary relationship among the many "ethnic groups (or nationalities)" of China that "have lived and worked in a pluralistic organic whole for thousands of years." Much of this third paper argued for the need for the dominant Han population to help the fifty-five minority groups modernize for the benefit of "the pluralistic whole" but without self-degradation.

Discussion of official, articulated cultural policies tended to be about "the nation" and its "minority populations." Their connections to "culture" were treated as self-evident. The paper on the media, on the other hand, treated nothing as transparent, except for the fact that many Chinese scholars and intellectuals were constantly invoking culture in comments and essays referring to Confucianism, Marxism, Westernization, Chinese tradition(s), "national character," and Mao Zedong. For some of these scholars, culture is an object of discourse, for others an analytic concept, and for still others the empirical attributes and properties of bounded populations.

Lest we think that this range of answers to the question of the state of cultural policies and national identity is peculiarly "Chinese," let me mention that the variety in the subject matter and scope of the other papers paralleled the case of the People's Republic of China. The paper on Thailand concentrated on the unitary view of Thai society continuing to be asserted by the state; this meant material on the historical development of the Thai Buddhist Polity, an ideology of nationalism, and the ethnic and religious conflicts resulting from the implementation of specific national cultural policies. The position paper on Japan made Japanese identity its subject matter, pointing out that this is the best way to understand the constant talk of Japaneseness among the Japanese (best known these days as the discourse on Nihonjinron); the link to culture here was one made simultaneously by my colleague and some of the many participants in the public discourse on Nihonjinron. Public discourse was my colleague's primary data and subject matter. Explications of social, historical, economic, technological, and health data in terms of culture constituted its content.

The paper on the United States was triply illuminating. First, I found myself wondering, before reading the paper, what it was someone would write about when asked to write about "cultural policies and national identity" in the United States. The answer was far from clear to me. Second, it was instructive to see that the paper turned out to be about folklore, the profession of folklore, and changes in public institutions' attitudes to "folk" artists, "community," and "traditions." There was no discussion of cultural studies, multiculturalism, the canon debate, the media, or the issue of censorship in the arts. And yet it was a perfectly plausible topic through which to answer the question he was asked to take on. The paper mentioned tension between "elitism" and "cultural pluralism," it broached the institutional tendency to equate "cultural conservation" with the foregrounding of "the arts," and it situated many of these processes and movements within federal granting agencies, professional organizations, and public and private institutions at regional, state, and municipal levels of organization.[20]

The variety of "things" my colleagues took on for this workshop at the East-West Center may surprise people who primarily work with others who share their own specific sense of culture. The fact, though, is that there is very little guarantee that scholarly essays on culture will have much in common, even when you think you are putting together a working group of like-minded researchers.

I don't think I'm exaggerating the point. For a much-used word, culture has little communicative efficiency. And yet it is clear, from the frequency of institutional and public invocations of culture around the world, that it is perceived to have communicative value.

(3) *Governmental influence on the shape of a country's culture.* Cultural policies are not innocuous. They are after all governmental policies, even if of a particular kind. If I have called attention earlier to the objectification of the cultural as something we need to examine and not take for granted, I want also to call attention to assumptions embedded in the policy side of cultural policies. Governments do not have a public say in everything about the practice of everyday life. Governments that come close are considered totalitarian, invasive, and excessively regulatory.[21] That many governments, political movements, and public institutions assert the belief that they have a say in the shape of a country's culture suggests that culture is highlighted as something of special value, in addition to being objectified and presumed.

If we look, in particular, at activist governments seeking to shape a country's culture, we see different degrees of investment in invoking culture. Some countries have clearly articulated, discursively visible cultural policies; others do not. Some countries—not all—have clearly articulated cultural policies that explicitly invoke issues of national identity. Some countries have clearly articulated, discursively visible policies on national identity that explicitly invoke issues of culture.[22]

Activist cultural policies and activist nationalist policies are common among postcolonial countries of the twentieth century, especially those whose territorial boundaries have more to do with European politics than with a precolonial sense of shared peoplehood. While many of us may be accustomed to thinking that "peoples" are "peoples" to a large extent because they share "a culture," there is simply no logical reason to privilege that view of peoplehood.[23] And yet most postcolonial countries of the twentieth century adopt the policy that a cultural policy and a national identity go hand in hand, even when the explicit policy is seemingly contradictory—such as when the government actively promotes cultural pluralism as a way of diffusing tension that could presumably tear the country apart.[24] Both the conceptualization of and the stress on national identity and cultural policy reflect a particular European historical experience, which has enabled them to be thinkable and to be thought necessary.

It is clear that there are different levels of consciousness, interventionism, and activism, if we look comparatively. Unlike many other countries, the United States does not have a department or ministry of culture. Where are we to look to determine the federal government's policy on culture or cultures in (or of) the United States? A colleague of mine in the arts had no trouble mentioning the existence of national-level, federally funded institutions, such as the National Endowment for the Arts and the National Endowment for the Humanities, when I asked her if she thought the United States has a cultural policy. But, like the folklore scholar I mentioned above, anthropologists and perhaps historians would have trouble with my colleague's implicit equation of culture with the arts, even if she meant that our government equates culture with the arts. Such an equation buys too unproblematically into an elite Eurocentric view of culture that would ignore issues of language, public rhetoric, immigration policy, education, class, race, and ethnicity that provide both support and challenges to that elite sense of culture as refinement and aesthetic achievement. Should or shouldn't those other policies be looked at as well by researchers of cultural policies? The United States simply does not have an institutional mechanism for developing, implementing, and debating a single, coordinated set of policies perceived to be about the country's culture and its national identity. Arguably, related policies in different spheres of life are developed through a decentralized institutional system usually lacking a single, stated, societal vision or longitudinal plan.

It may, in fact, be analytically useful to have countries like the United States without a single, clearly articulated and official cultural policy, because it forces us to grapple with the analytic problems embedded in the notions of culture and cultural policy and the practices of invoking them. It is cases like this that compel us to pose questions about the conditions under which countries may or may not develop and highlight official cultural and national identity policies.

Here are some suggestions. I suspect that it is the perception of weakness relative to other countries—however conceptualized and felt—that triggers and drives some official cultural policies. I suspect that high-level government officials become active participants if they believe that sectors of the country's population not well represented in major levels of government pose a serious threat to a vision of the country they care about or to a social group with which they identify. Likewise, we should then also consider what it means for a country not to have an activist cultural policy. Does it make sense, for example, to interpret the absence of an explicit cultural policy as a sign of national consensus with regard to national identity? Or perhaps as a sign that state institutions are particularly effective and experienced at exercising control in a less visible, more ideologically hegemonic manner reminiscent of Antonio Gramsci's comments about class domination?[25]

I have argued so far that a good part of the reason governments assert their say over the shape of their populations' cultures is that they link the idea of culture with respectability, necessity, unity, and the minimization of divisiveness, especially vis-à-vis the rest of the world. One particular aspect of this linkage requires special mention: the widespread acceptance of the assumption that it is culture that defines a nation as the socially, economically, and politically situated product of the latter half of this particular century.

Independent countries in the late twentieth century apparently feel the need to justify (rationalize? legitimate?) their claims to statehood by invoking a cultural argument. Other things have indeed been invoked in the past. A culturalist form of legitimation (or means of attempted unification) takes over in the late twentieth century—the contemporary counterpart of "racial" theories, spiritual theories, economic/class theories, and naturalist theories that dominated previous centuries. Is it somehow linked to conditions currently theorized as "postmodern"? Or perhaps more a reaction to those conditions, or a reflection of those conditions? A push toward global culturalism has been particularly evident in the work of UNESCO since the late 1960s: the sponsorship of two world conferences on cultural policies (the first in 1970, the second in 1982) and the commissioning and publication in the 1970s and 1980s of well over forty country-by-country reports on cultural policies.

The "ethnicization" of American society over the last twenty years (by which I mean the labeling of many group phenomena as ethnic and the promotion of certain things associated with each group as issues of ethnic pride) is a good example of recent culturalism. The switch from talk of races and immigrant groups to talk of ethnic groups and ethnic identity carries with it what I call the culturalization of difference. A public discourse that promotes intergroup tolerance employs the notion of cultural pluralism, not biological diversity, multilingualism, or class harmony. There appears to be a belief that cultural differences are valid and must be acknowledged. Other conceivable and prior perceptions of difference are treated, by contrast, as at best problematic. By implication, we learn to explain and validate the existence of collective identities by invoking cultural differences and, in the process, promote the view that all legitimate group entities—official "nations" among them—can and must be able to be identified by their cultural characteristics.[26]

It is hard to assess exactly just how much governments with activist cultural policies implicitly adopt these assumptions of legitimacy, rights, and value, but it seems clear that at this historical juncture they are at least semiconsciously responding to the fact that other countries in the world operate under those assumptions.

═══

When I set out ten years ago to do research in Israel, I saw myself studying "the Israeli obsession with ethnicity," not some Israeli obsession with culture.[27] By 1984, however, I had become convinced that a particular objectification of culture was implicated in the Israeli obsession with ethnicity, and was instrumental in perpetuating it. Changes in both the United States and Israel had made me wary of people who invoke culture to explain social, political, or economic phenomena, but they also drew my attention to the frequency with which that happened and the circumstances in which it tended to happen.

By the early 1980s, both the United States and Israel were in the midst of what I call "the ethnic revolution"—a discursive insistence on the celebration of ethnicity conceptualized as the celebration of cultural diversity. As cultural pluralism became the motto for this new public stance toward the nature and maintenance of certain (nonthreatening) social differences, "ethnic culture" typically became essentialized, celebrated, and pinpointed as the source of difference we would have to learn to live with and value.[28] Holism had returned as an instrument of liberal politics seeking an ideological way to counter the devaluation and continued underclass status of large sectors of a country's population.

I had gone to Israel to explore the way in which social, political, and economic domination of one half of Israeli Jews by the other half took place ideologically—without most people knowing or noticing.[29] I had not set out to study cultural differences, or even cultural similarities among Jews in Israel. But the more I heard Israelis make references to cultural differences the more I heard a discourse on culture intersecting the persistent discourse on ethnicity in a highly patterned way: when people talked about there being cultural differences, culture was invoked to explain (justify?) continuing social, economic, and political inequalities.

These perceptions were in step with the work of Iraqi-born Israeli sociologist Sammy Smooha, who had begun to rail against social scientists and politicians for increasingly highlighting cultural differences in discussions of "the persistence of ethnicity" in Israeli society, thereby perpetuating the view that it was culture and not political economy that had created and continually re-created ethnic differences in Israeli society.[30] I also found support in the work of Argentinian-born Israeli sociologist Shlomo Swirski, who showed that one could get mileage out of asking questions of the structure of Israel's political economy and the distribution of Ashkenazi (European-origin) Jews, Sephardi ("Middle Eastern"-origin) Jews, and Israeli Arabs within that structure, following the model of earlier "dependency theorists."[31] These writers encouraged my impulse to avoid treating culture as some independent variable. I hypothesized that the ongoing public discourse on ethnicity in Israel was a social and political phenomenon that needed to be examined as constructing, much more than reflecting, its referents.

Indeed, the intersection of the discourse on ethnicity with the discourse on culture was powerful and invidious. The alleged backwardness of some sectors of Israeli society was frequently attributed to some aspect of "their culture" or even to the force of "traditionalism" in "their culture." A form of liberal paternalism exonerated individuals, but blamed "the culture" with which they were identified.

So strongly entrenched is this theme in public discourse that when liberal commentators—foremost among them our fellow anthropologists—have sought to counter it, developing an alternative explanation has become de rigueur. Shlomo Swirski's 1981 book, for example (*Orientals and Ashkenazim in Israel: The Ethnic Division of Labor*), was deliberately entitled *Lo Nekhshalim, ela Menukhshalim* in Hebrew, better translated as "not people who have failed, but rather people who have been made to fail." Nitza Droyan, Maurice Roumani, Harvey Goldberg, and the many contributors to the journal *Pe'amim* have taken the strategy of writing the histories of non-European Jewish communities to show how flat and oversimplifying are the images entailed in the charges of cultural traditionalism.[32] Harvey Goldberg, Yoram Bilu, Henry Abramowitz, Shlomo Deshen, Moshe Shokeid, and Alex Weingrod have all taken the tack of analyzing customs, festivals, and rituals deemed "traditional" in Israel and showing how many central features of these "traditions" are really the product of the immigrants' encounter with discrimination in Israel, the Israeli bureaucracy, and the material conditions of their lives in Israel.[33] But in all cases the nemesis is the culturalist argument that continues to be invoked in the dominant discourse on "the persistence of ethnicity" in Israel.

Note some of the vivid illusions fostered by that pattern of invoking culture. It is tempting to read the use of "culture" to refer to nonelite circles or to large, diverse communities as an adaptation of a populist, anthropological sense of culture. But the fact is that in these situations "cultures" are being evaluated and placed on some hierarchical scale of comparative value with an objectified European culture sitting pretty at the top. This is the elite European/Eurocentric sense of culture masking itself as populist.

The intrinsic hierarchy of the culturalist argument becomes even more evident if we notice what happens when culture is invoked to provide praise, rather than to denigrate. Especially in the context of state institutions, we see a pattern of calling material objects, music, customs, and values of European Jewry *culture* (*tarbut*), while relegating the same kinds of things to the discursive status of *heritage* (*moreshet*) when they come from non-European Jewry.[34] A few activist Sephardi intellectuals have called this distinction the "folklorization" of non-Ashkenazi cultural life, identifying it as yet another ideological way in which the Ashkenazi population structured discrimination into Israeli society. At stake in this stream of public discourse is the question of the future—of what is "good enough" to be valued and continued in contemporary society vs. what can be praised safely as long as it stays in the past. Institutionally, in schools, books, museums, and funding offices, the canon remains overwhelmingly Eurocentric. Only in the still-marginal Sephardi intellectuals' movement called East for Peace, and their magazine *Apirion*, have I seen any serious discussion in the past decade of how Middle Eastern and North African values and perceptions could be used as the basis for understanding value in the present-day and future Israeli society (regardless of the "ethnic" distribution of the population).[35]

As I encountered this intersection of the discourses on ethnicity and culture, I became increasingly convinced of the enormous hegemonic power of the concept of culture itself and of the practices of invoking it (as well as of not invoking it) in Israel. Pierre Bourdieu's recent work corroborates that finding in the context of French society, by sensitizing us to the ways the upper socioeconomic crusts of contemporary French society employ "taste," "aesthetics," and "culture" as signs of social distinction whose referents get redefined and adjusted, seemingly unconsciously, so that they always differentiate between the social classes of French society.[36] Note that, in such a setting, it isn't just the alleged content of the culture that differentiates; it is the concept of culture itself that carries in its continued discursive usage a huge social, economic, and political value.

But as I turn to other countries, even to other regions, for perspectives on Israeli discourse about culture and the theoretical questions it has compelled me to ask, I am further struck by the apparent success European countries have had over the past 100 to 150 years convincing the rest of the world that culture is a "thing," that it has value, and that any self-respecting group of people must have it. People may contest the extent to which the content of their culture must be European in origin in order for it to be of value, but they are still overwhelmingly buying into the elite European idea that there is such a thing as culture and that it is through one's culture that one's value is judged. We need only think about China's current "culture fever" or Japan's ongoing Nihonjinron or Papua New Guinea's panic about developing a national culture or the Quebecois insistence on Quebecois cultural identity,[37] or even the fact that most countries of the world today have official ministries of culture, to see my point.

What is, I think, most revealing is the way in which the very idea of hierarchies of value, inherent in the old elite European (and Eurocentric) concept of culture, manifests itself, though differently, in different countries' discourses on culture. This is where global culturalism and societal culturalism intersect but still need to be differentiated. There is a pattern here. In much of the third world—in those countries that are seen as both economically and culturally poor or underdeveloped, whether recently postcolonial or not—we find that the public discourse on culture is part of a broad-ranging collective self-criticism. Cultural policies in these countries don't just describe what there is that the government, the elites, or even the nonelites seek to value; they usually prescribe a particular direction the country should take "culturally" in order to correct for some perceived societal flaw, such as internalized oppression, technological backwardness, destructive intergroup fighting, or a lack of historical awareness.

Such discourses on culture imply that any and all characteristics of the "collective self" are proper and necessary subjects of societal self-criticism. But note that they frame themselves as discourses on "culture." A culturalist argument is implicit in this type of discourse. Asking why it is that "we" are not "better," or "more stable," or "more self-sufficient," or "more independent," or "more influential," and framing one's answers in terms of "culture" implies comparing "cultures," seeing culture as something of value, and perpetuating an objectification which is, by definition, a comparative statement of value. What is interesting is that participants in these discourses of collective self-criticism around the world seem to be unwittingly letting that elite European, Eurocentric notion of culture-as-value serve as the preeminent criterion of value.

The Israeli case provides a useful contrast not because it is a Jewish society or a Middle Eastern society or a plural society or even an embattled society, but because it is (was) a European settler society. A significant segment of the population sees itself as European, not just as aspiring to be European. The still-dominant view is that the value of the society rests on its being Jewish and "Western" (read: European and Eurocentric). Any positive reference to culture almost always implies a European and Eurocentric culture, which they claim as their own and in contrast to which they disparage others. Criticism of it can seemingly only be specific—in the narrowest sense of culture as art, music, literature, philosophy, and theater. For criticism of other, wider-ranging social, political, or economic referents to be couched in terms of culture would be, I think, to suggest the need for much more of a break with European societies than the majority (or at least the dominant) population seems to want. To engage in major collective self-criticism and attribute problems to the (presumably mainstream Eurocentric) culture would be to criticize this thing they call culture that they objectify, aspire to, and claim as their own. A broad cultural criticism can take only two forms: either criticism of the cultures of "others," or criticism of individual performers and artists whose execution or reproduction of "culture" may not be quite up to snuff.

The most poignant illustration of this constraint is the flourishing of a discourse on Jewish racism among Israeli Jews since the mid-1980s and the almost total absence of references to it in Israel as a problem of Israeli culture. Here is an example of collective self-criticism employing terms other than "culture." Judaism, the Holocaust, morality, Jewishness, Jewish values, secular humanism, tolerance, rights, and mutual respect are the terms and frames of that heated and often pained discussion: culture is not, except when it intersects with the politics of ethnicity, as when someone seeks to "explain" the unworthiness or backwardness of a Sephardic Jew's views or behaviors by attributing their "racism" to "their culture." "Racism" is not, however, ever presented as a criticism of the culture of that Israeli society still hegemonically controlled by Ashkenazi Jews. A particular objectification of culture that is, in the Israeli case, both substantively and conceptually Eurocentric makes it highly unlikely that Israeli discourses on culture would ever be coextensive with its discourses of collective self-criticism.

=====

What does all this mean? We might all already agree that framing certain things as cultural and others as not is neither accidental nor innocent, but I worry that in conceptualizing cultural politics too substantively, empirically, or regionally or locally, intellectuals, community activists, and politicians are, even in acts of resistance against European hegemony, perpetuating the very terms—of hierarchies of differential value—that constitute that hegemony. And in the process we may well be missing the more significant phenomenon—that these struggles are taking place now not because of existing or expanding or narrowing "cultural" differences among groups of people, but because at this point in time much of the world has internalized culture as the marker of difference. In the end, where others see cultural politics as leading to chaos, I see it as homogenizing. And where others bemoan cultural politics as divisive, I bemoan it as consolidating a *single* vision of privilege and difference that remains elite and European in origin and Eurocentric in conception.

Interlocking patterns of global and societal culturalism are late-twentieth-century phenomena. They give the appearance of equality of value and multiplicity of form. They project positive images, unlike invocations of race and racism, class and classism, development and underdevelopment, barbarism and civilization, which have long been thought to project only negative images. They imply decentralization. They also tease. They promote a concern held by European elites and extend it throughout much of the world. They centralize and focus discussion of a particular sort when many other sorts had previously coexisted and are logically just as conceivable. And they continue to be used by populations in power to dominate, persuade, control, and justify—taking advantage of the simultaneous communicative inefficiency and community valorization of the cultural.

Notes

1 The department's official title; in 1988 the Duke administration split the anthropology department up into a department of cultural anthropology and a department of biological anthropology and anatomy.

2   In the spring of 1991 a session I organized for the annual meetings of the American Ethnological Society, entitled "Is Culturalism an Improvement on Racism?" drew a standing-room-only crowd. And just six weeks later at a working meeting of heads of area studies programs funded by the Rockefeller Foundation, I discovered that one of my colleagues at the University of Pennsylvania, anthropologist and editor of *Public Culture* Arjun Appadurai, was himself in the middle of drafting a paper on what he is calling culturalist movements. See also Jean Jackson, "Is There a Way to Talk about Making Culture without Making Enemies?" *Dialectical Anthropology* 14 (1989): 127–43.

3   For perspective, see George Stocking, Jr., *Race, Culture, and Evolution: Essays in the History of Anthropology* (New York, 1968), as well as the history of anthropology series that he presently edits for the University of Wisconsin Press.

4   The quickly canonized texts on this subject are George Marcus and Michael Fischer, *Anthropology as Cultural Critique: An Experimental Moment in the Human Sciences* (Chicago, 1986); and *Writing Culture: The Poetics and Politics of Ethnography,* ed. James Clifford and George Marcus (Berkeley, 1986).

5   A representative older collection of such work is *Cognitive Anthropology,* ed. Stephen Tyler (New York, 1969). An up-to-date version is *Cultural Models in Language and Thought,* ed. Dorothy Holland and Naomi Quinn (Cambridge, 1987).

6   I still find Clifford Geertz's *The Interpretation of Cultures* (New York, 1973) to be his seminal work, though his more recent book *Works and Lives: The Anthropologist as Author* (Palo Alto, Calif., 1988) extends the analysis to the present-day struggles over ethnographic interpretation. For a broader and interdisciplinary perspective, see *Interpretive Social Science: A Second Look,* ed. Paul Rabinow and William Sullivan (Berkeley, 1987).

7   For decades the field of anthropology in Great Britain has been dominated by the Association of Social Anthropologists, which has stressed social, political, and economic processes, functions, and structures. Of course, many of their earlier ethnographies are among those that have come under critical scrutiny.

8   An earlier generation of anthropologists emerging on the scene in the 1950s and 1960s shared some of the current misgivings when they chose to work on peasantries, urbanization, and political economy, rather than on "tribal" or "primitive" cultures.

9   I mean "self" in several senses: individual identity and subjectivity as well as collectivity/community identity and subjectivity, as in struggles for group self-determination. See Virginia R. Dominguez, "How the Self Stacks the Deck," *Anthropology and Humanism Quarterly* 16 (March 1991): 11–14.

10 Peircean pragmatics can fruitfully complement Foucauldian analyses of the link between knowledge and power. See, for example, *Semiotic Mediation: Sociocultural and Psychological Perspectives,* ed. Elizabeth Mertz and Richard Parmentier

(Orlando, Fla., 1985) in conjunction with Michel Foucault, *The Order of Things: An Archaeology of the Human Sciences* (New York, 1970).

11 Etymological evidence situated in social and politcal history makes a strong case for this claim, illuminating what James Clifford has called *The Predicament of Culture* (Cambridge, Mass., 1989).

12 Intersecting points of view appear in Edward Said, "Representing the Colonized, Anthropology's Interlocutors," *Critical Inquiry* 15 (Winter 1989): 205–25; James Clifford, Virginia R. Dominguez, and Trin Min-ha, "The Politics of Representations," in *Discussions in Contemporary Culture*, ed. Hal Foster (Seattle, 1987); and Benedict Anderson, *Imagined Communities: Reflections on the Origin and Spread of Nationalism* (London, 1983).

13 Useful references are the series on country-by-country cultural policies published by UNESCO and those specifically on European countries published by the Council of Europe. Over forty separate volumes of this sort published in the 1970s and 1980s are part of Duke University's library holdings. They include socialist and nonsocialist countries, European, Latin American, African, Middle Eastern, and South and East Asian countries.

14 Especially insightful is *Nationalist Ideologies and the Production of National Cultures*, ed. Richard Fox (Washington, D.C., 1990).

15 Pierre Bourdieu, *Outline of a Theory of Practice*, trans. Richard Nice (Cambridge, 1977), 171–83.

16 See Pierre Bourdieu, *Distinction: A Social Critique of the Judgment of Taste*, trans. Richard Nice (Cambridge, 1984); and Uli Linke, "Folklore, Anthropology, and the Government of Social Life," *Comparative Studies in Society and History* 32 (January 1990): 117–48.

17 Participating were Harumi Befu, Walwipha Burusratanaphand, Chua Beng-Huat, Allen Chun, Burt Feintuch, Lawrence Foanaota, Wari Iamo, Lamont Lindstrom, James Ritchie, Ma Rong, Yos Santasomba, Jacob Simet, David Whisnant, Geoffrey White, David Wu, and Haiou Yang. Revised drafts of the position papers will be published in a volume I am coediting with my East-West Center colleagues Elizabeth Buck and David Wu.

18 For a published version, see David Wu, "Chinese Minority Policy and the Meaning of Minority Culture: The Example of Bai in Yunnan, China," *Human Organization* 49 (March 1990): 1–13.

19 I am grateful to Haiou Yang at the East-West Center for this information and the sources she called to my attention: Wang He, "Traditional Culture and Modernization: A Review of the General Situation of Cultural Studies in China in the Recent Years," *Social Sciences in China* (Winter 1986); and Greremie Barme, "The Chinese Velvet Prison: Culture in the New Age, 1976–1989," 1989.

20 An expanded version of such an exposition can be found in *The Conversation of Culture: Folklorists and the Public Sector*, ed. Burt Feintuch (Lexington, Ky., 1988).

21 We in the United States like to call attention to that problem in other countries, though, as Michel Foucault aptly articulated in *Discipline and Punish: The Birth of the Prison*, trans. Alan Sheridan (New York, 1977), it doesn't take a notoriously totalitarian regime to develop a system that is invasive and highly regulatory.

22 Variants of note are described in Teodor Shanin, "Ethnicity in the Soviet Union: Analytical Perceptions and Political Strategies," *Comparative Studies in Society and History* 31 (July 1989): 409–24; David Whisnant, "Sandinista Cultural Policy: Notes toward an Analysis in Historical Context," in *Central America: Historical Perspectives on the Contemporary Crisis*, ed. R. Lee Woodward, Jr. (New York, 1988); and Wari Iamo, "Culture in Papua New Guinea Nationalism" (Proceedings of the Symposium on Nationalism in Papua New Guinea, Association for Social Anthropology in Oceania Meetings, Kauai, Hawaii, 20–25 March 1990).

23 See my book *People as Subject, People as Object: Selfhood and Peoplehood in Contemporary Israel* (Madison, Wis., 1989).

24 Singapore, Lebanon, Canada, and Yugoslavia have all spent much of the post–World War II era promoting intercommunal coexistence and intercultural tolerance in order to survive as unified national entities. The experience of Lebanon and, increasingly, Yugoslavia make it valid to wonder how successful that policy can be in the long run.

25 Antonio Gramsci, *Selections from the Prison Notebooks*, trans. Quintin Hoare and Geoffrey N. Smith (New York, 1971).

26 Two critically insightful takes on the ethnicity literature are Brackette Williams, "A Class Act: Anthropology and the Race to Nation across Ethnic Terrain," *Annual Review of Anthropology* 18 (1989): 401–44; and Phyllis P. Chock, "The Landscape of Enchantment: Redaction in a Theory of Ethnicity," *Cultural Anthropology* 4 (May 1989): 163–81.

27 Dominguez, *People as Subject, People as Object*.

28 A very different counterargument articulated by Fredrik Barth in *Ethnic Groups and Boundaries* (Boston, 1969) was highly influential in certain scholarly circles but not in the most public, popular discourses on ethnicity. Review essays on the Israeli "ethnic revolution" include Harvey Goldberg, "Introduction: Culture and Ethnicity in the Study of Israel," *Ethnic Groups* 1 (1977): 163–86; and Alex Weingrod's introduction and conclusion to *Studies in Israeli Ethnicity: After the Ingathering* (New York, 1985).

29 European-origin Jews (except for most of those from Spain and the Balkan Peninsula, who are not considered Ashkenazi) have dominated economic, artistic, and political life in Israel for decades, although by the mid- to late 1970s they stopped being the demographic majority among Israeli Jews. More than half of the Jewish population of Israel comes from North Africa, the

Middle East, South Asia, and the Balkan Peninsula and are dubbed Oriental or Sephardic Jews.

30 See, for example, Sammy Smooha, *Israel: Pluralism and Conflict* (London, 1978).

31 Shlomo Swirski, *Orientals and Ashkenazim in Israel: The Ethnic Division of Labor* (in Hebrew) (Haifa, 1981).

32 A fair amount of this literature, including the journal *Pe'amim*, is published in Hebrew, not English (the preferred language for academic publications within the Israeli academy). A good example is Nitza Droyan, *Without a Magic Carpet: Yemenite Settlement in Eretz Israel* (1881–1914) (in Hebrew) (Jerusalem, 1981).

33 For example, Shlomo Deshen and Moshe Shokeid, *The Predicament of Homecoming: Cultural and Social Life of North African Immigrants in Israel* (Ithaca, N.Y., 1974); Harvey Goldberg, "The Mimuna and the Minority Status of Moroccan Jews," *Ethnology* 17 (1978): 75–87; and *Studies in Israeli Ethnicity*, ed. Alex Weingrod.

34 See chaps. 4 and 5 of my *People as Subject, People as Object*. See also my article "The Politics of Heritage in Contemporary Israel," in Fox, ed., *Nationalist Ideologies and the Production of National Cultures*, 130–47.

35 Alternative publications periodically surface and touch on the issue, but rarely succeed in the long run. The magazine *Iton Akher* is a promising recent example.

36 Bourdieu, *Distinction*.

37 See Richard Handler, *Nationalism and the Politics of Culture in Quebec* (Madison, Wis., 1988).

The Politics of the "We"

MARIANNA TORGOVNICK

T here is a kind of "we" in cultural criticism that seems utterly convincing—rounded, magisterial, confident—and enough to make you
want to die if you can't be part of it. This "we" is more than a pronoun. In fact, the actual pronoun is only the most obvious marker,
the sign and symbol of how the circle of culture gets drawn: who's in,
who's out, why, and to what effect.

Here, for example, is critic Georg Lukács, using an impressive "we" in
his 1922 essay on reification, the process by which people become alien-
ated from their work, cut off from psychic development, and turned into
objects:

> man can[not] bring his physical and psychic "qualities" into play
> without their being subjected increasingly to this reifying process.
> We need only think of marriage, and without troubling to point to
> the developments of the nineteenth century we can remind our-
> selves of the way in which Kant, for example, described the situa-
> tion.[1]

I admire Lukács's essay for its insights; I envy its intellectual power and
ability to compel other critics to cite it.[2] Yet the "we" in this passage in-
timidates readers by testing knowledge and background, some of it fairly
detailed. What *did* Kant say about marriage? In which text? What other
nineteenth-century developments does Lukács have in mind? If these
questions make you even the tiniest bit uncomfortable, that is one reason
the critical "we" and its equivalents are so effective: they make readers
want to pass the test, to be part of the community addressed, part of the

in-group the writing defines. Academics are especially vulnerable to the pressure this kind of "we" exerts: when references are unfamiliar, they have learned to smile, noncommitally.

"We" has traditionally been the pronoun of choice for popes, kings, and queens; it comes with the territory of office. For critics, the trick in using it as a source of authority seems to be believing that the litany of great names comprises an aristocracy of its own, a line of descent as yet incomplete, awaiting one more name: "one of us" is about to enter the conversation, and the new arrival is the writer himself. Whether or not the writer agrees fully with the powerful ancestors matters less than the fact of essential conversational relationship. The writer needs to feel a part of the "we" as naturally, as inevitably, as royal heirs entitled to the throne: born to it, no special effort involved.

But though Lukács's "we" asserts membership in a unified European intellectual community, he did not fit comfortably into any such community, as some compelling facts from his life make clear. Lukács was a twentieth-century Hungarian Jew in Christian Eastern Europe, the son of a wealthy banker.[3] The original family name was Lowinger, transposed into the Magyar tongue by Lukács's father, an assimilated Jew who sent his children to schools for upper-middle-class gentiles. Lukács experienced throughout his formative period a vivid sense of alienation that culminated in his first major work, The Theory of the Novel, which defines modernity as a state incommensurate with the premodern condition of harmony and grace between individuals and their surroundings he called "immanent totality."[4] In his early work, Lukács felt considerable nostalgia for this lost condition of unity; in his later work, he believed a new source of unity had been found in the project of Marxism.

This philosopher and critic was also a political leader and government figure. But when he did not actually hold office, he usually lived outside Hungary, in political exile, in embattled relationship to the existing government or certain forms of Marxism.[5] Despite being a political leader, Lukács felt considerable concern about the meaning of Hungarian national identity within the shifting political contexts of twentieth-century Eastern Europe. His concerns were exacerbated by the fact that Hungarians who wrote literature or philosophy (including Lukács himself) normally did not write in their native language.[6] In itself, Hungarian identity was an issue upon which awareness of German intellectual traditions (like those represented by Kant) and the German language (in which Lukács wrote) always impinged as "father" and devourer.

Lukács claimed that his early background and personal history had little influence on his writing. It seems more likely that concepts such as "transcendental homelessness" and "reification" were connected to his outsider experiences: to have arisen in part from being Jewish by birth, being a member of the "homeless race" in philosophical traditions, and the essentialized object of anti-Semitism. For many European writers, especially at the beginning of the twentieth century, the concept of race is highly fragmented, politically charged, and determined by factors not generally considered racial in the United States—language group, political history, religion, and national origin, for example—so that allusions to the Anglo-Saxons, the Slavs, or the Jews as a race are common. For writers like Lukács, who belonged to "races" deemed exotic but often inferior, the urge to be part of some collective European "we" was extremely powerful.[7]

A Jew without religion or heritage, a politician without a secure national identity, a Marxist censored by many Marxists: Lukács's history of difficulty in fitting comfortably within larger groups is manifest. But so too is the desire for identification. Lukács's "we" affirms the privileges of membership; it omits what must have been a vivid sense of exclusion. So that while his writing sounds confident and may arouse anxieties in readers, it also and simultaneously masks the writer's potential concerns and insecurities. Both sides of the circuit are energized by the rage to be part of the "we," to be a cultural insider.

Lukács bears comparison on this point to other writers, of whom Dante and T.S. Eliot can serve as examples. During an audacious scene near the beginning of the Inferno, Dante has just been ushered by Virgil into Limbo, the anteroom to Hell, where the virtuous pagans are housed. There, amid "a blaze of light which was enclosed in a hemisphere of darkness," he sees a party of four great classical poets and thinkers conversing. The group sees Virgil and Dante and interrupts its conversation to "make a sign of greeting" that marks Dante as "the sixth among those high intelligences."[8] Dante is crowned with laurel even here, just a few pages into his epic Commedia. The poet affirms his greatness in advance; his welcoming reception by the prior poets has the force of certainty rather than daydream.

T.S. Eliot, a great admirer of Dante, reproduces the poet's moment with the great masters in his essay "Tradition and the Individual Talent." Eliot was thirty-one when he wrote this essay, which is riddled with anxious allusions to the question of how a poet can sustain himself after the age of twenty-five. Eliot's answer is establishing rapport with what he calls "the mind of Europe," the mind of "the nation," broadened beyond national boundaries by being linked to the "critical turn of mind" of "the race." Here is Eliot's version of the same incomplete circle that Dante invokes at the beginning of Inferno:

> [T]he historical sense compels a man to write not merely with his own generation in his bones, but with a feeling that the whole of the literature of Europe from Homer and within it the whole of the literature of his own country has a simultaneous existence and com-poses a simultaneous order. . . . The existing monuments form an ideal order among themselves, which is modified by the introduc-tion of the new (the really new) work of art among them. The existing order is complete before the new work arrives; for the order to per-sist after the supervention of novelty, the whole order must be, if ever so slightly, altered.[9]

Eliot identifies with the great names of the past as one in an immortal but expandable line of descent. Like Dante and Lukács, Eliot writes as if he has no doubts, no doubts at all, that his poems—and the very essay at hand—are effecting the subtle, inexorable readjustments he describes in the Western tradition.

Yet as for Lukács, even the briefest of biographies shows that the criti-cal "we" was likely to have assuaged feelings of doubt and exclusion. Dante was a thirteenth-century Florentine, a believing Christian and a fierce patriot, living in bitter exile at the end of his life and writing his Commedia, the work that will justify himself, his political cause, and the divine order to a world in which neither fellow citizens nor popes could be trusted. Eliot was a twentieth-century American from St. Louis, Mis-souri, seared by marital unhappiness, beset by religious doubts (though soon to experience conversion), living voluntarily in England, with little acknowledged intellectual identification with the United States.

Even rendered schematically, the life histories of Lukács, Dante, and Eliot are not only different from each other but from what was considered normative in their cultures. Those differences would multiply if the descriptions brought other categories to bear, such as class origins, wealth, sexuality, parenthood, and temperament. Their expressed political allegiances varied enormously, spanning a spectrum from revolutionary (Lukács) to conservative (Eliot). Their strongest shared experience was, perhaps, exile from their homelands. Yet in each case, the writer positions himself within a "we" that effaces particularities and affirms identification with a larger body whose common features are relatively bloodless—consisting mostly of maleness, European origin, and education in literary and philosophical traditions. Some might call this unblinking allegiance to what Eliot calls "the historical sense," to the Western tradition in its most abstract form, transcendence—and see it as the proper goal of education. But it is also a shortcut to authority that precludes an honest relationship to existing traditions.

In "The Mark of Gender," Monique Wittig says that the personal pronoun, the "I," marks "the pathways and the means of entrance into language" and asserts, in philosophical terms, the subject status of the speaker or writer.[10] Wittig further says that the plural form multiplies the effect of the singular personal pronoun: "[E]ach new class that fights for power must, to reach its goal, represent its interest as the common interest of all the members of the society."[11] As an affirmation of subject status, the "I" is strategic; the "we" amplifies the same strategy, with a leap into the universal that allows the writer to speak for the culture—hence its special lure for cultural critics.

The "we" I have described so far betrays the spirit of the first person at both levels. It offers the bribe of authority and tradition, and the security of belonging—but at the cost of losing touch with the "I" behind the "we." It establishes false alliances that cover up the writer's sense of isolation or pain. It coerces and assumes the agreement of the "you" it addresses. And it masks the multifaceted complexity of group identities. Critics have been sensitive to the political dangers of the "we" as a rhetorical device that either ignores or demonizes individuals or groups it excludes—no trivial danger.[12] But the "we" also effects a repressive politics of inclusion, in which those who identify with it must surrender crucial aspects of themselves.

I began this essay thinking that my resistance to the politics of the "we" came from the desire to participate as Dante, Eliot, or Lukács did, and from a certain frustration that I could not. I identified my inability to use their "we" with being Italian American and especially with being female, for many of the passages I have quoted suggest that this voice comes most naturally to a man, not a woman—"a man" who feels "his generation" in "his bones," whose intellectual fathers welcome adopted sons. Part of my resistance to the politics of the "we," part of the reason that I notice it at all, no doubt has to do with being outside some of the traditional "we's" unmarked assumptions, most of all its assumption of masculinity.

But I am not, when all is said and done, barred from using the cultural "we" in any definitive way—my education and profession guarantee that, as well as the existence, by 1991, of numerous women's traditions with which to affiliate. I have even used the "we" extensively in my writing.[13] My resistance, even hostility, to the "we" as it has generally been used must have additional sources. I believe it to be in part temperamental, having to do with the fear of being a joiner that I have cultivated since adolescence, when I both wanted to be part of the in-crowd and felt that what I wanted was mean-spirited. But the phenomenon is not limited to adolescents. And it has consequences for writing by intellectuals.

I do not object to the "we" voice in and of itself. What I object to is the easy slide from "I" to "we" that takes place almost unconsciously for many users of the first-person plural or its equivalents—and is often the hidden essence of cultural criticism. This slide can make the "we" function not as a device to link writer and reader, or as a particularized group voice, or even the voice of "the culture," but rather as a covert, and sometimes coercive, universal. I would like to slow down that slide to appreciate the full deceptiveness of the false cultural "we," and then its relationship to some current issues.

But first I need to come closer to home, to the immediate contexts for me. I never met Dante or Lukács or Eliot. I did meet Lionel Trilling, at least slightly, when I was a graduate student at Columbia University during the 1970s. Trilling illustrates with unusual clarity the dynamics of the "we" in cultural criticism, a term with which his name was synonymous for several decades.[14] People associate the cultural "we" with Trilling and, when the people are women, they almost always criticize it as an exclusionary device.[15] For me, Trilling remains a touchstone of the "we"—a critical voice I wanted both to emulate and avoid.

In The Opposing Self (1955), Trilling says that the "we" reveals a "writer's notion of what constitutes the interesting and the valuable . . . what constitutes 'us'"—and this is a bald statement of the "we's" exclusionary bent.[16] When he was accused of addressing a changeable "we," but most often the narrow "we" of New York intellectuals, Trilling disagreed, but defined further.[17] Yes, he said, his "we" changes from essay to essay, but it is never narrow. Most often, he said, it refers to "the temper of our age," a temper embodied in New York intellectuals because of the "assiduity" with which this group pursues ideas. Even more strongly, Trilling claimed that this group represented all others: "The structure of our society is such that a class of this kind is bound by organic filaments to groups less culturally fluent which are susceptible to its influence."[18]

For Trilling, the "we" was powerfully, almost infinitely expandable. He advocated a Mandarin or Brahmin system—other groups being, in Trilling's words, "less culturally fluent"—but not really what he thought of as an exclusionary one. Anyone not part of the intelligentsia was "organically filamented" with it; anyone could rise from one group to another. Someone could be born into a "less culturally fluent" class yet learn to speak as an intellectual.

Trilling's idea of "organic filamentation" was part of his belief that universities are sites of acculturation and advancement that serve in the United States what we might call for short the "melting pot" project of American culture. His intentions were democratic. But in presiding over the mechanisms by which "cultural fluency" was achieved, his "we" could produce chillingly coercive effects, as in the following sentences, which are typical of his style:

> Emma is more difficult than any of the hard books we admire [Proust or Joyce, for example].

> If we speak of encyclopedias, there is one actual encyclopedia which we must have in recollection—the great Encyclopedie itself.

> Which brings us to the third book of Gulliver's Travels.[19]

In the 1980s and 1990s, the use of the canon of great books as Trilling uses it in these sentences—as the medium of "cultural fluency"—has often been linked to a repressive intellectual politics. But the canon existed for critics like Trilling in a different spirit. It was a gatekeeper of sorts—but one thought of as genial and generous. Anyone who took the trouble to read great books would be admitted through the gate; more, anyone willing to take the critic's version of things on provisional faith could be admitted to the "we," could come along with "us" to the third book of *Gulliver's Travels*. Belief in the open gate of tradition is one reason some critics have been so hostile toward what they call "canon busting": these recent tendencies seem to besmirch an educational mission they find noble and socially useful.

Ultimately, Trilling's view of the canon as the very thing that will make culture cohere dovetails with recent critiques. There is no question of the canon coming to the masses: the masses must come to the canon. But it's important to catch the open invitation in Trilling's sentences, the way that all readers are welcome to read the texts to which he refers and the way that the reading will suffice. Trilling's sentences present themselves as the Ellis Island of intellectual life, and are the product of an immigrant culture. The canon is like the Statue of Liberty, transforming the huddled masses into an intellectual community.

This assimilationist metaphor cuts to the bone of the politics of the "we" in writing about culture today. As a working-class child whose parents did not go to college, I believe in the difference education makes in a person's life. As an undergraduate and graduate student I felt, and even now as a professor, I feel the power of the model that says that reading the same books, the great books, will make intellectual and social life fulfill the desire for seamless community. This faith in books, this hunger for wisdom and harmony to come from books, retains its allure. Yet the model was always utopian, as Trilling's history reveals.

Thinking of Trilling, I recall immediately certain facts: his immigrant origins, his Jewishness, his embattled status as a young professor at Columbia, which had not previously tenured Jews and told Trilling, when it tried to terminate his contract, that he would be more comfortable somewhere else.[20] These well-known aspects of Trilling's history may well have mediated his predilection for the "we." As Russell Jacoby and others have noted, Trilling tended to be "always amazed and appreciative of his good fortune" in the profession—even though he had to negotiate his relationship to "the tradition" and fight, tenaciously, for what he got.[21] All too humanly, he identified with the forces that once threatened to exclude him. And he became their defender and embodiment after the student activism of 1968, which accelerated his move from liberalism to reaction.

All his professional life, Trilling tended to separate his "uptown" exis-

tence as an Anglophile professor at Columbia from his "downtown" existence writing first for Jewish and then for liberal periodicals.[22] He didn't
leave a memoir, or any fully autobiographical writing, and his critical
prose rarely contains allusions to his personal history outside his life as
a teacher.[23] When I attended his class in the early 1970s, near the end of
his life, Trilling had taken to reading aloud long passages from his essays
and praising them as "elegant" or "well-put" without—and this was the
curious part—ever identifying them as his own.[24] Looking up at the ceiling and not at his students, reading his own prose aloud, Trilling made
himself into the anonymous third person that his "we" always resembled.

It was a puzzling and disturbing performance. Here was this man, so
famous, so intellectually powerful—with a wiry elegance of mind that
also marked his physical appearance. Yet the man had disappeared into
the tradition, a tradition he felt that most of the students before him
no longer respected and therefore no longer deserved. His manner was
effete and distant—and, finally, both defeated and hostile. His "we" was
directed toward the ceiling, not toward his students, sitting there before
him. We were the barbarians inside the gates; he wanted none of us. He
was a teacher who didn't see us; a role model who would share and be
generous with just a chosen few. At the time, I was incompletely aware
of what Trilling meant to me; after a lecture or two, I dropped his course
and forgot about the possibility of working with him. Now, years later,
I can feel both the poignancy and the insult in the scene. I can imagine
how pained Trilling must have felt on these occasions. I can also feel
my sense of rejection and—even more strongly—my unwillingness to be
rejected.

It might make sense at this point to launch a fuller and fiercer attack on
Trilling—to use him to the end as a negative model for writing cultural
criticism today. But I find I simply cannot do that. For Trilling had certain
qualities I very much admire. Today, his essays can seem old-fashioned
and, sometimes, embarrassingly complacent—as when he unblinkingly
assumes that culture is, and should be, the sole property of the middle
and upper classes.[25] But I still love his definition of culture which, said
Trilling, is not just books, social institutions, and political activity, but the
"hum and buzz of implication . . . the whole evanescent context in which
statements are made . . . the half-uttered or unuttered, or unutterable expressions of value . . . the things that for good and bad draw the people of

a culture together." [26] The terms "good and bad" in this definition mark one of Trilling's many allusions to the ideal of the critic as "adversarial" to the culture—as an intellectual gadfly, not just a spokesperson or passive supporter—an ideal that continues to motivate today's cultural critics. [27]

Most of all, Trilling at his best was a critic who had a public voice. He had the ability to make educated people—often years after they had obtained their bachelor's degrees—care about phenomena like Austen's *Mansfield Park* and the nature of the modern self. His best-known and most respected book, *The Liberal Imagination*—a collection of close readings and essays on scholarly topics—sold over 100,000 copies the year it was issued in paperback. Few cultural critics, even today, achieve that level of acceptance among academics and in the general readership, and those who do often encourage the public's skepticism about universities and their mission—a move very different from Trilling's affirmation.

The "we" Trilling used—in the terms he conceived it—may be gone forever. Since the mid-1950s, when Trilling did his best work, things have changed and often through the confluence of circumstances whose full results no one really could have predicted. [28] In the academy today, when awareness of multiple group memberships within the larger culture has proliferated, and (from another direction), when all notions of subjectivity are criticized, it might seem best to get rid of the cultural "we" entirely—to simply stop using it. [29] But I don't believe that to be either necessary or desirable, especially when writing cultural criticism. The "I" marks experiences, facts of life, emotions, and beliefs; the "we" marks positions, group identifications, allegiances, and political configurations. Both perspectives operate simultaneously, fluidly, and multiply in a culture. I want the "we" to be an option for critical writers—along with the "I" and criticism's normative third person. But I want a "we" that is different from Trilling's—more open and personal, more fluid and tentative, more aware of differences as well as common ground.

———

There is no escaping the politics of the "we." Again and again, it turns up in public debates. As I finished different versions of this essay, some of the latest examples were multiculturalism and gay rights. [30] There was also an emerging polemic over how, and whether, the United States should return to ideas of "community" lost since the 1960s. There will be other examples by the time this essay is read. In these debates, conservatives usually want to preserve some core idea of identity, to circle the wagons and keep "them" out; liberals usually celebrate diversity and difference.

But ultimately the "we" is not just an intellectual issue or a rhetorical one. It affects us all where we live—on our streets, in our communities. "Can't we all get along?" asked Rodney King in 1992, during the Los Angeles riots. A month later and for a long time after that, King would be a debated, contested figure—a hero to some, a troublemaker to others. But at that moment, before the cameras, he reached out to all Americans. He went to the core of emotion—feelings for all the families whose fathers or sons would not be coming home, the shared sense of impotence and sadness.

Differences and shared experiences, the personal and the communal, what divides and what brings together—the essence of the "we." The "we" is more than a pronoun. Who uses the "we," and how they use it matters. It is a state of mind that establishes who counts and who doesn't, what can or cannot be thought and done.

=====

Now I need to come all the way home, to my role as the writer of this essay. What does my obsession with the "we" have to do with my specific status as an Italian American woman who teaches English and lives in Durham, North Carolina? The examples of Lukács, Dante, Eliot, and Trilling say that the answer is: a great deal. To me it is axiomatic that Italian American females can and do write in many ways, about many topics, and with varied politics. There is no special identity, no natural sisterhood, between Camille Paglia and Sandra M. Gilbert, for example, or Barbara Grizzuti Harrison and Mary Gordon, though all are Italian American females and writers. Still, and above all, writing as an Italian American woman means an awareness of paradox: reading, thinking, writing, finding a voice; imping onto a tradition of active intellectual life which has no branch marked Italian American and female.

I am not alone in seeing the Italian American tradition in stark terms as hostile to its intellectual women. Helen Barolini puts it this way in her Introduction to The Dream Book, an anthology of Italian American women's writing: "The Italian woman's soul was in her consecration as core of the family, upholder of its traditions and transmitter of its values." But writing, says Barolini, means breaking away and produces "the sense of being out of line with one's surroundings, not of one's family and not of the world outside the family: an outsider."[31]

When she describes taking her first trip to do research—her first trip ever without parents or husband—Louise De Salvo makes the same point with grim humor:

> I come from a family, from a cultural heritage, where women simply don't go away to do things separately from men. . . . Women sit around and wait for their men. Or they watch their children and wait for their men. Or they work very hard and watch their children and wait for their men. Or they make a sumptuous meal and they work very hard and watch their children and wait for their men. But they don't go anywhere without their men. Or do anything for themselves alone without their men. Except complain. About their men and their bad luck in having been born female.[32]

When Italian American females want professions, books, learning, independence, writing, they face all the obstacles women traditionally face, plus one: often they have to leave the culture of their childhood. It is clear that men can feel the book deprivations of Italian American culture too: witness Mario Puzo in *The Godfather Papers*, who describes how his decision to be a writer was viewed as madness in Hell's Kitchen, and he himself as someone who "had gone off his nut." But intellectual men are more likely to feel and stress the attractiveness of the culture, its robust plenitude and girth.

When I think of Italian American girlhood, I think above all of being parceled and bound. I think of the little brides of Christ, all lined up in identical white veils and dresses, waiting to be confirmed at age thirteen. We file down the aisle of the church with our adult "sponsors." We walk in silence, careful not to turn our heads or smile at our friends and relatives. We do not want to stand out—the nuns have told us above all to avoid doing that. Beneath my veil, I smell the residue of perm fluid in my hair; I feel stiff crinolines around my hips and legs. Although I am not to stand out, I feel acutely conscious of being watched—and I hope I look beautiful.

No one has made the comparison out loud, but confirmation is a dress rehearsal for marriage and the girls understand it that way, in white dresses and veils, walking down the aisle. At confirmation, Catholics affirm allegiance to God, their willingness to be "soldiers of Christ." It is strong, thrilling rhetoric and seems egalitarian, since the boys are there too, dressed in suits and ties, walking down the other aisle in the church. But the aura of equality is a dodge, and we know it. The boys will be soldiers; we will be wives. We are really agreeing to be obedient and virtuous—the same values we have always been taught in relationship to males: stay in place, keep quiet, make a gesture of submission at the appropriate moment.

Before confirmation, the priests quizzed and confessed us; now, at the end of the aisle, the bishop will bless us. A row of boys precedes each row of girls to the altar: none of us even questions the order—first male, then female. If they wish, the boys can become the priests and bishops; the girls can only observe that kind of power. The priests and bishops stand in for our male relatives—our fathers, brothers, and later husbands, to whom we owe earthly allegiance, rendering unto Caesar.

At the altar I kneel at the cardinal's feet, receiving his blessing—a hand placed briefly on my head, then a rapid cross made above it. Not a word spoken that is not according to ritual and formula. No speeches or commentaries like those that would impress me years later at Bar or Bat Mitzvahs. Not a sign of individuality, except for the confirmation name, my "sponsor's" name, now ecclesiastically (but not legally) added to my own: Marianna Bernadetta De Marco, Bernadetta being the real name of my "sponsor," whom I have always called Aunt Minnie.

But the new name did not fool me into feeling special on this occasion, and I dropped it almost immediately. Before me, that day in church, there were dozens of girls. After me, there were also dozens—all wearing identical veils and white dresses. Even our brand-new garter belts and stockings—the ball and chain of womanhood—were standard department store issue. I wanted to be done with that kind of femininity, that kind of conformity. With confirmation behind me, I was ready to make my move.

———

The day before confirmation, as the Church required, I made confession. But as the priest shut the gate that separated my face from his, I said to myself: Well, that's that; after tomorrow I won't be back. I had made my last confession. I sauntered out to the porch of the church and announced my resolution to my friends. They doubted I would make it stick. "What about your parents?" some of them said. But I was sure I could handle them. "What about getting married?" my friend Connie asked triumphantly. "Maybe I won't get married," I said, shocking them all—then, hedging my bets, "or maybe I'll have a civil ceremony."

I kept my vow. I had that civil ceremony. I've never been back to confession. I returned to that church only for one uncle's funeral, then another's, and then, just last year, for my father's. So it wasn't the church that drew me. It was the family, the way that tradition expresses itself most for Italian Americans. Still, recently, I have become aware of a certain feeling beneath my bravado for what I cast away: not the church, but the belonging, not the submission, but the participation in ritual. Richard Rodriguez has called Catholics the people of the "we"—with an instinct and training for effacing the self and embracing group emotion. I had to confess: it is true, even years after I had willed something different.

When Italian American daughters rebel, their "I-ness" comes through loud and strong—but so too does their remembrance of the "we." They feel the lure of family and community, the thrill of self-sacrifice. The "I" is a heady release conflicted by a potent nostalgia. I want the "I" with its hunger for difference and freedom. But I want the "I" to linger along with the "we"—to be part, somehow, of our collective memory.

Notes

1   Georg Lukács, *History and Class Consciousness: Studies in Marxist Dialectics*, trans. Rodney Livingstone (Cambridge, Mass., 1971), 100. Lukács's original German text uses "man" and "wir" ("man"/"one" and "we") interchangeably. In German, this specific passage uses "man" where the "we" appears in translation; still, the translator is entirely true to the passage in using the English "we." In fact, many other passages in the German essay use the "wir" voice throughout or in tight alternation with the German "man." When I refer below to Lukács's "we," I include both actual uses of the "wir" and equivalents like the universal "man" in this passage.

After this note, my essay does not attempt to take account of how the "we" form functions in different languages. Among the complications would be the reflexive forms typical of certain languages and the connotations of different forms of address, neither of which is important in English. Another factor would be whether a language is rich in pronouns (like Japanese) or poor in pronouns (like English). For reflections on the "we" in different languages, see Emile Benveniste, *Problems in General Linguistics*, trans. Mary Elizabeth Meek (Coral Gables, Fla., 1971); and Monique Wittig, "The Mark of Gender," in *The Poetics of Gender*, ed. Nancy K. Miller (New York, 1986), 63–73.

2   The encroachment of "things" on people is an outstanding theme in the late work of Dickens, for example, in *Our Mutual Friend*. In the twentieth century, D. H. Lawrence continues to explore the theme obsessively. Lukács's essay is helpful in naming and understanding the phenomena that their fictions and other modernist documents record.

3   See Lee Congdon, *The Young Lukács* (Chapel Hill, N.C., 1983), for biographical information. See also *Georg Lukács: A Record of a Life*, ed. Istvan Eorsi (London, 1983), a set of interviews with Lukács himself. A rich pictorial record of Lukács's life is available in *Gyorgy Lukács: His Life in Pictures and Documents*, ed. Eva Fekete and Eva Karadi (Budapest, 1981).

4   Georg Lukács, *The Theory of the Novel*, trans. Anna Bostock (Cambridge, Mass., 1971); originally published in German in 1920.

5   Lukács was minister of culture in 1956, at the time of the failed Hungarian Revolution. Along with Imre Nagy, who led the Hungarian government, Lukács was interned in Romania for many years—his most notorious period of exile, which many Hungarians failed to survive. Although Lukács was invited throughout these years to denounce Nagy (with whom Lukács had often disagreed in public statements), he refused to do so. Lukács was denied Communist party membership from 1957 to 1967, and even after 1967 was regarded as a "chief ideological risk." His growing international reputation in the 1970s protected him near the end of his life. The interviews in Eorsi, ed., *Georg Lukács: A Record of a Life*, detail the Romanian exile and other periods of exile in Vienna, Berlin, and the Soviet Union.

6   See Congdon, *Young Lukács*, 8–9.

7   I have in mind here writers such as Henry M. Stanley, Joseph Conrad, Bronislaw Malinowski, and Sigmund Freud. Stanley was a Welshman who claimed he was an American from the South and idealized in his writing the racial type of the Anglo-Saxon; Conrad and Malinowski were Slavic Poles who aspired to being part of an English-speaking "us"; Freud was an Austrian Jew who idealized the model of the Roman citizen. I discuss each of these figures and their relationship to a European "we" in *Gone Primitive: Savage Intellects, Modern Lives* (Chicago, 1990).

8   Dante Alighieri, *Inferno*, trans. John D. Sinclair (New York, 1961), 63.

9   T. S. Eliot, "Tradition and the Individual Talent," in *The Sacred Wood: Essays on Poetry and Criticism* (London, 1948), 47–59.

10 Wittig, "Mark of Gender," 65.

11 Wittig is actually discussing at this point her use of "elles" in Les Guérillères, a plural third-person feminine that does not exist in English. Her point remains applicable to the first-person plural in English (see "Mark of Gender," 69).

12 See especially Edward Said, Orientalism (New York, 1978).

13 In Gone Primitive I summarize general ideas about "the primitive" using the "we" voice. I call attention to the levels of resistance that statements made in this voice are likely to produce in certain readers.

14 The terms cultural criticism and cultural studies are often used as synonyms. The term cultural studies originated in British left politics and hence is often associated with the left—but this is by no means always the case in this country. At an earlier point, cultural criticism would have confined itself to "high" and cultural studies to "mass" or "popular" culture. That distinction is no longer fully viable.

15 See Carolyn Heilbrun, "Presidential Address," PMLA 99 (May 1984): 408. Heilbrun's story has an ambiguous ending: in 1992 she resigned from Columbia, citing its old-boy mentality and her frustration as a feminist (see Anne Matthews, "Rage in a Tenured Position," New York Times Magazine, 8 November 1992, 46–47, 75, 83). See also Nancy Miller, "Decades," in this volume. A female character in the recent film Metropolitan argues with a man who insists on quoting from an essay in which Trilling uses the "we."

16 Lionel Trilling, The Opposing Self: Nine Essays in Criticism (New York, 1955), ix.

17 See "Preoccupations of a Critic," Times Literary Supplement, 26 August 1955, 492; and Graham Hough, " 'We' and Lionel Trilling," Listener 75 (1955): 760. Hough found Trilling's "we" "monotonously apocalyptic."

18 Lionel Trilling, Beyond Culture (New York, 1965), ix–xi.

19 The first two quotations are from Beyond Culture, 52, 36; the third quotation is from The Opposing Self, 180.

20 For two accounts of these matters, see Diana Trilling, "Lionel Trilling, a Jew at Columbia," Commentary 67 (March 1979): 44; and Russell Jacoby, The Last Intellectuals: American Culture in the Age of Academe (New York, 1987).

21 Jacoby, The Last Intellectuals, 84.

22 See Mark Krupnick, Lionel Trilling and the Fate of Cultural Criticism (Evanston, Ill., 1986).

23 Trilling's single novel, The Middle of the Journey (1947; repr. New York, 1980), does contain covert autobiographical references.

24 As a graduate student, I recognized Trilling's prose and some of the specific essays from which he read; I suspect the undergraduates were baffled by this aspect of his classes.

25 For example: "[I]n a complex culture there are, as I say, many different systems

of manners and since I cannot talk about them all, I shall select the manners and attitude toward manners of the literate, reading, responsible middle class of people who are ourselves" (Lionel Trilling, "Manners, Morals, and the Novel," in The Liberal Imagination [New York, 1950], 207). This essay was originally a lecture delivered to a largely middle-class group—a partial excuse. And Trilling is of course right that culture was, and continues to be, largely associated with the middle classes and above. It is only his lack of reflectiveness on this state of affairs, as in his use of the word "responsible," that seems insufficiently thoughtful.

26 Trilling, "Manners, Morals, and the Novel," 205–6. This view of culture, which is widely shared by critics of the novel, may explain why such critics often also write cultural criticism.

27 The idea derives from Matthew Arnold's Culture and Anarchy (1869); Arnold wanted intellectuals to leaven Philistine culture. Edward Said articulates a later version of the same idea, using the terms "secular criticism" and "oppositional criticism" in The World, the Text, and the Critic (Cambridge, Mass., 1983).

28 Among them would be the wide availability of scholarships and fellowships after Sputnik, the civil rights movement, feminism, the gay rights movement, awareness that the "melting pot" has not worked for racial minorities, and the increased influence of certain ethnic groups, like my own group, the Italian Americans.

29 The unity and coherence of the "subject position" have been attacked by various forms of post-structuralist thought as "essentialist." Many feminists and African-American scholars disagree, though they otherwise belong to forms of post-structuralism. These critics argue for the strategic necessity of retaining the subject position in discourse. See, for example, Nancy Hartsock, "Rethinking Modernism," Cultural Critique 7 (Fall 1987): 187–206; and Henry Louis Gates, Jr., "The Master's Pieces: On Canon Formation and the African-American Tradition," SAQ 89 (Winter 1990): 89–111. Defense of the discursive subject can also be said to assume that no writing (even writing in the third person) can really avoid the subject position—so that the post-structuralist point can be both conceded and seen as having no consequences.

The literature on this issue is extensive. See also Gayatri Chakravorty Spivak, "French Feminism in an International Frame" Yale French Studies 62 (1981): 154–84; and Paul Smith, Discerning the Subject (Minneapolis, 1988). Smith makes a useful distinction between the word "agent" and the word "subject." He wants to redeem the idea of the acting or writing being who claims no absolute power on the world or absolute coherence of being. See also Diana Fuss, Essentially Speaking (New York, 1989).

30 The original version of this essay, published in SAQ (Winter 1991), discussed the multiculturalism debate extensively.

31   Helen Barolini, ed., *The Dream Book: An Anthology of Writings by Italian American Women* (New York, 1985), 12, 19.

32   Louise De Salvo, from "Portrait of the *Puttana* as a Middle-Aged Woolf Scholar," in Barolini, ed., *The Dream Book*, 94.

Notes on Contributors

JANE COLLINS is Associate Professor of Anthropology at the State University of New York, Binghamton. Her publications include *Unseasonal Migrations* (1988) and *Work Without Wages* (coedited with Martha Gimenez) (1990).

CATHY N. DAVIDSON is Professor of English at Duke University and Editor of *American Literature*. She is the author of *Revolution and the Word: The Rise of the Novel in America* (1988), *The Book of Love: Writers and Their Love Letters* (1992), and *Thirty-six Views of Mount Fuji: On Finding Myself in Japan* (1993).

VIRGINIA R. DOMINGUEZ is currently Professor of Anthropology at the University of California at Santa Cruz and author of *White by Definition: Social Classification in Creole Louisiana* (1986) and *People as Subject, People as Object: Selfhood and Peoplehood in Contemporary Israel* (1989).

MARK EDMUNDSON teaches English at the University of Virginia and is Contributing Editor to *Harper's* and *Raritan*. He is the author of *Towards Reading Freud: Self-Creation in Milton, Wordsworth, Emerson, and Sigmund Freud* (1990) and editor of *Wild Orchids and Trotsky*.

GERALD GRAFF is the George M. Pullman Professor of English and Humanities at the University of Chicago. He is the author of *Professing Literature: An Institutional History* (1987) and *Culture Wars* (1992).

RICHARD INGLIS is Head of Anthropology at the Royal British Columbia Museum and has done extensive fieldwork among the Nuu-chah-nulth on Vancouver Island.

ALDONA JONAITIS is Vice President for Public Programs at the American Museum of Natural History and has published widely in the field of Northwest Coast art history. Her books include *Art of the Northern Tlingit* (1986), *From the Land of the Totem Poles* (1988), *Chiefly Feasts: The Enduring Kwakiutl Potlatch* (1991), and *A Wealth of Thought: Franz Boas on Native American Art* (forthcoming).

ALICE YAEGER KAPLAN teaches French at Duke University, where she is also a member of the Literature Program. She is author of *Reproductions of Banality: Fascism, Literature, and French Intellectual Life* (1986) and *French Lessons: A Memoir* (1993).

CATHERINE LUTZ is Associate Professor of Anthropology at the State University of New York, Binghamton. She has published *Unnatural Emotions* (1988) and *Language and the Politics of Emotion* (coedited with Lila Abu-Lughod) (1990).

NANCY K. MILLER is Distinguished Professor of English at Lehman College and the Graduate Center, City University of New York. Her most recent book is *Getting Personal: Feminist Occasions and Other Autobiographical Acts*.

LINDA ORR is Professor of Romance Studies at Duke University. She published *Headless History: Nineteenth-Century French Historiography of the Revolution* in 1990.

ANDREW ROSS is Director of the American Studies Program at New York University. His most recent book is *Strange Weather: Culture, Science and Technology in the Age of Limits* (1991). He is also the author of *No Respect* (1989) and *The Failure of Modernism* (1986).

HENRY M. SAYRE teaches art history at Oregon State University. He is the author of *The Visual Text of William Carlos Williams* (1983) and *The Object of Performance: The American Avant-Garde Since 1970* (1989).

JANE TOMPKINS teaches English at Duke University. Her books include *Sensational Designs: The Cultural Work of American Fiction, 1790–1860* (1985) and *West of Everything: The Inner Life of Westerns* (1992).

MARIANNA TORGOVNICK is Professor of English at Duke University. Her books include *Closure of the Novel* (1981), *Gone Primitive: Savage Intellects, Modern Lives* (1990) and *Crossing Ocean Parkway: Readings by an Italian-American Daughter* (1994).

Index

Library of Congress Cataloging-in-Publication Data
Eloquent obsessions : writing cultural criticism / edited by Marianna
Torgovnick.
Rev. and expanded version of the South Atlantic quarterly, v. 91, no. 1 (winter
1992) special issue, "Writing cultural criticism," edited by Marianna Torgovnick.
Includes index.
ISBN 0-8223-1455-X (cloth).—ISBN 0-8223-1472-X (pbk.)
1. Popular culture—United States.   2. Arts, American.   3. Arts, Modern—20th
century—United States.   4. Culture.   5. United States—Intellectual life—20th
century.   I. Torgovnick, Marianna, 1949–   .   II. South Atlantic quarterly.
III. Title: Writing cultural criticism.
E169.04.E46   1994   306.4'0973—dc20   93-43530 CIP